THE
CELTS

THE CELTS

JOHN DAVIES

BASED UPON THE S4C TELEVISION SERIES

CASSELL&CO

I Beca

Based on the series *The Celts*
produced by Opus Television for S4C
in association with Comataidh Craolaidh Gaidhlig.

Distributed worldwide by S4C International.
Producer - J Mervyn Williams
Director - Caryl Ebenezer

First published in the United Kingdom in 2000 by Cassell & Co
A Member of the Orion Publishing Group
Reprinted 2001,(twice)

Distributed in the United States of America by Sterling Publishing Co., Inc.
387 Park Avenue South, New York, NY 10016-8810

A CIP catalogue record for this book is available from the British Library

ISBN 0 304 35590 9

Designed by Richard Carr
Map artwork by Roger Courthold
Printed and bound in China by Dah Hua Printing Press Co Ltd

Cassell & Co
Wellington House
125 Strand
London WC2R 0BB
United Kingdom

Half-title page: *A bronze fitting based on a horse's head, dating from the first century* BC. *It may have been part of a chariot and was found at Stanwick, Yorkshire, England. (British Museum / Erich Lessing / AKG)*

Title and this page: *Celtic crosses in the landscape, Llanddwyn, Anglesey. (Jean Williamson / Mick Sharp)*

contents

▦ introduction

I TAKE THE N85 out of Ennis, a pleasant town in County Clare, graced by a memorial to Daniel O'Connell, and by the De Valera Museum, housed in the former Presbyterian church. I pass two hitch-hikers with German flags sewn to their rucksacks; a few miles down the road, there are three beflagged Swiss and, a little further on, two Austrians. I give the Austrians a lift. 'Why', I ask, 'are there so many hitch-hikers on this road?' 'We're all going to Doolin,' they reply. 'Why?' I say. 'Because', I am told, 'there'll be real music and singing and dancing and drinking and camaraderie and trips to the Cliffs of Moher and the Burren and the ferry to the Aran Islands.' I suggest there were other places in Europe where the young can find August jollity – Ibiza, for example, or Corfu or Torremolinos. 'But here it is Celtic,' they say, 'and Celtic is wonderful.'

An evening of music in a Dublin pub.

There seemed to be something ironic in all this. Here they are, teens and twenties from Germany, Switzerland, Austria and, also, so I was told, increasingly from Hungary and the Czech Republic, converging on the distant shores of Munster to become engrossed in the charms of Celticity. They come from Mitteleuropa, the region traditionally considered to be the original heartland of the Celts, and yet to them that heartland is in the furthest reaches of Europe on the coasts and islands down from Galway Bay.

'What is so wonderful about this Celtic thing?' I ask. The answers come thick and fast, not only from the Austrians but from a Belgian to whom I also give a lift. Adjectives tumble out: anarchic, spiritual, unmaterialistic, companionable, romantic, unregimented, soulful, unhurried, instinctive – all qualities, it seems, that their own societies have come to lack. This then is what they want to find, these pilgrims from the valleys of the Danube and the Rhine. They are seeking, as one of them put it, 'the world we have lost and should not have lost'.

It is one definition of Celticity and, judging by the world's appetite for books on Celtic spirituality, music, myths, art, magic and landscapes, it is the definition most widely held today. It may not have much relevance to the real history of the Celts, but it does confirm an abiding feature of Celticity: that the word, to quote Humpty Dumpty, means what those who use it choose it to mean. Like many of the protean heroes of Celtic legends – Gwydion in the Mabinogi, for example – it can change into a myriad shapes.

When the word Celt was first used – and that was by Greek writers in the sixth and fifth centuries BC – it was as the name of a people or peoples inhabiting the region to the north of the Greek colony of Massalia (Marseille); indeed it may originally have been the name given by the Greeks to a tribe living in the vicinity of Massalia. Such may have always been the fate of the Celts; that is, they were never allowed to define themselves – others did that for them. To later classical writers, Celts denoted the inhabitants of a wider territory; as a result, it can sometimes appear to have become the name applied to all European peoples not part of the literate and more politically advanced societies of the Mediterranean world. This leads to the initial metamorphosis of the Celts – from being a single tribe to being the first historically documented civilization on a European scale, or, as the great exhibition on the Celts held at Venice in 1991 had it, the first Europeans. The Celts came to be portrayed as the precursors of the Common Market and the European Union, a concept which my Austrian and Belgian friends latched on to with enthusiasm.

A peaceful scene on the Hallstättersee near Salzburg, Austria.

Yet some classical writers acknowledged the existence of the Scythians, the Thracians and, later, the Germans, thus acknowledging that the Celts were a recognizable people or group of peoples rather than the undefined mass of Europeans dwelling beyond the boundaries of classical civilization. So the Celts went from definition to definition; from tribe to 'the Europeans' to an ethnonym, the term for a specific ethnic group.

Two thousand years passed before Celtic was endowed with a further four definitions. That came about as a consequence of the work of the brilliant Welsh scholar, Edward Lhuyd. His careful analysis of the Irish, Breton, Welsh and Gaulish languages, partly published in 1707, allowed him to identify a linguistic group within what would later be known as the Indo-European family of languages, although it was not until 1853 that the group was fully acknowledged to be a member of that family. With some hesitation, Lhuyd called the group Celtic. By extension, those peoples who in modern times speak a Celtic language came to be known as Celts, although, before the researches of Lhuyd, none of them had ever applied the term to themselves; neither had any classical writer described the inhabitants of Britain and Ireland as Celts. In addition, the word Celtic was applied to the body of myth created by medieval speakers of Celtic languages. Thus, the earliest Irish literature came to be considered as offering a unique portrayal of the European Iron Age. In the same way, the Brythonic cycle of stories, particularly those concerning King Arthur, came to be acclaimed as the essence of Celtic imagination and refinement. Furthermore, through the researches of William Stukeley (1687–1765), the term Celtic came to be applied to any material evidence of the pre-Roman era. Stonehenge, Avebury, chambered tombs and standing stones all became Celtic, a development also evident in France and Germany. Thus, in its seventh metamorphosis, Celtic came simply to mean prehistoric.

Nearly a century and a half after Lhuyd's work, Johann Georg Ramsauer began his epoch-making investigations at Hallstatt near Salzburg. His excavations, begun in 1846, continued until 1863; a thousand graves were uncovered, yielding artefacts dating from the eighth to the fifth centuries BC. Objects, belonging to what was coming to be known as the Iron Age, discovered earlier in western Europe, had often been described as Celtic, and it seemed natural to apply the same name to the Hallstatt material. Excavations in eastern France from 1865 onwards produced artefacts with affinities to those of Hallstatt, giving rise to the belief that a Hallstatt 'Celtic' culture had been widely present in western and central Europe in the early centuries of the Iron Age. Thus, in addition to the seven definitions already advanced, Celtic came to mean an archaeological complex.

A decade after the first discoveries at Hallstatt, explorations began at La Tène on Lake Neuchâtel in Switzerland. They brought to light a large quantity of weapons, personal objects, vessels and parts of vehicles, apparently thrown into the lake as part of a ritual act. Other sites, as far apart as the Thames valley, Champagne and the Po valley, came to yield similar material. Objects in the La Tène tradition date from c. 450 BC to the beginning of the Christian era. Highly sophisticated in their construction and decoration, they are in a style congenial to modern taste and one which is in marked contrast to the styles of the classical world. Although the region in which La Tène objects have been found was not necessarily coterminous with the regions believed to have been inhabited in the Iron Age by speakers of Celtic languages, the La Tène style has come to be considered the art of the later prehistoric Celts, indeed as the quintessence of Celtic art. Thus Celtic was given yet another meaning, this time as the name of an art form.

With the increasing appreciation of the achievements of early Christian Ireland, the word Celtic came to be applied to masterpieces such as the Tara Brooch (c. AD 750), *The Book of Kells* (c. AD 800) and the stone crosses of Monasterboice. (c. AD 950). The other Celtic-speaking countries also produced illuminated manuscripts, metalwork and stone crosses in the same tradition, thus giving substance to the concept of a Celtic art brought into being a thousand years and

Part of a page from The Book of Kells. *(Trinity College Library, Dublin)*

more after the heyday of La Tène. This, it could be argued, gave Celtic a tenth meaning. The ecclesiastical milieu of these achievements had its own marked character. The churches of the Celtic-speaking countries, with their decentralized organization, their detachment from Rome, their emphasis on ascetic monasticism, their distinct body of legends and their intimate relationship with the world of nature, gave rise to an entity to which it would be pedantic to deny the name Celtic Church. Thus, Celtic became the name for what A. J. Toynbee considered to be the Far Western European Civilization.

While evidence of the bygone Celts of the European heartland was being discovered and analysed, the living Celts of Ireland, Wales, the Scottish Highlands and Brittany were stirring. Nineteenth-century Ireland was particularly troublesome to the British authorities; the Welsh proved restive on numerous occasions; Highland Scotland was not without its troubles and Brittany, with its dogged defence of its venerable religious practices and its tenacious social traditions, was clearly a very distinctive part of the French state. Among the dominant peoples of the states inhabited by the Celts – the English and the French – a new definition of Celticity arose. To be Celtic was to be backward, subversive, lacking in organizational talents, superstitious, impractical and deficient in intelligence and enterprise. Above all, it suggested peripheral peoples out of touch with the modern world. Such a definition carried with it feminine overtones. Consistent with the patriarchal ideas of the time, peoples with feminine characteristics needed to be ruled by peoples with masculine characteristics – people such as the English. Yet, some of the members of the dominant nations, Matthew Arnold in particular, found in what they considered to be the imaginative, sensitive, otherworldly and idealistic spirit of the Celts a valuable antidote to the crass materialism which they believed to be the chief characteristic of their own nation.

At the same time, the Celts themselves were forging links with each other, although it is doubtful whether, outside certain intellectual circles, a widespread sense of a shared Celticity has ever existed. By the 1890s, there were those among the Irish, the Welsh and the Highland Scots who had come to believe that they had aspirations in common. Ironically, they were aspirations which ran counter to attributes that had characterized the Celts ever since they had first appeared on the stage of history. By the end of the nineteenth century, it was claimed that to be Celtic was to be egalitarian, radical in politics and contemptuous of all manifestations of aristocracy.

The redefining of the Celts continued throughout the twentieth century. By the end of that century, they had become, at least for the Doolin pilgrims, the cynosure of Europe. It is all very odd indeed.

A scene from the Gundestrup Cauldron. Made from embossed silver gilt plates, the cauldron dates from the first half of the first century BC and was discovered, dismantled, in a Danish bog. As the feet of the riders almost reach the ground, the horses of two thousand years ago were obviously much smaller than those of today. (Nationalmuseet, Copenhagen, Denmark)

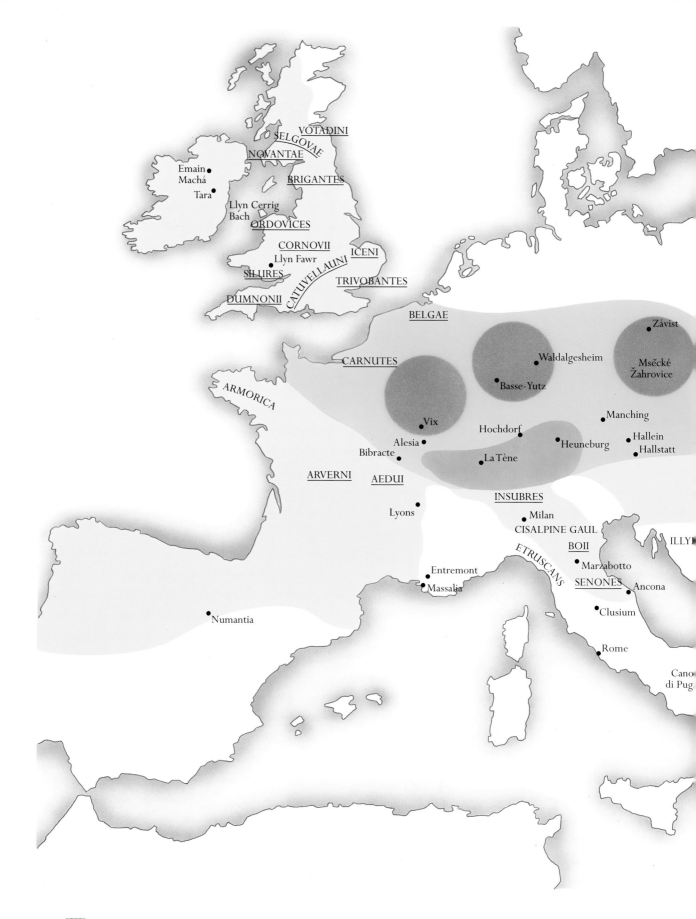

VOTADINI
SELGOVAE
NOVANTAE

Emain
Machá
Tara

BRIGANTES

Llyn Cerrig
Bach
ORDOVICES

CORNOVII
Llyn Fawr
ICENI

SILURES
CATUVELLAUNI

TRIVOBANTES

DUMNONII

BELGAE

CARNUTES

ARMORICA

Závist

Waldalgesheim

Mšecké
Žahrovice

Basse-Yutz

Vix

Manching

Hochdorf

Hallein
Hallstatt

Alesia
Bibracte

Heuneburg

La Tène

ARVERNI

AEDUI

INSUBRES

Lyons

Milan

CISALPINE GAUL

ETRUSCANS

BOII

ILLYR

Marzabotto

SENONES

Ancona

Entremont
Massalia

Clusium

Numantia

Rome

Cano
di Pug

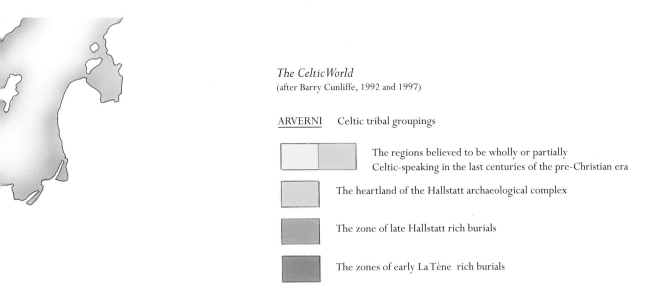

The CelticWorld
(after Barry Cunliffe, 1992 and 1997)

ARVERNI   Celtic tribal groupings

The regions believed to be wholly or partially
Celtic-speaking in the last centuries of the pre-Christian era

The heartland of the Hallstatt archaeological complex

The zone of late Hallstatt rich burials

The zones of early La Tène rich burials

NNONIA

SCORDISCI

THYLIA

TROCMI

TECTOSAGES

•Bâlâ

Pergamum

TOLISTOBOGII

Phocaea

Delphi

chapter one

In the Beginning

Yr Eifl, the triple peaked mountain in Gwynedd, Wales, was the legendary site of Caer Arianrhod, described in Math fab Mathonwy, the fourth of the tales of Y Mabinogi, the greatest prose work in medieval Welsh. (Jean Williamson / Mick Sharp

The village of Hallstatt on the shore of the Hallstättersee. It was in the hills above the village that Ramsauer excavated the graves of the salt-workers of Hallstatt.

The Hallstättersee from the hills above Hallstatt.

IN 1980, Hallein, sixteen kilometres south of Salzburg – the site, like its neighbour Hallstatt, of an Iron Age salt production centre – was the setting of an ambitious exhibition of Celtic art. A considerable number of speakers of Celtic languages travelled from the far west of Europe to the Salzkammergut to admire what many of them considered to be the achievements of their distant ancestors. They went in search of the birthplace of their culture and their language. It was probably a vain exercise, for it is unlikely that the present-day Celticity of Britain, Ireland and Brittany owes its origins to waves of invaders from some imagined Celtic heartland. Yet, as Celticity is more an intellectual construct than a verifiable fact, it would be well to seek to give an account of its history in terms of the development of the construct. From that point of view, Celticity has its roots in the Salzkammergut, in Hallstatt above all, and it is there that it is fitting to start.

Hallstatt is an enchanting place. Demure and remote on its lake shore, its church and huddle of houses represent the ideal of a lakeside alpine village. Above the village lies the site of the graves excavated by Ramsauer, graves dug in the salt deposits laid down there by the great sea which covered the region in the Permian era, some 260 million years ago. It was in order to exploit the salt deposits that people originally settled at Hallstatt and it is the effectiveness of salt as a preservative which gives the place its significance. In the late Bronze Age, c. 1000 BC, Hallstatt was already a centre of importance, producing the salt which ensured that people over a wide area of central Europe could eat palatable

meat following the autumn cull of cattle, sheep and pigs. The area's successive Bronze Age cultures, categorized as Hallstatt A and B, developed by *c.* 750 BC into phase C, a phase characterized by the coming of iron. Iron-making had been pioneered by the Hittites of Anatolia around 1500 BC. The technique had been adopted by the Greeks by 1000 BC; it reached the Alps two and a half centuries later, an early example of the way in which the Mediterranean world would impact upon the world of the Celts.

In what sense can the term Celt be applied to the people of the Hallstatt C culture? The name of the village and that of Hallein might offer a clue, for halwyn, haloin and holenn are the early words for salt in Welsh, Cornish and Breton. Yet, for the discoverers of the Hallstatt C culture, language was not the most important of the considerations which led them to assume that this culture was Celtic. More significance was attached to the belief that some at least of the artefacts of Hallstatt C offered correspondences with what Greek writers had described as the accoutrements of the people they called Celts. Chief among them was the lengthy slashing sword, sometimes made of bronze and sometimes of iron, used by Celtic mounted warriors. The richest of the Hallstatt graves yielded numerous examples of such swords, some of which are meticulously illustrated in the watercolours of Ramsauer's excavations painted by his friend Isidor Engel. Daggers and the appurtenances of feasting and horsemanship also feature in the graves of the Hallstatt élite; and an élite there certainly was, for this early Iron Age community was in no sense egalitarian.

Johann Georg Ramsauer (above), who undertook excavations at Hallstatt before the age of photography. Realizing the need to record his remarkable discoveries, he commissioned his friend Isidor Engel to prepare meticulous water- colour paintings as a record of the graves and their contents. (Naturhistorisches Museum, Vienna)

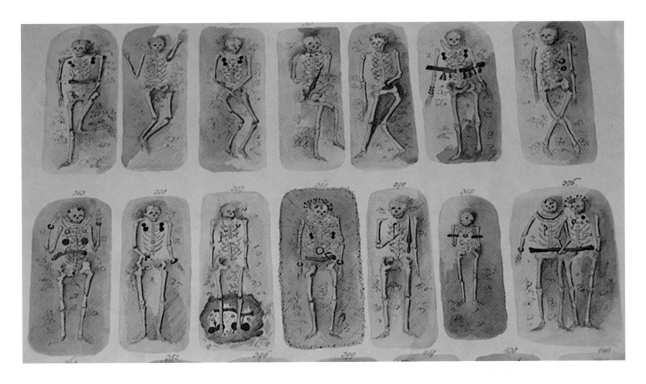

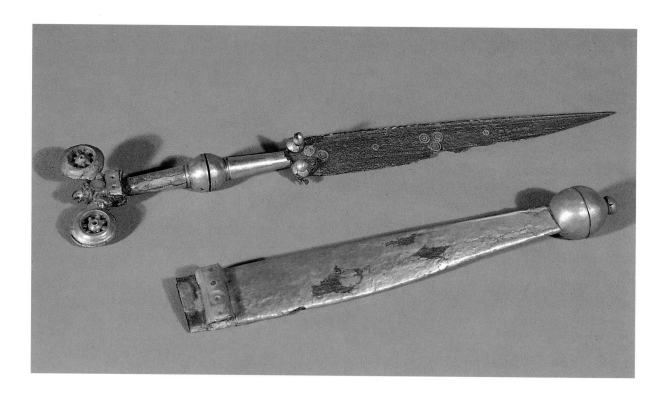

This dagger, with its iron blade and its handle and scabbard of sheet gold was found in tomb 696 at the Hallstatt site. (Naturhistorisches Museum, Vienna / Erich Lessing / AKG)

An analysis of the contents of the two thousand and more graves which have by now been excavated shows that about a quarter of the dead went to the afterlife with no grave goods at all; these, presumably, were the slave labourers of the salt mines. The majority, probably skilled artisans, were buried with at least a dagger and a shoulder ornament. The graves of the élite represent some 5 per cent of the burials. Of these salt barons, the males went to their graves with an array of weaponry, ornaments and vessels, while the females – a surprisingly high proportion of the élite – were accompanied by rings, belts, bracelets and headdresses.

In terms of opulence, the objects excavated from the Hallstatt graves pale into insignificance compared with the splendours later unearthed in princely tombs such as Hochdorf (*c.* 530 BC) in southern Germany and Vix (*c.* 500 BC) in eastern France. But, as Hallstatt was the first site of the early Celtic Iron Age (750–450 BC) to be systematically excavated, the Swedish archaeologist Hans Hildebrant in 1872 successfully advocated Hallstatt as the name which should be applied to all the sites of that age. Thus, the wide swathe of Europe from Bohemia to France and from Slovenia to Belgium in which early Iron Age artefacts of the Hallstatt type are recurrently discovered became the territory of the Hallstatt archaeological complex.

The evidence from Hallstatt, and even more so from cognate sites in France and Germany, is proof of the existence of a society of considerable sophistication. Although Hallstatt C is seen primarily as the era which ushers in the Iron Age, its salient feature, perhaps, is the skill of its bronzesmiths. The making of copper, which is 90 per cent of the content of bronze, was one of the great discoveries of prehistory. With copper smelting, metallurgy was born, and the experience of working the metal led to a knowledge of other materials. Bronze came into existence when it was discovered that copper is hardened by the addition of tin. Before that discovery, copper was largely restricted to the making of adornments, cult objects and status symbols, but with the coming of the harder bronze, it was possible to use it to make weapons and tools. Copper ore was widely available, but tin had to be brought to central Europe from western Britain, Brittany, Italy or northern Spain. A bronze-making society was therefore one involved in long-distance trade. Such a society was emerging in central Europe between 2500 and 1200 BC. Its expansion was greatly stimulated by the opening up of the east alpine copper mines. That began around 1200 BC, and the thirty-two mineshafts at Mitterberg in western Austria eventually produced as much as twenty thousand tons of crude copper. This increasing exploitation was undertaken by the peoples of the Urnfield Culture, a culture which had come into existence in the middle Danube valley by about 1300 BC. By 800, it had become general from Hungary to France. The culture was so named because the Urnfield People cremated their dead and placed the ashes in urns, with sometimes as many as ten thousand inhumations in a single site.

Details of the Engel watercolours of the Hallstatt graves and their contents. (Naturhistorisches Museum, Vienna)

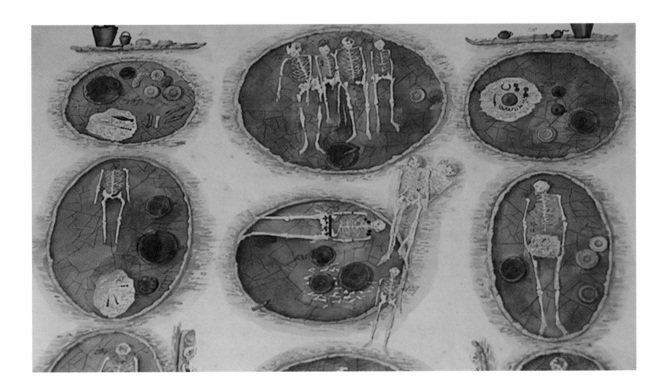

This gold torque from Broighter, County Down, is one of the finest La Tène artefacts to have been discovered in Ireland. (National Museum of Ireland, Dublin)

It is generally accepted that the Hallstatt culture evolved from that of the Urnfield People; indeed, the earliest phases at Hallstatt itself are considered to be very much in the Urnfield cultural tradition. Along with the growing use of bronze, that tradition offers evidence of increasingly skilful horsemanship. The horse was domesticated in the Ukrainian Steppes somewhere around 4000 BC, initially as a source of food; of the animal bones found at Dereivka on the Dneiper River, 74 per cent were those of horses. Over the following millennium, horse-riding was mastered, permitting the development of nomad pastoralism, the context, according to some prehistorians, of the early dispersal of the Indo-European languages. There is some evidence of migration from the Pontic Steppe to the Great Hungarian Plain, although further west horsemanship was probably learnt through example rather than migration. In the last pre-Christian millennium, vehicles and the appurtenances of horsemanship loom large in the archaeological record of the Celts. Indeed, as Barry Cunliffe put it, late prehistoric Europe is 'swamped with bronze horse-gear'.

Early Hallstatt sites extend from eastern Hungary to southern Germany and offer little evidence of contact with the more advanced societies of the Mediterranean, although the metal technology, the main plant crops and the domestic animals of the inhabitants of those sites had their origins in those societies. In the years after 600 BC, the centre shifts westwards and Mediterranean influences multiply. That may partly be explained by the establishment *c.* 600 of a Greek colony at Massalia (Marseilles). Founded by the citizens of Phocaea on the Ionian coast, Massalia became the centre of trade between the peoples of the Mediterranean and those of the European hinterland. The main arteries of the trade were the valleys of the Rhône and the Saône and onwards to those of the Rhine, the Seine and the Danube. The Hallstatt people traded, not only with the Greek colonies of the western Mediterranean, but also with the Etruscans of the region between the rivers Po and Tiber. Etruscan civilization was at its height between 700 and 500 BC, and attracted artists from Corinth and other Greek cities. Rich in tin and copper, the Etruscans were distinguished for their metalworking, pottery and architecturally sophisticated tombs. Enemies of the Phocaeans of Massalia, they eventually made direct contact with the Hallstatt zone via the alpine passes north of the Po valley.

The products of central and western Europe sought by Mediterranean peoples included the tin of Cornwall and Brittany. The mention of the 'tin islands' in the writings of Pytheas of Massalia may refer to Cornwall. Archaeologists postulate the existence of an Atlantic trading system. It became bound up with that of the Mediterranean via the valleys of the Loire and the Garonne and their links with that of the Rhône. In addition, trade passed through the Strait of Gibraltar, a route dominated by the Phoenician port of Cadiz. The furs of forest animals and the amber of the Baltic were also prized, and these imports into the Mediterranean world involved trade routes up the valleys of the Elbe and the Oder, along the Danube and over the Alps. But perhaps the main export of the Hallstatt zone was people, for the Mediterranean products sought by the northerners were frequently bartered for slaves.

Those products were luxury goods to satisfy the palates of the aristocracy, or to enhance their prestige in life and death. They included glass and coral for the making of jewellery, rich fabrics and ornaments and, above all, wine. Classical authors are unanimous about Celtic enthusiasm for wine. They craved it, wrote Plato. 'They sate themselves with unmixed wine,' wrote Diodorus Siculus. 'Their desire makes them drink it greedily and when they become drunk they fall into a stupor or into a manic disposition. And therefore many Italian merchants in their usual love of lucre look on the Gallic love of wine as their treasure trove. They transport the wine by boat on the navigable rivers and receive in turn for it an incredibly high price; for one jar of wine they receive a slave – a servant in exchange for a drink.' This last comment may be an exaggeration; Cunliffe believes that 'a trader might expect to get the equivalent of half a dozen *amphorae*

Detail of a gold torque of the second half of the fourth century BC, found at Waldalgesheim in the Rhineland. (Rheinisches Landesmuseum, Bonn)

for a healthy Gaul'. *Amphorae* of the period 700 to 450 BC have been found in large quantities in the vicinity of Massalia, in the middle and upper Rhône valley, in the Rhineland and in the upper Danube valley; there have been isolated finds in the Loire, Seine, Meuse and Elbe valleys, and even in that of the Severn.

Chieftains located along the trade routes succeeded in controlling and manipulating the transfer of goods, thus gaining for themselves riches and power. In the archaeological record, the most conspicuous way of displaying that wealth and power was through opulent burial, a practice which may owe something to Etruscan traditions and possibly to those of Mycenaean Greece and to Egypt. Thousands of Hallstatt burials have been discovered in central and western Europe, but those containing a wide range of luxury objects are restricted to a fairly narrow zone extending from the upper Danube to the upper Seine. The zone is seen as the core area of later Hallstatt culture and is considered to have been dominated by substantial principalities ruled by Celtic-speaking warrior élites enriched by their control of trade.

Opulent graves of the Hallstatt C era (750–600 BC) are found in the east of the zone – at Hradenin and Lovosice in Bohemia, for example, or in southern Germany, where at least ninety élite burials of the period have been discovered. The graves contained pottery and bronze vessels holding food and drink, objects either symbolic of the feasting the deceased had enjoyed in this world, or intended to provide them with the means of feasting in the next. The richest of the graves are vehicle burials; the corpse was taken to the grave in a four-wheeled vehicle which was buried with it in a timber-lined pit crowned with a barrow. So cumbersome were the vehicles that they had presumably been built specifically for the funeral rite.

Elite burials of the Hallstatt D era (600–450 BC) have not been found in the easternmost part of the Hallstatt core area; there are none, for example, in Bohemia. Vehicle burial continued in southern Germany and spread to eastern France. The greater opulence of the Hallstatt D burials suggests a concentration of power with larger and fewer principalities, and the objects they contain indicate increasing contact with the Greek colonies and with the Etruscans.

Among the most remarkable of the Hallstatt D burials is that of Eberdingen-Hochdorf, one of a number of tumuli in the vicinity of Hohenasperg near Stuttgart. Excavated in 1978–9, it was created for a six-foot (1.83 metres) man in his forties and is dated to around 530 BC. Although there were probably richer tombs, Hochdorf is remarkably well preserved and, unlike many, was not disturbed or looted in antiquity. The tomb chamber is 4.7 metres square and is enclosed in a barrow nearly sixty metres across. The most outstanding object it contained was a three-metre-long bronze couch on which the corpse was

The most outstanding object found in the Hochdorf tomb was this three-metre (9.75 foot) long bronze couch bearing the body of a man who was in his forties when he died in about 530 BC. (Württembergisches Landesmuseum, Stuttgart)

laid. The back of the couch is decorated with depictions of chariots and stick-like male figures, who are apparently dancing; its sides are turned up in the manner of a Biedermeier sofa. The most fascinating feature of this astounding creation are the eight caryatid-like figures whose heads and arms support the couch and whose feet rest on the castors which allow the couch to be easily moveable. The grave contained other marvels. The body was adorned with a gold torque, a bracelet, shoes and a leather belt with gold mounts, a

The Hochdorf tumulus near Stuttgart. Excavated in 1978–9, it proved to contain a tomb of extraordinary richness.

The back of the Hochdorf couch was decorated with depictions of a chariot and stick-like male figures (left). It was supported by bronze human figures whose feet rested on the castors which enabled the couch to be moved. (Württembergisches Landesmuseum, Stuttgart)

The replication of the Hochdorf tomb showing the body of the chieftain, the couch, the cauldron and the chariot. (Keltenmuseum, Hochdorf-Enz)

gold-plated dagger and a conical birch bark hat similar to those crowning the heads of the stone statues found in other Hallstatt sites. Most of these objects were probably of local manufacture, although the couch was decorated with coral which may have come from the Bay of Naples. However, a bronze cauldron, adorned with lions and capable of holding five hundred litres of liquid, came from a Greek workshop and is indicative of the far-flung contacts of the lord of Hohenasperg.

The Grächwil hydra or waterpot with detail (right) of the elaborate and symbolic metal-work on its rim. (Historisches Museum, Bern)

Even more astonishing than the Hochdorf grave is the later tomb at Vix, the most westerly of the known Hallstatt D élite burials. Strategically located on the upper Seine in Burgundy, the tomb was discovered in 1953 and has been dated to *c.* 500 BC. The most spectacular object it contained was a bronze krater or huge vase, 1.64 metres high and weighing 208 kilograms. Of Greek manufacture, it was so large that it was transported to Vix – presumably from Massalia – in sections and was perhaps put together there by its Greek maker. Vix also yielded a dismantled funerary vehicle, a superb diadem, perhaps Europe's finest prehistoric object in gold, and a gold collar of exceptionally fine filigree. In addition, there were basins and other vessels of Etruscan origin. The krater has no parallel, and is therefore unlikely to have arrived at Vix through trade. It is more plausible to interpret it as a specially made diplomatic gift bestowed by some authority upon a Celtic chieftain whose goodwill was sought. The ultimate fascination is that the tomb is that of a woman. A recent analysis of her remains indicates that they are those of a diminutive woman who had suffered from diseases which had caused her to have a twisted face and an unusual gait. Originally known as 'the princess of Vix', there is now an increasing readiness to consider that she was some kind of priestess with shaman-like attributes. For a woman to have so rich an interment was unusual but not unique, for later elaborate tombs at Rheinheim in Saarland and at Waldalgesheim in the Rhineland are also those of women. The prominence of women in the

The replication of the Vix burial showing the diminutive female body and the huge bronze vase or krater. Dating from about 500 BC, the figure, when discovered in 1953, was called 'the princess of Vix'. She is now thought to have been a priestess or shaman. (Musée Archéologique, Châtillon-sur-Seine)

The great krater from the Vix grave is over a metre-and-a-half (five foot) in height and weighs more than 280 kilograms (620 pounds). (Musée Archéologique, Châtillon-sur-Seine)

This bronze wine jug dates from about 430 BC and was found in a tomb at Reinheim in Saarland. (Landesmuseum für Vor-und Frühgeschichte, Saarbrücken)

Hallstatt cemetery has already been noted. Later evidence – the role of Boudica and Cartimandua in the Britain of the first century AD and the status of women as defined in the Irish and Welsh law codes, for example – offers further grounds for believing that Celtic societies held women in comparatively high regard.

Other Hallstatt D graves have yielded objects of remarkable workmanship and provenance. An elaborate Greek-made hydria or water pot was found in a burial at Grächwil in Switzerland. The Grafenbühl tomb near the Hochdorf grave was originally fabulously wealthy; robbed in antiquity, the remnants overlooked by the robbers provide evidence of imports from Etruria, southern Italy, Greece, Syria and the Baltic. Even more remarkable evidence of contact with far distant lands comes from the double grave at Hohmichele on the upper Danube. The tomb contained a man and a woman and the fabric of the woman's dress was embroidered with Chinese silk. Yet another trade route is indicated by a discovery in a princely tomb in Magdelenberg in the Black Forest; a belt-hook of about 550 BC, it was probably made in the upper Douro valley in northern Spain. Tombs at Dürrnberg near Hallein have also yielded very significant discoveries. By about 580 BC, Hallein was overtaking Hallstatt as the centre of salt production in the eastern Alps. Burials at Dürrnberg became increasingly elaborate and some contain complete assemblages of objects from the neighbourhood of Venice. A discovery in grave 112 is particularly fascinating. Dated about 480 BC, it is a locally produced bronze wine flagon with a long slanting spout. Its shape was borrowed from the Etruscans, but the fantastical animals and human head on the handle and the rim may have associations with the art of the Steppes. Thus, in the very last phase of the Hallstatt era, native craftsmen were drawing upon influences from the south and the east and creating an art which was distinctly their own. It was a development of great promise and significance.

Rich tombs were built in association with elaborate habitations. Thus, *Fürstengräber* or princely tombs are discovered in conjuction with *Fürstensitze* or princely residences. Hochdorf and Grafenbühl are burial sites associated with the hillfort of Hohenasperg, Vix with Mont Lassois, Hohmichele with Heuneburg and Dürrnberg with Ramsaukopf. Of these hilltop princely residences, the most remarkable is Heuneburg, the only Hallstatt fortified site in central Europe to have been thoroughly excavated. Its walls enclose three hectars; they were built in about 530 BC, and are unique in temperate Europe. Constructed in mud brick on a stone foundation and with a series of rectangular bastions, they are so Mediterranean in their conception that it would be reasonable to assume that they are the work of a Greek architect. Mont Lassois, situated at the point at which the Seine becomes navigable by small vessels, was also strongly fortified with ramparts up to three metres high. Some sites were so well chosen that they came to be occupied by later settlements. The remains of the six-hectar hillfort of Hohenasperg, for example, lie beneath an imposing Renaissance château. Evidence of iron smelting, bronze casting, jewellery making and a range of other craft activities within the hillforts indicates that they were more than the private residences of chieftains, a presupposition strengthened by the orderly rows of houses which some of them contained. They were in fact proto-cities, the first example of towns in Europe beyond the Alps, and the forerunners of the *oppida* which would loom so large in the story of the Celts in the last century or two of the pre-Christian era. Occupied hillforts declined in number as they became larger, suggesting a concentration of power which, as has already been suggested, is also indicated by the increasing richness of burial sites. For example, of the twelve hillforts of the Hallstatt D1 era (600–530 BC) in the Breisgau district of the Black Forest, only one was occupied during Hallstatt D 2–3 (530–450 BC).

Prehistorians have been mesmerized by the riches of the Hallstatt D sites of the Danube–Seine Zone. Furthermore, as many of them began their studies as classicists, they are equally entranced by the zone's links with Mediterranean

A replication of a bronze wine flagon of about 420 BC, found at the hilltop stronghold of Dürrnberg near Hallein. It has an animal-headed handle and a long slanting spout. (Keltenmuseum, Hallein, Austria; the original is in Museum Carolino-Augusteum, Salzburg)

Archaeologists at work on a section of the wall at the Heuneberg hillfort near Stuttgart, Germany.

civilizations. The zone of an elaborate upper-class culture, it would seem, must be the heartland of an ethnic and linguistic group. Thus, the core area of Hallstatt D sites has been seen as the area in which a Celtic *koine* or lingua franca developed. Such ideas are highly speculative. They owe much to early twentieth-century thinking, which assumed that an archaeological complex is the equivalent of a culture and that a culture is the product of a specific people – indeed, in the opinion of some writers, of a specific race. The concept of a people carried with it the presumption that they had a specific language and thus the territory of the Hallstatt archaeological complex became the territory of the speakers of Celtic; in turn, the territory of the speakers of Celtic became the territory of the Hallstatt archaeological complex. There was more than a tacit assumption that all 'Celtic' artefacts were produced by Celtic-speakers, and that all Celtic-speakers produced 'Celtic' artefacts. It therefore followed that the Celtic language must have evolved in the Hallstatt zone – the 'Celtic heartland'. Later evidence of its presence in regions beyond the boundaries of that zone was interpreted as the result of invasion of those regions by people from the 'heartland'.

Such theories are now viewed with suspicion. There is a realization that they involve a considerable degree of circular argument; archaeologists have taken on trust notions from linguists, as have linguists from archaeologists, causing each to build on the other's myths. The Hallstatt archaeological zone was not necessarily coterminous with the region inhabited by speakers of Celtic languages. Some of those with a Hallstatt culture could have spoken languages which were not Celtic. There may be a parallel here with the Gothic architecture of the Middle Ages; although Gothic cathedrals were first built in northern France, they are not restricted to French-speaking regions. During the early Iron Age, Celtic-speakers could have long been living in regions lacking a Hallstatt material culture. Germany has a rich heritage of Baroque architecture, but there are extensive German-speaking regions in which the style is virtually absent. These arguments are particularly pertinent when considering those lands in which Celtic languages are spoken today. Up to the 1950s, it was generally accepted that the Celtic language or languages were introduced into Britain and Ireland in the centuries after 700 BC, and that the introduction represented the invader ethos of the dynamic Hallstatt culture and its La Tène successor. Yet, the Irish archaeological record for the centuries after 700 BC offers no evidence of significant immigration, and, apart from some localized exceptions, neither does the British. There is an increasing readiness to accept that the belief that cultural change must necessarily be caused by invasion is the offspring of the imperialist mentality of the nineteenth century.

Invasionism lost favour from the 1950s onwards – the era, significantly

Another view of the wall at the Heuneberg hillfort near Stuttgart, Germany.

An astonishing bronze mount of the third century BC found at Malomeříce near Brno. It originally crowned a wooden drinking vessel. (Moravské Zemské Muzeum, Brno)

perhaps, of rapid decolonization. Instead, emphasis was placed upon the capacity of indigenous societies to innovate and develop. The change of emphasis, together with the chronological revolution brought about by the discovery of the Carbon-14 dating system, shattered the accepted portrayal of European prehistory. In 1973, Colin Renfrew lamented that 'it will be decades before we have a really persuasive prehistory of Europe that carries the same conviction … as the old diffusionist picture once did'. There was still a readiness, however, to accept that the appearance by about 2000 BC of distinctive beakers in burials was evidence of a major migration of people to Britain and other parts of western Europe. The Beaker Folk were believed to have migrated from the Rhineland and to have brought with them a culture which contained elements originating in central Europe, or perhaps from as far to the east as the Ukraine.

To Myles Dillon, writing in 1967, these migrants could reasonably be considered to be Celts, or at least proto-Celts, a notion which had originally been aired by John Abercromby in 1912 and by scholars such as Henri Hubert and Joseph Loth. Assuming that they had their origins in the area north of the Black Sea, that would mean that they sprang from the region widely assumed to be the cradle of the Indo-European languages. Thus the Celts could conceivably have carried the Indo-European inheritance westwards at much the same time as the Aryans carried it eastwards to India. This would help to

The Celtic Language Tree

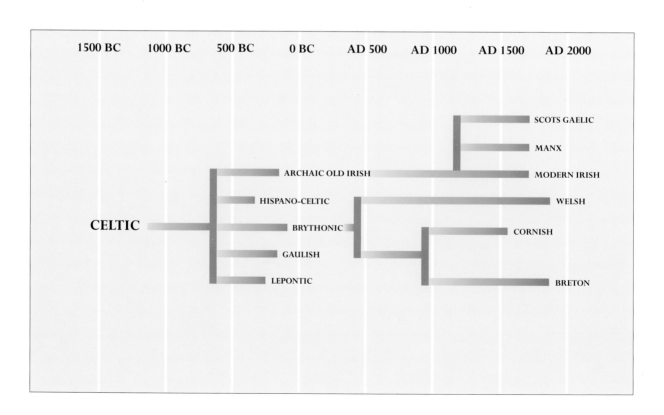

explain the apparent similarities between the social organization, law and poetic conventions found in early Ireland and in Vedic India, a matter which had excited the scholarly world ever since Joseph Vendryes had ventilated it in 1918. Thus, although the eastern Alps of the eighth century could reasonably be considered to have been the place of origin of a material culture specifically associated with the Celts, it was not necessarily the wellspring of the Celtic language; that language or its ancestor could plausibly be considered to have been widely spoken over much of central and western Europe twelve centuries earlier.

By the 1980s, even the notion that the spread of the Beaker culture represented a migration was under attack. The only indubitable major migrationary movement in European prehistory, it was argued, was that associated with the spread of agriculture which began in the seventh millennium BC. In 1987, Renfrew offered the bold thesis that the Indo-European language or languages became prevalent over most of Europe in the wake of the Agricultural Revolution, just as, in recent centuries, the spread of agriculture was the engine for the spread of Indo-European languages in the Americas and Australasia. Renfrew noted that, on productive land, a hunter-gatherer society can sustain one person per ten square kilometres, while agriculture can sustain five persons per one square kilometre. No dramatic invasions need to be postulated. The practice of farming can be discerned in Turkey around 7000 BC; it had reached the Orkney Islands by 3500 BC. Over those three and a half millennia, agriculturalists could have made their way, a few kilometres in each generation, to the furthest reaches of Europe from the Indo-European heartland. That heartland, argued Renfrew — and on this matter he is in agreement with some earlier scholars — should be considered to be Anatolia, where the essential elements of western agriculture — wheat and barley — are indigenous. Pre-European languages, specifically Basque, could have survived because their speakers had embraced agriculture and had therefore thrived, unlike the peoples wedded to hunter-gathering who had been overwhelmed by the greater peopling power of agriculturalists.

If undifferentiated Indo-European had spread throughout Europe between the seventh and fourth millennia BC, it is not necessary to seek a localized cradle for the Celtic language. In Britain, Ireland and Gaul and elsewhere, there could have been what Christopher Hawkes described in 1973 as 'culminative Celticity'. Proto-Celtic could have crystallized out of Indo-European *in situ*. Thus, the ancestor of Brythonic could have been spoken in Britain as early as 4000 BC, and that could also be true of the ancestor of Irish in Ireland and of Gaulish in Gaul. J. R. R. Tolkein's reference to Welsh as 'the senior language of the men of Britain' may therefore be considered a very modest claim indeed.

Býčiskála

ONE OF THE MOST intriguing archaeological sites of the Hallstatt period is that of the Býčiskála Cave in Moravia, fifteen kilometres from Brno. It won fame because its discoverer claimed that in it ceremonies were held of a bizarreness highly appealing to the more fervent Celtic enthusiasts. Jindrich Wankel, a local doctor, explored the cave in 1872 and interpreted the human remains he found as those of a rich man surrounded by his ritually murdered wives and female slaves. He claimed that the arms of some of the deceased had been chopped off and that skulls had been severed or shaped into drinking cups. The eerie setting of the cave and the presumed evidence of a powerful bloodthirsty chieftain provided much ghoulish delight and inspired a painting reconstructing the scene. It was assumed that the chieftain was a Celt and that the evidence from Býčiskála corroborated classical writers' comments on human sacrifice among the Celts. Recent interpretations are more prosaic. The cave contained the remains of as many males as females; evidence of chopped off limbs is unsubstantiated and, of the forty or more individuals, no more than two can be shown to have suffered a violent death. Perhaps the most appealing object found in the cave is a superb bronze bull of exquisite workmanship.

This argument would fit in with the comments of the classical writers, who offer no suggestion that the great majority of the people of western Europe in the last centuries of the pre-Christian era had traditions that located their origins in any region other than that in which they lived. Diodorus Siculus stated that the British regarded themselves as autochthonous, and Julius Caesar made the same comment about the inhabitants of the island's inland areas. Thus, if Renfrew's theory is to be accepted, it would be misleading to restrict Celtic origins to the Hallstatt archaeological zone; that need not be the unique and original homeland of the Celts and their language.

Renfrew's thesis that the Indo-European language or languages were spread concurrently with the diffusion of agriculture – a thesis in which he gives particular prominence to the Celts – has not received universal acceptance. In accord with the acerbic character of much of the discussion among prehistorians and linguists, one commentator on the thesis stated that, rather than putting a cat among the pigeons, Renfrew had put a pigeon among the cats. It is likely that early farmers were egalitarian subsistence peasants. How therefore did cognate elaborate social structures come into existence in widely separated Indo-European-speaking societies? How can similar words for king – *raj* in the Sanskrit of India, *rex* in the Latin of Italy and *ri* in the Goidelic of Ireland – be explained if those languages were crystallizing out in far-flung locations long before their speakers had kings? The question is equally pertinent when considering the words for other ranks and objects unlikely to have been familiar to the earliest practitioners of agriculture – words which the painstaking reconstructors of proto-Indo-European maintain had been inherited by Indo-European's daughter languages. Renfrew deals briskly with these objections. Similarities between ancient Ireland and ancient India may be accounted for by coincidence. Many pre-literate communities have shared characteristics; some features once considered to be specifically Indo-European can be found among such peoples as the Japanese, the Polynesians and the Meso-Americans. The word for king may originally have meant little more than a prominent man and could by chance have come to mean king in some, but not all, Indo-European languages.

Renfrew's answers have not satisfied everyone. Indeed, some of his critics believe his whole approach to be fatally flawed. J. P. Mallory argued that his work has 'strayed light years away from whatever consensus the general run of Indo-European studies has managed to achieve'. Europe, stated Mallory, offers ample evidence of agriculturalists speaking pre-Indo-European languages. As a term, proto-Celtic is so imprecise as to be virtually meaningless. If the ancestor of Celtic had been spoken over much of western Europe as early as 4000 BC, the differences between its daughter languages would, by the opening of the historic era, have been far greater than in fact they were. The attack on migration and invasion has been carried too far. There is hardly any archaeological evidence for migrations of Gaelic speakers to Scotland and of Brythonic speakers to Brittany in the immediate post-Roman period, but the historic record confirms that they occurred. The arguments of Mallory and others can be seen as insuperable obstacles to the acceptance of Renfrew's thesis. Yet that thesis is worth discussing, if only because it draws attention to the wide variety of explanations offered for the origins of the Celts.

That wide variety makes it necessary for any statement about those origins to be hedged around with doubts and qualifications. The scholarly writings on the issue sometimes seem to dissolve into arcane minutiae. As Cunliffe put it: 'Specialized works should be approached only by those of a resilient disposition.' Linguists are in a particularly difficult situation, for the Celtic languages on which they are best informed – those which are currently spoken – are precisely those languages totally bereft of any early stone or metal inscriptions. They are also languages about which the classical authors have almost nothing to say. On Celtic origins, the only fixed reference points are the writings of those authors; they are by no means objective, but the archaeological identity of the Celts becomes more and more speculative the further enquiry is pushed back into centuries earlier than their composition. Central to the issue is the fact that the archaeology of pre-literate societies can offer virtually no evidence about linguistic change.

An open-work disc 12.5 centimetres (five inches) in diameter found at Cuperly near Epernay, France. Dating from the early fourth century, its creation involved sophisticated compass work. (Musée des Antiquités Nationales, St-Germain-en-Laye / RMN / DBP)

Thus, although there is a widespread recognition that the Hallstatt archaeological zone is the heartland of a distinct Celtic material culture, answers to more general questions concerning the origin of the Celts are in a state of flux. As has already been noted, the traditional view that the Celtic language or languages were spread westwards by invaders in the centuries after 700 BC has been largely set aside. Invasionism – originally suspect on archaeological grounds – has been further weakened by studies comparing the genes of the present inhabitants of western Europe with those of the region's inhabitants thousands of years ago. In view of the way in which simplistic accounts of prehistoric linguistic origins were used in the twentieth century to underpin vicious racial theories, scholars are understandably reluctant to place too much emphasis on biological archaeology. Nevertheless, the studies undertaken so far, very slight though they are, indicate that the genetic make-up of the peoples of the western Europe of today is very similar to that of its late Stone Age and Bronze Age inhabitants. Not too much should be made of this very tentative work, but if larger-scale studies yield similar results, they

could perhaps offer support for Renfrew's thesis that the inhabitants of much of western Europe became Celts *in situ*.

Yet, if there is a majority scholarly view at all at present, it is that Celtic evolved between 1500 and 1000 BC, probably in the region between the Danube and the Rhine, and that the language and its associated culture spread westwards, not by invasion but by acculturation – the process whereby one group assimilates the cultural traits of another. The scholars who favour this interpretation are increasingly prepared to accept that the process was in train in an era earlier than that of the full vigour of the Hallstatt culture. Details in a sailing manual of about 600 BC, the *Massilliot Periplus*, preserved in later texts, refer to Britain as Albion and Ireland as Iernè. These names are in an early form of Celtic and there is no reason to doubt that versions of Celtic were established in the two islands well before the compiling of the manual. In about 500 BC, Hecateus of Miletus provided evidence that much of southern Gaul was inhabited by Celts and he gave no suggestion that they were newcomers to the region. Herodotus, 'the father of history', writing in about 450 BC, noted that Celts lived beyond the Pillars of Hercules (the Strait of Gibraltar) and were among the most westerly peoples of Europe, thus establishing that parts at least of the Iberian Peninsula were lands of the Celts. Cisalpine Gaul, which included much of northern Italy, has traditionally been considered to have been Celticized through invasions from the 390s onwards. Yet, there is a growing readiness to accept that the language, or one of the languages, of the Golasecca culture of the Italian

P and Q Celtic

Irish	Welsh	
CEANN	PEN	(head)
CÉ	PWY	(who)
CEATHAIR	PEDWAR	(four)
MAC	AP	(son of)

Examples illustrating one of the most remarked upon differences between the Brythonic (P-Celtic) and the Goidelic (Q-Celtic) groups of the Celtic family of languages.

Lakes, which flourished from the ninth to the fifth centuries BC, was the form of Celtic known as Lepontic.

Furthermore, hillforts, which are so prominent a feature of the Hallstatt D Zone, had long been constructed in regions well beyond the boundaries of that zone. The earliest ramparts on the Dinorben fort in Wales have been dated to around 1000 BC, and in England hillforts such as Harting Beacon, Norbury and Borough Hill were under construction by the eighth century BC at the latest. In the Iberian Peninsula and in Atlantic France also, the antiquity of many hillforts is increasingly recognized.

It would not therefore be unreasonable to suggest that the Celtic language or languages seeped into Atlantic Europe and possibly into Cisalpine Gaul at least as long ago as the earliest centuries of the last pre-Christian millennium. It is assumed that this process happened in the context of trade and that Celtic was the lingua franca of the Atlantic trade routes and of those of the alpine region. It can be posited that Celtic played the same role as Swahili was to play in East Africa and Malay in the islands of south-east Asia. If these notions are accepted, it would follow that Celtic became widespread in Atlantic Europe in the context of the vigorous trading system of the late Bronze Age. Originally, the speakers of Celtic may not have been as numerous as those speaking non-Indo-European languages, and any notion that those languages were somehow inferior is surely nonsense. After all, as the linguistic history of Hungary and Turkey proves, Indo-European has not always won. As Mallory argues, new languages tend to be adopted when they offer better access to goods, status, ritual or security than those which are abandoned. It is reasonable to assume that, in the Atlantic Europe of the last pre-Christian millennium, Celtic offered such better access. Nothing is known about the languages Celtic displaced, although some remnants of them may survive in place-names, and they could possibly have had some influence upon their displacer; for example, the mutations which are such a feature of modern Celtic languages may conceivably be the consequence of the impact of earlier speech patterns.

The question of whether or not the language seeping westwards was a single, broadly uniform Celtic has been much discussed. By the dawn of the Christian era, when evidence becomes more extensive, it is apparent that the Celtic languages of Ireland and the Iberian Peninsula were more archaic than those of Britain and Gaul; the distinction is generally summed up by the terms Q-Celtic and P-Celtic. Whether this means that Ireland and the Iberian Peninsula absorbed one form of Celtic and Britain and Gaul another is open to doubt. A more likely explanation is that the Celtic languages of Ireland and the Iberian Peninsula experienced less evolution because the communities which spoke them were

The pair of bronze wine flagons found at Basse-Yutz near Metz, France. Decorated with coral and red enamel, they date from the early fourth century BC. (British Museum, London)

more isolated from innovative developments than were the Celtic-speakers of Britain and Gaul.

The archaeological record indicates that the economies of Gaul and Britain were much more closely integrated into that of the Hallstatt zone than were those of Ireland and the Iberian Peninsula. The Gaulish and British élites actively sought prestige objects of Hallstatt provenance, and craftsmen proved adept at creating local versions of such objects. Atlantic France has yielded many hoards rich in the long swords so characteristic of the Hallstatt tradition. In Britain, the contacts with the Hallstatt zone are, perhaps, even more evident. Among the earliest examples of an object made of iron to be found in Britain is a Hallstatt C sword recovered from Llyn Fawr above the Rhondda in Wales. Thrown into a lake, it was found in association with a locally made iron sickle, a precise imitation of a native bronze prototype, indicating that the technology imported from mainland Europe was rapidly being adopted to serve local needs. Other metal objects from the Hallstatt zone found in Britain include horse trappings, cart fittings, razors, bronze buckets and cauldrons, pins and *fibulae* (safety-pin-like brooches). Evidence from Ireland and the Iberian Peninsula is much sparser. It consists of a few variants of Hallstatt C swords and buckles and virtually no Hallstatt D material at all. In the case of Ireland this is particularly ironic. It would later be acknowledged as the Celtic country *par excellence*, but in the early Iron Age its contacts with the most dynamic Celtic centres seem to have been minimal.

Those centres underwent great changes in the period 450–400 BC, changes which mark the end of the Hallstatt era. In the Hallstatt D core zone, rich burials came to an end and the elaborate hillforts were abandoned. Judging by the burial evidence, new and rather different élites arose in areas to the north of that core zone. There, the dead were accompanied to the afterlife, not by the ceremonial weapons of the Hallstatt tradition but by real weapons, and not by cumbersome four-wheeled vehicles but by usable two-wheel war chariots. Objects relating to feasting and wine drinking continued to be prominent, but they were mainly of Etruscan rather than Greek origin. In some places – Dürrnberg, for example, or Hohenasperg – the new order seems to have been an evolution from the old, but by 400 BC the regions with the richest material culture offer evidence, in social organization and in art, of a society both original and innovative.

Much has been written about the causes of this change. The decreasing contacts with the Greek colonial cities – Massalia in particular – may have been the consequence of a reorientation of Mediterranean trade. The greater contacts with the Etruscans can be seen as the result of their expansion towards the Po valley, possibly caused by the pressures placed upon Etruria by the rising power of Rome. The abandonment of the elaborate hillforts is more problematic. The economy which sustained them may well have been undermined by the tradition of ritually expunging the fruit of the community's surplus by burying it alongside deceased chieftains. Military conquest was probably more significant. In about 460 BC, Heuneburg was destroyed by fire, an accident possibly, although it is more likely that it, and other richly endowed hillforts, had become the envy of aggressive neighbours. Indeed, the increasingly warlike tomb deposits of the following centuries suggest that the wealthy centres of the Hallstatt D core zone were overwhelmed by warrior peoples dwelling to the north of that zone.

These developments provide the context of the new core areas which would set the scene for the opening of the last phase of the Celtic Iron Age. The richest of them lay in the middle Rhineland and the Mosel valley where, in the century after 450 BC, numerous opulent warrior burials took place. A large number of the tombs were looted in antiquity and many of them were opened in the nineteenth century by excavators in pursuit of treasure and curios rather than precise archaeological data. Subsequent scientific excavation has established the importance of the region. It is especially rich in the beaked flagons and the *stamnoi* (bronze wine holders) of Etruria and in objects adorned with local adaptations of Etruscan motifs. Perhaps the most magnificent object found in the region is the bronze wine flagon excavated at Basse-Yutz on the Mosel; like the Dürrnberg flagon, it is Etruscan in inspiration and its even more fantastical

Detail of one of the Basse-Yutz wine flagons with its fantastical animal-shaped handle and spout. (British Museum, London)

animal heads indicate the direction in which Celtic art was evolving.

Among the most significant of the burial sites of the middle Rhineland is that at Waldalgesheim near Bingen; it was there in 1870 that artefacts in the so-called vegetal style were first recognized, giving rise to the concept of Waldalgesheim art.

Equally revealing are the fifth and fourth century tombs of the Marne valley in Champagne. The valley, some hundred kilometres north of the Hallstatt stronghold of Mont Lassois, had important Hallstatt sites, in particular that of Les Jogasses near Épernay, but so numerous in the valley are the tombs of the immediate post-Hallstatt era that it has been claimed that 'no other region can boast as many traces of the Celtic world as Champagne'. From the 1860s onwards, grave robbing became an important local industry there, with thousands of tombs opened in order to prise from them bronze and pottery objects for which there were eager purchasers. A small minority of the graves – about a hundred and fifty of those so far discovered – contained two-wheeled chariots, and the élite warriors buried in them were also accompanied by their swords, lances, knives and helmets. In addition, more lowly warriors were buried with their daggers, spears and javelins. Imports loom less large in Champagne than they do in the Rhineland, leading to speculation that the Marnians were a community dependent upon the more richly endowed peoples of the Rhineland.

The third of the immediate post-Hallstatt core areas was in Bohemia, a region which had its own links with Etruria via Dürrnberg, the Alps and the region

A panel from the Gundestrup Cauldron. On the right, warriors are blowing the trumpets which were a central feature of Celtic warfare. (Nationalmuseet, Copenhagen)

around Venice. The Celtic presence in Bohemia is a matter of great interest to its present inhabitants and some of the leading works on the Celts, in particular the contributions of Jan Filip, have been written in Czech. The influence of Etruria is particularly evident in the settlement at Závist near Prague, which contains a ritual centre strongly reminiscent of an Etruscan temple. As Celtic religious ceremonies were generally held in groves or by watersides, Závist is unique in the temperate Europe of the period and represents the earliest interpretation north of the Alps of the Mediterranean concept of a sacred enclosure. More characteristic of Celtic Bohemia, however, are weapon-rich burial sites, comparable with those of the Rhineland and the Marne, with the tombs of the male members of the dominant social group almost invariably containing full panoplies of swords, lances, armour and shields.

The emphasis on weaponry suggests a society geared for war. This is precisely the portrayal offered by classical writers. 'The whole race … is war mad,' wrote Strabo, 'high-spirited and quick to battle.' Writing of one engagement, Polybius described how their enemies 'were terrified by the fine order of the Celtic host, and the dreadful din, for there were innumerable horn blowers and trumpeters and the whole army was shouting their war cries'. Diodorus Siculus concurred: 'They blow into [their trumpets] and produce a harsh sound which suits the tumult of war … They loudly recite the deeds of valour of their ancestors and proclaim their own valorous quality, at the same time abusing and making little of their opponent and attempting to rob him beforehand of his fighting spirit.'

These descriptions are reminiscent of those of Bronze Age Homeric Greece and have at least an echo in the earliest Irish and Welsh poetry. In both those traditions, and presumably also in that of the Iron Age Celts of mainland Europe, members of the élite upheld their position through their success as raiders, success which allowed them to reward their followers with feasts and with prestige objects. Indeed, it was probably their prowess as raiders which allowed the Rhineland and Marne élites to overwhelm those of the Hallstatt core zone. As Cunliffe has pointed out: 'Once the raid had become an established part of the status system, there was an inbuilt imperative to intensify,' for the more successful a raid leader, the larger the number of followers and the greater their expectations. Although the immediate post-Hallstatt core areas appear to have been inhabited by communities enjoying a high degree of stability, the 'inbuilt imperative to intensify' could lead to ever-larger bands of marauding warriors increasingly divorced from any territorial base. It was this development, it could be argued, which triggered the dynamic peregrinations of the Celts in the fourth century BC. And in their journeyings, they carried with them an art more sophisticated than anything hitherto seen in temperate Europe.

Detail of the trumpets and the trumpeters on the Gundestrup Cauldron. (Nationalmuseet, Copenhagen)

chapter two

The Celtic
Heyday

'The Early Celtic Lands' (The Stock Market)

I N the winter of 1857, Hans Kopp, an enthusiast for antiquities, noticed, when walking along the banks of the northernmost tip of Lake Neuchâtel in western Switzerland, a series of wooden piles in the shallow waters of the lake. He investigated, gathered up some forty iron objects lying in the mud around the piles and showed them to his patron, the collector Friedrich Schwab. Thus began the exploration of the prehistoric site of La Tène (which means the shallows), work which was conducted with varying degrees of intensity from 1857 to 1917. The waters and the boggy land representing the ancient bed of the River Thiele, a stretch of some 115 metres, produced an astonishing number of artefacts, including 269 spearheads, 166 swords, 41 axes, 29 shields, 8 cauldrons and 382 *fibulae*. Initially, La Tène was believed to be a settlement of pile dwellings, but the overwhelming preponderance of weapons among the objects discovered there gave rise to the belief that it was an arsenal. However, by the early twentieth century, the realization that La Tène lacked evidence of metalwork production caused it to be seen as a military encampment. By mid century, increasing knowledge of the votive deposits found in many parts of Europe led to the notion that it was a cult centre at which warrior pilgrims dedicated weapons to the gods. Perhaps all the interpretations have an element of truth.

The finds from Hallstatt were already known when the La Tène discoveries burst upon the world. The La Tène objects were recognized as being in a more developed and elaborate style of workmanship than those of Hallstatt. Thus the Hallstatt artefacts were assigned to the early phase of the Celtic Iron Age (750–450 BC) and those of La Tène to its late phase (450 to the end of the pre-Christian era). In 1872, when Hans Hildebrant successfully advocated that Hallstatt should be the name of the first phase, he also ensured that the later phase should be known as La Tène. It

Lake Neuchâtel, Switzerland
with the town of Neuchâtel
on its shore.

*The site of La Tène on Lake
Neuchâtel.*

soon became apparent that the La Tène objects had their predecessors, particularly
those discovered in the three immediate post-Hallstatt core zones of the Rhineland,
the Marne and Bohemia. By 1902, discussions among archaeologists had led to the
classification of the La Tène era: A (450–400 BC), B (400–250 BC), C (250–150 BC),
D (150–0 BC); a further category was later added to take account of British and
Irish artefacts of the first and second centuries AD.

Of the finds at La Tène itself, the great majority were dated to period C, with
some 10 per cent belonging to period D, which indicates that the site was in use for
at least two hundred years. It yielded nothing belonging to periods A and B. Thus,
although La Tène gave the style a name, western Switzerland cannot be considered
its birthplace. The Rhineland offers many examples of period A, and there are those
who advocate the claims of that region, and stress in particular the innovativeness
of the designs associated with Waldalgesheim. But where La Tène art originated is
unknown and unlikely to be known. It is difficult to sum up its essence other than
to emphasize that it is in marked contrast with the art of classical antiquity. The
adjectives used to describe it include abstract, curvilinear, non-narrative, sinuous,
fantastical, shape-changing, dream-like, voluted, elusive, triadic, phytomorphic and
zoomorphic. Asymmetry is sometimes mentioned, although the Battersea shield,
described as 'the noblest creation of late Celtic art', is superbly symmetrical. Frank
Delaney conjures up an image of the art: 'a tendril of a plant teased into itself, then
spun outwards until it becomes a pattern, a whorl, a whole inner world, leaping,
coiling, dancing'. In the last resort, the art defies definition, yet assemblages of La
Tène artefacts have a mysterious unity that is immediately recognizable.
Furthermore, they have, for modernists and post-modernists, an immediate appeal
beyond that of the formalism of classical art.

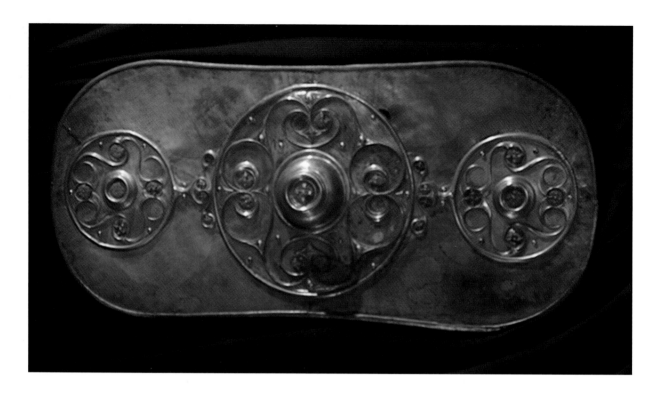

The Battersea shield. It is in fact the bronze face and binding of a shield which had probably been made of wood. Discovered in the Thames, it dates from the first century BC and has been described as 'the noblest creation of late Celtic art'. (British Museum, London)

Although large quantities of artefacts in the La Tène style have survived, only a partial appreciation of the art is possible. Examples of its usage in textile-making and wood-carving have almost all vanished. If there were painters among the artists, their work – apart from designs on pottery – no longer survives. Thus knowable La Tène art is primarily metalwork. To see it as a form of decoration, of art for art's sake, would be a gross underestimation of its significance. As Ruth and Vincent Megaw put it: 'Celtic art is the visible expression of a system of ideas, where even the most seemingly non-representational motifs may have a precise, perhaps religious, meaning.' Its modern appreciators cannot know what meaning the artists were seeking to communicate or whether the acquirer of an artefact was fully aware of that meaning. But indubitably, the skills of the artists were devoted to more than mere adornment. In addition, post-Renaissance distinctions between high art and folk art would have been meaningless to the La Tène practitioners. Although the most skilful artists were no doubt those who made the prestige objects sought by the rich, the artistry deployed in the making of mundane things – from buckets to fire-dogs – is central to the enduring appeal of La Tène art.

Much effort has been expended upon establishing its chronology and in analysing the influences upon it, with the work of Paul Jacobsthal (1944) and the Megaws (1989) offering the most authoritative framework. La Tène A is considered to owe something to the late Hallstatt tradition with its emphasis on abstract geometric forms. That tradition is also a forerunner of La Tène in the sense that it offers precedents for native adaptations of Mediterranean artefacts. Among such precedents is one of the lions on the Hochdorf Greek cauldron, which was locally replaced, not by an exact replica, but by an altogether more whimsical beast. Borrowings from the Etruscans and Greeks, plant-based motifs in particular, were also a potent influence. The Celtic affection for extravagantly fanciful zoomorphic shapes may have its ultimate origins among the Scythians, although the inspiration probably came via the Scythian elements absorbed by the Etruscans and the Greeks rather than directly from the people of the Steppes.

As the La Tène A style evolved into the styles of the B, C and D periods, these influences were brought together in a remarkable synthesis which culminates in the triumphs of later Celtic art. The masterpieces found in France include the superb

helmet of Agris, the bronze statue from Essonne near Paris, the *phalera* (an ornamental disc or plate) from the Marne valley and the disc from Auvers-sur-Oise. England can offer the Battersea shield, the Desborough mirror and the Waterloo Bridge helmet, Wales the Trawsfynydd tankard, the Capel Garmon fire-dogs and the fine metalwork recovered from Llyn Cerrig Bach, and Scotland the Netherurd Torque and the Torrs horse armour. As is the case with Hallstatt D, La Tène finds are rare in Ireland and in the Iberian Peninsula; it has already been suggested that this may have relevance with regard to the archaic character of the Celtic languages of those regions.

La Tène objects found in Italy range from the helmet from Apulia and the torques of Ancona to the elaborate *fibulae* from Padua and Brescia. Germany has yielded magnificent torques, such as those from Trichtingen and Waldalgesheim, as well as the *fibulae* from Parsberg and elsewhere. Switzerland offers a range of La Tène material in addition to those found in the type site, and Austria too has its riches, such as the plethora of grave goods from Mannersdorf, east of Vienna. Further to the east and the south-east, La Tène objects are widely distributed, with the Czech Republic, Hungary, Slovakia, Slovenia, Croatia, Serbia, Moldova, Ukraine, Romania, Bulgaria and Turkey all yielding significant finds. So rich is Hungary in Celtic gold objects that an entire room of the National Museum at Budapest is devoted to them. Romania offers perhaps the most astonishing of all La Tène objects: the helmet from Ciumeşti crowned by a bird with moveable wings. Furthermore, much of

The parade helmet found at Agris near Angoulème, France, in 1981. Dating from the fourth century BC, gold, iron, bronze, silver and coral were used in its creation. Combining geometric patterns and elements of the vegetal style, it is one of the finest examples of Celtic art. (Musée de la Société Archéologique et Historique de la Charente, Angoulème)

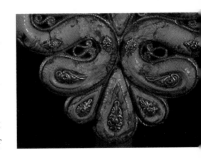

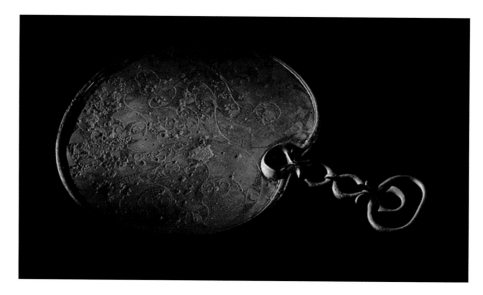

The superbly symmetrical mirror found at Desborough, Northamptonshire, England, dates from the late first century BC. (British Museum, London)

temperate Europe is awash with coins bearing designs based upon those of the coins of the kingdom of Macedonia; they illustrate the way in which Celtic metalworkers could transform the precise representational images of Greek tradition into a bewildering array of abstract forms.

The artefacts noted above were all made of iron, bronze, gold or electrum; unalloyed silver was rarely used by La Tène artists. There is, however, evidence of the ability of the artists to work skilfully with other materials. The dearth of evidence of woodworking has already been noted; the craft was undoubtedly practised, for hoards prove that almost every tool used by a modern woodworker was available in the La Tène era. A few wooden votive objects deposited in ritual shafts have survived remarkably well. The timbers lining the shaft at Fellbach-Schmiden near Stuttgart have been dated to 125 BC and the shaft has yielded animal carvings of great charm. Stone sculptures of considerable merit have also come to light; they include a joined pair of heads and a seated figure from the Rhône estuary and a curious head of a deity from Heidelberg. Work in glass shows sophistication and the rare textile survivals offer at least a suggestion that weavers making cloth for that Celtic invention, the trousers, favoured patterns resembling those of Scottish tartans.

Apart from metal, the medium which offers ample proof of the skills of La Tène artists is pottery. Although some Celtic-speaking regions – Ireland and highland Britain, for example – were virtually aceramic in the last pre-Christian centuries, other regions had rich traditions of pottery-making. Among the most aesthetically pleasing objects discovered in the cemeteries of the Marne valley is a fourth century BC vase painted in what seems a very modern manner. Stamped decorations of a distinctly La Tène character have been found on flasks from Slovakia and vases from

Dobova in Serbia. From Pavia in northern Italy and from near Berne in Switzerland come handsome banded vases, cups and bowls. Brittany has yielded attractive terracotta objects with decorations which seem to be an adaptation in ceramic of motifs popular among metalworkers. The example of metalworkers also seems to have inspired the maker of a vase from Czobaj in Hungary, with its rams' head handles, and the maker of the zoomorphic handle of a terracotta pot from Peçine in Serbia.

The fact that artefacts in the La Tène tradition have been found over so extensive an area and in such far-flung regions raises a number of questions. Were all those regions occupied by Celtic-speakers? Were all La Tène objects made by Celts and did all Celtic communities produce La Tène objects? The answer to the last question is no, for – as has been seen – Ireland and the Celtic-speaking regions of Spain were largely outside the La Tène tradition. It is unlikely also that La Tène art was exclusively produced by the Celts; such was its appeal that it is probable that it was adopted by other peoples.

The primary question is the first one. Can it be assumed that, by the third century BC, Celtic-speakers occupied the whole of the wide band of territory in which La Tène artefacts have been found – a band extending from Scotland to Turkey? 'Occupied' is probably a misleading word, for it should not be considered that the territory was exclusively inhabited by Celtic-speakers or even that all Celtic-speaking regions were necessarily contiguous. However, other evidence – place-

The head and antlers of a wooden stag found in a cult pit in Felbach-Schmiden in Baden-Württenberg, Germany. It dates from the early first century BC. (Landesmuseum, Stuttgart)

names for example — makes it possible to assert with some confidence that Celtic-speakers inhabited, or at least were at some time present in, all the regions in which La Tène artefacts have been found in some quantity.

It has been suggested that the Celtic language or languages spread westwards through acculturation. Should it be assumed that they spread southwards and south-eastwards through the same process, or, in this case, can invasion and migration be invoked? They can indeed, for on the southward and south-eastward expansion the classical authors are unequivocal. Their evidence makes sense; raid-based communities such as those of the La Tène élite were far more likely to direct their invasions southwards and south-eastwards to lands containing rich cities and sanctuaries replete with prestige objects — the lands of the wine they craved — than westwards to regions of subsistence agriculture.

The bottom panel of the Battersea shield. The decoration is based upon interlocking s-motifs and includes swastika patterns surrounded by red glass. (British Museum, London / Werner Forman Archive)

Naturally enough, the Roman authors were chiefly concerned with Celtic incursions into Italy. Latin writers viewed the incursions as attacks specifically upon the growing Roman state, although it is probably more correct to view them as part of a power struggle involving not only the Romans but also the Etruscans and the Greeks — indeed as part of the complex politics of the Italian Peninsula as a whole. As has been seen, there is reason to believe that the Italian Lake region had long been the home of Lepontic-speaking Celts. The invasions of the decades after 400 BC, however, brought far more extensive parts of northern Italy under Celtic control. Livy, writing *c.* 20 BC, drew upon a mass of writings and memories concerning the invasions. 'There is a tradition', he wrote, 'that it was the lure of Italian fruit and especially of wine ... that drew the Gauls to cross the Alps ... [They] collected the surplus population ... and set out with a vast host.'

The lure of fruit and wine is also mentioned by Pliny the Elder writing *c.* AD 79. References to surplus population occur in the work of Pliny's contemporary, Pompeius Trogus, while the Greek historian, Polybius, writing in about 150 BC, stressed the warlike nature of the invaders, their mercenary bands and the numerous followers of the leading warriors. The archaeological record confirms the written evidence. The lure of wine is amply corroborated. Innumerable burial sites, particularly in Champagne, suggest an overpopulated society, and the multiplicity of grave goods indicates that raiding warriors were an integral part of Celtic communities. Furthermore, the apparently rapid contraction in the population of the Marne valley after about 400 BC, and similar, although less definite, evidence from the Rhineland and Bohemia suggest that the early fourth century saw an exodus of people from the core areas of early La Tène culture.

In 391 BC, the invaders attacked the Etruscan city of Clusium — the modern Chiusi near Perugia. In 390, they defeated a Roman army on the River Allia, a tributary of the Tiber. Marching on Rome, they captured the entire city save for

This bronze statue of a warrior was found at St-Maur-en-Chausée near Beauvais and dates from the first century BC. (Musée Départemental de l'Oise, Beauvais)

the Capitol; that, according to tradition, was saved when its garrison was warned by the honking of geese. Bribed with a thousand pounds of gold, the attackers moved northwards to what would later be known as Cisalpine Gaul, or the Gaul south of the Alps. Increasingly a region of Celtic settlement, Cisalpine Gaul came to include not only the foothills of the Alps and the Lake region but also most of the Po valley and the lands along the eastern Italian coast as far south as Ancona. Among its inhabitants were the Insubres around Mediolanum or Milan, the Cenomani around Brescia, the Boii – possibly originating in Bohemia – around Bologna, and the Senones – migrants from Champagne, perhaps – north of Ancona. They were in contact with fellow Celts beyond the Alps, some of whom were to migrate southwards to join them in the late fourth and the third centuries.

Among the places colonized by the Celts was the ruined Etruscan city of Marzabotto between Bologna and Florence. Mid-nineteenth-century excavations there yielded a mass of material, *fibulae* in particular, which were seen in 1871 by French and Swiss archaeologists attending the International Congress of Prehistoric Archaeology at Bologna. They recognized that the finds closely paralleled those discovered in Champagne and Neuchâtel. That recognition, it has been claimed, was 'the turning point in Celtic Studies'. Assuming that the accounts of Livy, Polybius and others were correct, the Marzabotto material had undoubtedly been produced by Gauls or Celts. So close were the similarites between that material and the artefacts found at Neuchâtel and Champagne that the Celts must have been responsible for those artefacts also. Thus, it was at Bologna in 1871 that La Tène art was fully accepted as the art of the Celts.

The establishment of Celtic settlements in early-fourth-century Italy had widespread repercussions. Following Rome's humiliation in 390 BC, it took a generation for the city to reassert its authority over Latium. In 385 BC, Celtic mercenaries, sailing from the Syracusan port of Ancona, began serving Rome's enemy, Dionysius of Syracuse, and the presence of Celts in southern Italy is indicated by the superb La Tène helmet discovered at Canosa di Puglia. The Etruscans, already in decline, were further enfeebled by Celtic raids, enabling Rome to overwhelm Etruria by 309 BC. The weakness of Etruria and the recruitment of Celtic mercenaries by Syracuse, and later by the Carthaginians, together with the covetousness of the inhabitants of Cisalpine Gaul, fed the raid mentality central to the culture of the Celts. So numerous were their attacks upon Roman territory that it could be argued that the city was obliged to become a major military power – the first step towards becoming a world empire – because of its need to crush them. By 283 BC, Rome's nearest Celtic adversary, the Senones, had been decisively conquered and a vast army of Gauls were defeated at the battle of Telemon in 225. However, two hundred years were to pass before Cisalpine Gaul was finally subdued.

It was during the years of that long conflict, particularly in the period 390 to 285 when there was a close-range threat, that the Roman image of the Celt was created. That image would prove long-lasting; Cicero's anti-Celtic arguments in the courts of the Rome of the first century BC, and some of Julius Caesar's comments on his adversaries in the Gallic wars of that century can be traced back to the stereotypes created in the fourth century. Those stereotypes were primarily concerned with the Celts as warriors. The Roman writers were bemused by the fact that the Celts had a ritual concept of warfare: many of them went naked into battle; the issue between contending armies could, they believed, be settled through single combat; triumphant noise and bragging were as important as the fighting itself; the honour of a warrior demanded that in defeat he should commit suicide; attack involved initial ferocious onslaughts, which quickly led to wild despair if the onslaughts were checked. To the Romans, the Celts were barbarians lacking the methodical discipline which is the hallmark of civilization. Yet, in order to magnify the achievement of defeating them, they had to be portrayed as noble in their savagery, the theme of some of the finest sculptures of the ancient world.

Describing the fourth-century Celtic migrations, Pompeius Trogus wrote of 'three hundred thousand men seeking new territories. Some settled in Italy … some, led by birds, spread through the head of the Adriatic and settled in Pannonia' (essentially, eastern Austria, western Hungary and Croatia). The large quantity of La Tène B (400–250) artefacts found in Pannonia would seem to confirm the notion that a Celtic thrust into the central Danube basin coincided with that into northern Italy. Archaeologists have suggested that a series of cemeteries across western Hungary – including the celebrated graves at Sopron – denotes the route of the migrants. Some of them moved eastwards to the heart of modern Romania and others southwards, Pompeius Trogus noting that in 358 BC they were in conflict with the Illyrians of the Dalmatian coastlands.

The intensity of the Celtic colonization of the Danubian lands has been much debated. Contributors to the catalogue of the great Celtic exhibition at Venice claimed that, by c. 200 BC, the Carpathian Basin had been 'completely Celticized'. On the other hand, Colin Renfrew, while acknowledging the abundance of La Tène artefacts in the region, doubts whether 'numerous Celtic peoples ever settled in Pannonia'. Barry Cunliffe is more circumspect. He accepts that there were large-scale folk migrations, but believes that many of the region's La Tène artefacts could have been produced by other peoples who had adopted the style. The virtual omnipresence of the La Tène culture in the Danubian lands can also be attributed in part to trade, intermarriage or mercenary activities. With occasional La Tène finds occurring as far to the east as the Crimea and the Don Basin, the correlation between settlement and archaeological discoveries should not be pressed too far.

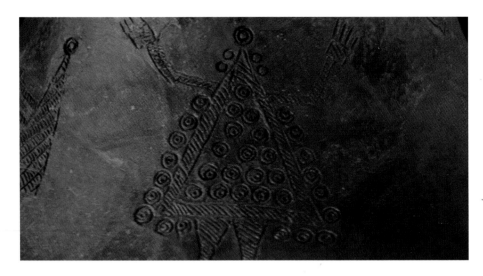

Schematic figures incised on pots dating from the fifth century BC and found at Sopron in Hungary. (Naturhistorisches Museum, Vienna)

While the concept that the Celts totally dominated the Danube Basin from the mid fourth to the mid second century BC is probably untenable, archaeological and literary evidence makes it difficult to reject the notion that, during those years, they were a powerful presence, at least in Pannonia and Illyria. Those regions were near enough to the Hellenistic world for their Celts to be objects of curiosity to the Greeks. The fighting skills of the Celts were known in Greece, for Dionysius of Syracuse had brought his mercenaries there in 367 to support Sparta in its war with Thebes. Their usefulness as mercenaries was commented upon by Xenophon (died 354), and Plato (died *c.* 348) discussed their characteristics as did Aristotle (died 322). Aristotle's pupil, the Emperor Alexander, met a deputation of Illyrian Celts in 335 when, instead of expressing their awe of him, they declared that their only fear was that the sky might fall upon them. In 323, following his extraordinary victories and shortly before his death, Alexander received at Babylon the greetings

An example of a Sopron pot. (Naturhistorisches Museum, Vienna)

of a group of Celts, whose travels had probably given them an opportunity to weigh up the looting possibilities of Greece and Asia Minor.

None of the Greek commentators of the fourth century BC give the impression that the Celts represented a threat to them. The situation changed as a result of the increasing chaos in the decades following Alexander's death. The Celts attacked Macedonia and Thrace in 298 and again in 281, when they killed the eldest son of Ptolemy, the founder of Egypt's Greek dynasty. The following year saw the great Celtic eruption when a vast horde moved southwards. Macedonia was pillaged and then, in the middle of the winter, some thirty thousand warriors attacked Greece itself. They were led by Brennus, a name which was probably a title. The leader of the attack upon Rome over a century earlier had also been called Brennus. They were lured, wrote Pausanius – a Greek of the second century AD, who drew upon earlier lost chronicles – by the riches of the great sanctuaries, particularly that of Delphi high on the slopes of Mount Parnassus. Initially, they had some success, but their depredations came to an end when they were foiled by thunder, hail and landslides. Terrified by nature's malevolence, which they interpreted as divine punishment, they withdrew. Brennus committed suicide and the retreating force suffered fearful retribution at the hands of the Greeks. After the events of 280–78, the fury of the Celts would be as deeply engraved upon the consciousness of the Greeks as it was upon that of the Romans.

Some of the survivors of the great incursion settled around Belgrade, where they became known as the Scordisci. Others established a Celtic enclave at Thylia on the east coast of what would later be Bulgaria. Many enrolled as mercenaries serving the rulers of the successor kingdoms of Alexander's empire. In 274 in Egypt, for example, there were Celts serving in the army of Ptolemy II, and there are references in 217 and 186 to their service in the armies of his successors. The most

The theatre at the Sanctuary of Apollo at Delphi. Built in the fourth century BC, it could accommodate five thousand spectators.

Further views of the Sanctuary of Apollo at Delphi. The Sanctuary had rich treasuries which were probably the objective of the raids of the Celts.

remarkable venture of the survivors of the incursion was that of the Tectosages, the Trocmi and the Tolistobogii, three tribes of invaders who, to judge from the number of women and children among them, were in search of land rather than loot. In 278, they agreed to enter the service of Nicodemus, king from 278 to 250 of Bithynia, just across the Bosphorus in Anatolia, an agreement which led to the establishment of a Celtic state in Asia.

Nicodemus sought mercenaries in order to enrich himself at the expense of his neighbours. However, the incomers, who came to be known as the Galatians — the Greeks' name for Celts — eventually established their own polity in northern Phrygia around what later became the Turkish capital of Ankara. A ruling class of semi-nomadic pastoralists with the native Phrygians as their vassals, they terrorized the rich cities of the coasts of Anatolia. In the 230s, the growing power of Pergamum resisted their demand for tribute and in 233 inflicted a severe defeat upon them. Over the following years, the Galatians, reinforced perhaps by further Celtic migrants, resumed their marauding. In the early second century, when Rome was being drawn into the affairs of Pergamum, a joint Roman and Pergame army defeated the marauders in 190 and sold forty thousand of them into slavery.

The Galatians seem long to have been successful in retaining their cultural distinctiveness. There was little that was unique in their material culture; this at least is the impression gained by a visitor to Ankara's wonderful Museum of Anatolian Civilizations. Classical sources, however, note their typically Celtic institutions — their tribal assemblies, for example, and the ceremonies conducted at the *drunemeton*, a word which offers at least a suggestion that there were Galatian druids. Place-names too are indicative; for a latterday Celt, passing through Bâlâ while travelling from Ankara to Cappadocia is an emotional experience. Galatia was still a meaningful term in the last century BC when its boundaries may have been wider than ever before. By then, however, it was subject to increasing Hellenization. When Paul wrote a letter to the Galatians *c.* AD 55, he was undoubtedly thinking in terms of a province rather than an ethnic group. Jerome's comment *c.* AD 385 that the Galatians spoke a language similar to that of the Treveri of the Mosel valley is fascinating; it can hardly have been true when it was made, but it preserves a folk memory of what had once been a real linguistic kinship.

The most significant legacy of the Galatians came, not from their triumphs, but from their defeats. Following Pergamum's victory in 233 BC, Attalus I commissioned a huge monument to celebrate its role as the defender of civilization against barbarism. Erected within the city's acropolis, probably in the sanctuary of Athena, a comment by Pliny the Elder suggests that it was made of bronze. Two of the finest statues in the museums of Rome were long considered to be marble copies of some of the Pergamum bronzes. One of them is the famous Dying Gaul in the Museo Capitolino; now known to have been made from Anatolian marble, there is growing acceptance that the original monument was not of bronze, and that the statue in Rome was part of the original composition completed at Pergamum in the 220s. The other is a statue at the Museo Nazionale Romano; it portrays a Celtic warrior who, in the moment of defeat, has killed his wife and is ending his own life by a sword thrust into the heart. The origin of its marble is unknown, and, for the moment at least, it is considered to be a Roman copy.

Pergamum's success in 190 inspired further monuments, including a great frieze, rich in images of Galatians, around the temple of Zeus, and sculptures of Celtic

The 'Dying Gaul'. The statue was part of a monument erected at Pergamum in the 220s BC to commemorate the victory of Attalus 1 over the Galatians. (Museo Capitolino, Rome)

Maiden Castle in Dorset, in southern England, and one of Europe's most magnificent hillforts. Its construction occurred in phases between about 350 and 50 BC. Extending over 120 hectares (forty-eight acres), it was captured by the Romans in AD 43. Skeletons of its Brythonic defenders were found during excavations.

trophies carved on the balustrade of the Temple of Athena. Remnants of these are exhibited at the Pergamon-Museum in Berlin. Of the five extant Roman copies of the Galatian figures, one is in Paris, one in Naples and three in Venice, all of them portraying the anguish of the vanquished. The commissioners of the monuments, Eumenes I and Attalus II, also presented a massive votive offering to the acropolis in Athens, where it was placed along the Wall of Kimon overlooking the Theatre of Dionysius. Even more than those at Pergamum, the Athens monument makes explicit the identification of the Celts with the Titans, the enemies of the Olympic gods of light and order, a theme emphasized in the work of the poet Callimachus, the third-century head of the Library at Alexandria.

Part of the fascination of the Pergame monuments is the virile, dignified pathos of the defeated Celts, particularly in the statues of the 220s, a portrayal which suggests that they were an enemy Pergamum was proud to have subdued. For the student of the Celts, however, more can be learnt from the apparently exact way the monuments delineate the appearance and the accoutrements of the Celts. The figures appear uncannily like north-western Europeans, a resemblance which would be heightened were they still to have their original paint; indeed, it has been suggested that, suitably dressed, they could well have been members of a Scottish regiment. Most of them are naked, a frequent feature of classical portrayals of the Celts, and based, it would appear, upon memories of the ferocious Gaesatae. All but one are beardless but most sport a heavy moustache, another characteristic frequently mentioned by Greek and Latin authors. They have lean, muscular bodies; obesity, noted Aristotle, was a punishable offence among the Celts. Some of them wear a torque, a distinguishing mark of the high-born Celtic warrior. The sculptures of trophies admirably illustrate Celtic war equipment – chain mail, shields, spears and trumpets – as does the armour beneath the figure of the Dying Gaul.

Although the Pergame monuments portray Celts in defeat, the era of their composition was the high-water mark of Celtic power. The traditional map of Celtic peoples inhabiting a huge expanse from Ankara to Galway and to Vigo was more meaningful in 250 to 200 BC than it had ever been before or would be in the future. By then, written sources were becoming more plentiful and they would take a quantum leap forward in the first century BC, particularly as the result of Julius Caesar's account of his years in Gaul. Archaeological evidence also becomes more abundant. Thus, it is possible to offer a portrayal of the Celts in the era of their greatest dominance.

In the presumably Celtic communities of the last pre-Christian centuries, a degree of unity may be discerned. Nevertheless, it would be wrong to assume that the Celtic lands had one uniform culture. As David Rankin commented, the characteristics of the Celts as described by the classical authors and as suggested by the archaeological record cannot be proved to have existed in their entirety in any Celtic community. As has been seen, La Tène art was rare in Spain and Ireland. With the exception of the Arras culture of east Yorkshire, cart burials are unknown in Britain. Cremation became the dominant funeral rite of most of the Celts of mainland Europe; it was not adopted in Britain and Ireland, and Spain offers evidence of practices similar to those of the Parsees of Bombay. Most mainland Celts built square houses, while those of the islands and parts of Iberia built round ones. Wheel-made pottery appears in the La Tène core areas from 400 BC onwards, but the technique was not used in Britain until the first century BC. Indeed, such were the distinctions between the mainland and the islands that it is perhaps not surprising that Strabo distinguished between the men of Britain and the Celti.

These are among the factors that have caused some scholars, John Collis, Simon James and Malcolm Chapman among them, to argue that the word Celt should not be applied to the inhabitants of Iron Age Britain. As they rightly stress, no classical author does so, and none of the inhabitants of the island called themselves Celts until Edward Lhuyd published his linguistic studies in 1707. Basic to their argument is their belief that the use of Celtic as a blanket term can force archaeological analysis into an overriding and predetermined Celtic straitjacket. They also suggest that the fascination with fine La Tène or Celtic metalwork obscures the fact that elaborate art is above all a marker of a wealthy ruling class rather than of an ethnic group. The debate has become somewhat acrimonious, particularly following accusations that the critics of Celticity are motivated by English hostility to demands for autonomy by the non-English inhabitants of the United Kingdom, and that their arguments are, consciously or unconsciously, an expression of Europhobia and 'Little Englandism'.

Such accusations are wide of the mark, especially in view of the fact that opponents of archaeological pan-Celticism do not suggest that Iron Age Britain had a uniform culture; rather is their emphasis upon the importance of regional diversity.

These are issues of substance, although the arguments of the anti pan-Celticists are not wholly convincing. Simon James in particular gives somewhat cavalier treatment to the undoubted fact that Iron Age Britain was Celtic-speaking. Perhaps the chief factor to consider when discussing the character of late Iron Age culture is not its divergence from some 'Celtic' norm, but rather the issue of how far from the Mediterranean the culture was located. Beyond the boundaries of classical civilization, there were successive bands of peripheries inhabited by communities of decreasing social and economic complexity. Britain, and even more so Ireland, was in one of the furthest of the bands.

The crux of the matter is the use of words. It is likely that none of the Celtic-speakers ever called themselves Celts. It is even more unlikely that they called themselves Gauls, especially in view of the possibility that, originally, Gaul meant stranger, or even enemy; the parallel here with the later word Welsh may be significant. Although there is much evidence that the words Celt and Gaul were interchangeable, Julius Caesar states that, in Gaul itself, only the peoples of the centre and the north-west – the region of the later Roman province of Gallia Lugdunensis – were truly Celts. The fact of the matter is that the classical authors were somewhat insouciant in their choice of names for their neighbours. Would all members of a widely dispersed people, although speaking a common language or a closely related group of languages, necessarily have had one single word to describe that people as a whole, or would they have identified themselves through a profusion of names for individual clans and tribes? As Miranda Green has argued, if the word Celt is to be proscribed, so should the word Greek be. 'The Greeks did not think of themselves as Greek, but as Athenian or Corinthian or whatever; it is because we see things in common between them that we call them Greek.' If sufficient 'things in common between them' may be discerned among the people traditionally defined as Celts, then the term Celt has validity. That means, of course, that it is not the Celts who do the defining; that is done for them. To quote Malcolm Chapman: 'The term Celtic carries with it the indelible connotation of "otherness".' The regional diversity of Britain – or for that matter of any of the other regions considered to be Celtic – is not a convincing argument against the use of the word Celt. As Simon James himself put it: 'Profound localism and strong cultural diversity on the one hand, and important linkages across wider areas on the other are not mutually exclusive … characteristics.'

Of 'the things in common', the most obvious must be the abundance of artefacts in the La Tène tradition present in most of the regions believed to have had Celtic inhabitants. Yet, a more fundamental definition of Celticity needs to have a linguistic base, for in the last resort, the Celts were those people who were Celtic-speaking – although few scholars would go so far as Joshua Whatmough, who attacked 'the extra-linguistic abuse of the word *Celtic*'. There have been valiant attempts to reconstruct 'Common Celtic', the ancestor of the Celtic languages spoken in the La Tène era, an exercise in reconstruction as theoretical as that involving Indo-European itself. Reconstructors face formidable problems. Evidence from the Britain and Ireland of the first Christian millennium provides some basis for the task. In comparison, mainland Europe yields little, for the surviving material is insufficient to allow a full understanding of the grammatical structure of the Celtic languages spoken there. Even if there were ample evidence, reconstructing an ancestor language is full of pitfalls; reconstructions of Latin from the plentiful material provided by its daughter languages result in constructs somewhat different from actual verifiable Latin. Even if it were possible fully to reconstruct 'Common Celtic', the result would not be a primal entity; it would, as Mallory put it, be 'a slice of one strand of a linguistic continuum'. As 'Common Celtic' was presumably spoken over very extensive regions, its character would have been complicated by the likelihood that its speakers were in close contact with speakers of a variety of other languages for, as Rankin has commented: 'It is not easy to assume the monolingual uniformity of any inhabited area in ancient times.'

Of the materials available for the study of continental Celtic, the most accessible are the names of places, tribes and individuals contained in the writings of the classical authors. The names that are Celtic can readily be recognized, allowing scholars to assert that Celtic names were borne by the invaders of Italy, Pannonia, Illyria, Greece and Anatolia and by tribes in Gaul, Switzerland, Britain and elsewhere – and it would be reasonable to assume that the bearers of Celtic names were themselves Celtic-speaking. Furthermore, there are the modern place-names which can be traced back to their Celtic roots. Among them are Lyons, Leiden, Carlisle and Laon, all commemorating the Celtic god, Lug. The modern Welsh word *dŵr* (water) descends from the word which gave Europe the rivers Dee, Douro, Dordogne, Derwent, Durance and Oder, and the word *pen* (head) is cognate with Pennine, Apennine and Pindus. Memories of Celtic mercenaries gave a name to the Gallipoli in Thrace and to that in Puglia. Celtic names for cities include Vienna, Milan, Paris and London, all evidence of the vast regions in which the Celtic languages were once spoken.

Several of the classical authors state that the Celts spurned the written word, but it would seem that such comments refer to the unwillingness of the Celtic priesthood to commit their lore to writing rather than to opposition to writing *per se*. The written materials produced by the Celts themselves include words on

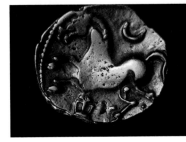

One of the coins minted during the revolt of Vercingetorix. Its obverse bears his likeness and name and the reverse depicts an interpretation of the horse motifs which featured on the coinage of the Macedonian kings. (Musée des Antiquités Nationales, St-Germain-en-Laye)

ceramics, weapons and coins, and inscriptions on metal and stone monuments. The scripts employed were borrowed from neighbouring peoples. The earliest examples of Celtic writing come from the region of the Golasecca culture around the Italian Lakes, in lettering based upon Etruscan characters. In Spain, the scripts of the Phoenicians and the Iberians were pressed into service, in southern Gaul and the Balkans that of the Greeks and in northern Gaul, Pannonia and Britain that of the Romans.

Inscriptions on ceramics include about a dozen sixth or fifth century word-bearing vases from the Golasecca region, and some two hundred pieces of pottery discovered in southern Gaul. Most of them offer little information beyond Celtic names, presumably those of the object's owner or maker. Switzerland has yielded a La Tène sword with an indubitably Celtic name, Kosisios, engraved on the blade, and a torque bearing the name of the Nitiobriges people has been unearthed in Champagne. More information comes from coins, which were probably first used by the Celts as a result of payments to mercenaries. By the third century BC, some at least of the Celtic peoples were minting their own coinage. They sometimes bore a name – that of either the location of the mint or the ruler who had authorized the minting. The Gaul of the first century BC produced coins bearing, among other names, that of the great Gallic hero Vercingetorix. Before the end of that century, Britain had produced its first examples of artefacts bearing lettering. They were the coins of the Atrebates, the Catuvellauni and the Trinovanti peoples; some of them carried the word Camu – Camulodunum or Colchester, the capital of

The Botorrita Tablet, discovered near Saragossa, Spain, in 1970. Made of bronze, it is engraved with some two hundred words. Their meaning has not been fully elucidated, but it is probable that they represent some kind of legal text. Employing a script developed from that of the Phoenicians, the tablet is proof that a Celtic language was in use in northern Spain in the first century BC. (Museo de Saragossa, Saragossa)

Cunobelinus, Shakespeare's Cymbeline and the Cynfelin of Welsh tradition.

Stone and metal monuments with inscriptions in Celtic have been found in Gaul, Italy and Spain. Southern Gaul is the most abundant source with some seventy inscriptions in Greek script; the information they offer is disappointing, for most of them are very brief dedications or epitaphs. Far more exciting is the bronze Botorrita Tablet discovered near Saragossa in 1970. A legal text dating from the first century BC, it consists of some two hundred words. Until its discovery, there was some doubt about the nature of the language of the so-called Celtiberians, who inhabited most of the northern half of the Iberian Peninsula. As the language of the tablet is indubitably Celtic, the discovery at Botorrita is of key importance in the history of Celtic studies. But even the Botorrita Tablet seems almost a minor find compared with the tablet which came to light at Coligny near Lyon in 1897. With 2,121 lines of lettering, it is by far the largest ancient Celtic document ever discovered. Engraved in Latin characters, it lists the sixty-two months of a five-year cycle and is a highly sophisticated attempt to adapt the phases of the moon to solar rhythms. As Venceslas Kruta put it: the Coligny Calendar displays 'a knowledge of celestial movements accrued over several centuries, as well as the ability to create mathematical models to express them'.

Thus, the linguistic evidence, fractured and incomplete although it is, permits the assertion that, in the later centuries of the pre-Christian era, Celtic was indeed spoken from Spain to Turkey, from Ireland to Pannonia and from Belgium to Italy. Linguists postulate that there were at least four forms of continental Celtic: the Celtiberian of the Iberian Peninsula, the Lepontic of northern Italy, an inadequately documented language spoken in the Danube basin and beyond, and the Gaulish of Gaul; furthermore, in view of Julius Caesar's celebrated comments on the three divisions of Gaul, the inhabitants of that region could well have spoken several

The Coligny Calendar, the most remarkable of all ancient examples of Celtic inscriptions. The bronze tablet, with its 2,212 words arranged in sixteen columns, was found broken into fragments, suggesting that it had perhaps been ritually destroyed. (Musée de la Civilisation Gallo-Romaine, Lyon)

markedly different versions of Gaulish. Brythonic, the P-Celtic language spoken in most of Britain, is believed to be closely related to the Gaulish of central and north-western Gaul. Pictland in north-eastern Scotland is also believed to have had P-Celtic-speaking inhabitants; one form of Pictish, however, may represent a pre-Indo-European survival. Ireland was certainly Celtic-speaking, although the traditions preserved in the *Leabhar Gabhála* (The Book of Conquests) – suggest that some of its inhabitants were more 'Celtic' than others. Q-Celtic was dominant in Ireland, but Ptolemy's list of place-names, compiled in the second century AD, indicates that the island had some P-Celtic-speakers. In the same way, evidence from Gaul – presumed to have been a P-Celtic-speaking country – suggests that it also may well have contained some Q-Celtic-speakers; there are linguists, however, who argue that too much significance has been attached to the P and Q distinction.

Of the other markers of Celtic identity, religious beliefs will be discussed later. Their methods of warfare have been mentioned already. It would be wrong, however, to assume that those methods were uniform throughout the regions of Celtic speech. For example, the war chariot, which looms large in the history of the Britain of the first century AD, had been abandoned in Gaul at least a century earlier. Ancient Irish texts have much to say about such chariots, but they are absent from the Irish archaeological record. Evidence of the way the Celts fed themselves is considerable. Lacking the heavy plough with its coulter which turned the sod, their light plough or ard merely scratched the soil. The ard's criss-cross ploughing created an agrarian landscape characterized by what became known as 'Celtic fields'; yet, as these are abundant in Scandinavia, they cannot be considered to be uniquely

Detail from the Gundestrup Cauldron.

Celtic. The fields were planted with spelt and emmer wheat, barley, millet, beans and lentils, together with flax for weaving. Little game was eaten, and the favoured meat was pork; it featured widely in ritual burials, and boars were revered, as the many statuettes of them testify. The Celts kept hens, a practice they had borrowed from the Scythians, but the cat and the ass were unknown among them. Their cattle were small, as were their horses; the Gundestrup Cauldron portrays a procession of horses with the feet of the riders almost reaching the ground.

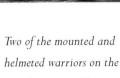

Two of the mounted and helmeted warriors on the Gundestrup Cauldron.

There are difficulties in interpreting sources which discuss the political and social organization of the Celts. The fullest classical source is that provided by Julius Caesar, but his writings are concerned with a brief timespan and do not offer a sustained account of Celtic society. There is some suggestion that Posidonius, the Greek polymath (died *c.* 50 BC), did provide such an account, but his voluminous works survive only in fragments copied by later writers. Furthermore, Greek and Latin writers imposed their own ideas on what they heard and saw, in particular by interpreting Celtic terms in the light of their own experience. Much can be gleaned from early Irish legal texts, and to some extent from the later Welsh texts also, but those texts were written down many centuries after the La Tène era and were often the work of ecclesiastics whose knowledge of ancient lore was filtered through their Christian world view. The value of those texts to a study of the island Celts of the first Christian millennium will be considered later.

To the extent that it is possible to portray the nature of La Tène society, it would appear to be highly hierarchical, although communities in more peripheral regions – inland Britain, for example – probably had a simpler, more egalitarian structure. Irish evidence suggests that Celtic rulers were originally semi-divine figures but by the first century BC power, in central Gaul at least, was in the hands of an aristocracy with one or more chief magistrates. Writing of that region, Julius Caesar noted that 'only two classes of men are of any account – the druids and the knights' – a statement which can, to some extent, be reconciled with later Irish and Welsh evidence. That evidence suggests that early Celtic polities in the islands had nothing approaching what could be called public administration, and that the workings of the law rested upon customary arrangements between kin groups. It may be presumed that this was also the case among the continental Celts, at least among those not greatly influenced by the classical civilizations. Indeed, it was presumably the absence among them of cohesive centralized state structures which obliged them eventually to accept the rule of Rome.

The usual portrayal of prehistoric temperate Europe is that of an intensely rural society, dotted with the 'Celtic' villages which museum curators delight in recreating. Yet, by the last centuries of the pre-Christian era, parts at least of Celtic Europe were able to sustain far larger units of population. As has been seen, there were quasi-urban settlements in the Hallstatt era – Heuneburg, for example – but, with the growing economic power of Rome, the trade and the wealth of adjoining Celtic lands increased, allowing the development of more fully urban centres. Indeed, it could be argued that Rome extended its political power northwards because, had Gaul, Rhaetia, Noricum and Pannonia remained outside the orbit of Roman power, the city and its territories would have been economically dependent upon regions over which they had no control.

Of the fortified towns or *oppida* of the last century or two of the pre-Christian era, among the most remarkable is Manching, some fifty kilometres north of Munich. It had an area of 360 hectars and was surrounded by a seven-kilometre wall, an example of the *murus gallicus* which so fascinated Julius Caesar. Built in its most complete form in 130–120 BC, the site itself and the ecology of the surrounding countryside have been intensely studied. Although only some 3 per cent of the immense interior has been fully excavated, the results have been astonishing. Its extensive industrial quarter has yielded proof of working in ceramics, metal, wood, leather, textiles, glass, bone and gemstones, and the inhabited areas have yielded sufficient evidence to indicate the existence of a large settlement of neat streets of thatched half-timbered houses. The need to fell timber for the houses, and above all for the wall, caused changes in the local vegetation. The rich local iron deposits were much exploited, in particular to produce the sixty tons of metal believed to have been deployed in making the nails securing the planks of the *murus gallicus*.

The stone foundations of the houses of the oppidum *of Numantia, Spain, captured by the Romans in 134 BC.*

The massive wall suggests that defence considerations were central to the establishment of Manching, although the construction of massive fortifications could have been inspired as much by a desire for flamboyant display as by real defensive needs. Manching's strategic position in the Danube valley also gave it a vital economic role; the 886 coins uncovered in the area already excavated are proof of the part Manching played in the trade between temperate and Mediterranean Europe.

Of the *oppida* defended by *muri gallici*, Manching was the most easterly. Regions beyond it, such as Bohemia and Pannonia, also had their *oppida*, for example the comprehensively looted settlement at

Stradonice from which thirty railway cars full of bones were removed in order to manufacture fertilizer, or the 150-hectar *oppidum* at Závist, superimposed upon a renowned Hallstatt site. It is calculated that in the last pre-Christian centuries, there were about a hundred and fifty *oppida* in Celtic-speaking Europe, with the largest number in Gaul. Julius Caesar listed twenty-nine Gallic tribes, some, such as the Helvetii, with up to twelve *oppida*, and all with at least one apiece. Bibracte, some fifty kilometres south-west of Dijon, has attracted the greatest attention. Extending over 135 hectares, it was the chief settlement of the Aedui tribe and was also a place of inter-tribal gatherings. Bibracte fascinated Napoleon III, and the studies he initiated there became central to the development of Celtic archaeological scholarship. The Iberian Peninsula also had its *oppida*. They were smaller than those of Gaul, which they probably predated. Among them was the 24-hectar *oppidum* of Numantia, halfway between Burgos and Saragossa. It contained rows of closely packed commodious houses, all with wine cellars and stone foundations. The rise of the *oppida* coincided with increasingly large-scale iron production, the use of the potter's wheel and a growing abundance of low-value coins – a key indicator of the emergence of a truly widespread money economy.

The footings of the buildings erected during the Roman reconstruction of Numantia.

The reconstruction of a Celtic house at Numantia.

By the era of the *oppida*, all the Celtic-speaking communities of mainland Europe were facing and succumbing to the power of Rome. Those of Cisalpine Gaul had already been severely weakened by Rome's victory at the battle of Telamon in 225 BC. During the early years of the Second Punic War (218–201), when Hannibal

An attempt at Butser Ancient Farm, Hampshire, England, to recreate the round houses of Iron-Age Britain.

A round house at Butser in the process of being built.

seemed master of northern Italy, many of the Celts of Cisalpine Gaul made common cause with him. Rome's eventual victory in the war brought Roman power to the River Po and beyond. Strabo stated that the Boii reacted by leaving the region around Bologna in which they had settled, and migrating beyond the Alps – a statement that finds some confirmation in the work of Pliny the Elder. The Romans seized Milan, the centre of the power of the Insubres, and established colonies at Cremona, Piacenza and Bologna. There was intense rural colonization too; even today, centuriation – a system of land-division based on decimal principles – is immediately apparent in aerial photographs of the Po valley. As a result of Roman expansion, many of the great estates of central Italy were worked by Celtic-speaking slaves; but slavery is not a condition conducive to language maintenance, as the fate of west African languages in the Americas amply proves.

By the first century BC, artefacts in the La Tène style were giving way to those acceptable to classical taste, local religious cults were being subsumed into the official Roman religion and Celtic personal names were yielding to Latin ones. In 81 BC, Cisalpine Gaul became a Roman province. Despite the turbulence caused by Spartacus's slave revolt of 73 to 71 BC – a revolt in which Celts were much involved – the inhabitants of the province were granted Roman citizenship in 49 BC. Although their Celtic-accented Latin gave rise to sarcasm in Rome, some of the greatest Latin authors, Livy, Virgil, Tacitus, the Plinys and Catullus among them, had strong links with the Po valley. There is some evidence that Celtic was still spoken in Cisalpine Gaul as late as the second century AD, and there are suggestions that Celtic words long survived in the dialects of the inhabitants of the southern slopes of the Alps.

Rome's struggle with Carthage, one of the factors in the conquest of the Cisalpine Celts, was wholly central to the subjugation of the Celts of the Iberian Peninsula. Following their defeat in the First Punic War (264–241), the Carthaginians used their enclaves on the Iberian coast as bases for their conquest of Iberia, which they hoped would serve as a counterpoise to the power of Rome. By 219, on the eve of the Second Punic War, their control of the peninsula extended as far north as the River Ebro. Renewed war gave Rome the opportunity to invade Iberia, and by 206 BC armies under the elder and younger Scipio had destroyed Carthaginian power there. In 197, the peninsula – apart from the homelands of the unconquered Asturies and the Cantabri – was organized as two Roman provinces, Hispania Citerior and Hispania Ulterior. The inhabitants, however, showed no willingness to accept the replacement of Carthaginian sovereignty by that of the Romans, and the Roman general, Gracchus, was obliged to subdue the Celtiberians stronghold by stronghold; according to Polybius, he destroyed three hundred of their cities (probably their forts) in the year 179–8 alone. Resistance continued, centred upon the *oppidum* of Numantia. In 134, a third Scipio besieged the *oppidum* for eight months, reducing its inhabitants to cannibalism. When they surrendered, Scipio, an experienced destroyer of cities – he had obliterated Carthage in 146 – razed Numantia to the ground and condemned its citizens to slavery.

In Iberia, as in Cisalpine Gaul, Roman control eventually led to Romanization, although Tacitus claimed that Celtic was still spoken there in the first century AD, and Silius Italicus (died AD 101) wrote of how the Gallaeci delighted in their war songs. Again as in the case of Cisalpine Gaul, Latin literature was to owe much to the lands of the Celtiberians – the native place of Quintilian, Seneca, Lucan and, above all, of Martial, who consciously identified himself with the Iberians and the Celts. In north-west Iberia, the Galicians – undoubtedly a word of Celtic origin, although they lived beyond the boundaries of what have traditionally been considered the lands of the Celtiberians – today delight in what they believe to be their Celtic origins. The history of Galicia in the early Christian centuries offers some basis for that belief, although it probably owes much to the assumption that no lands thrusting out into the Atlantic could be bereft of Celts.

By the early second century BC, the territories under Roman control consisted of two non-contiguous parts: Italy and the Iberian Peninsula. The links between them were by sea; it was Roman control of the sea that had forced Hannibal, when invading Italy in 218, to take his army and his elephants on an overland route

The hillfort or Celtic castro *of Monte Santa Tecla near A Guarda on the coast of Galicia, Spain. It is clear that the Galicians, like the Britons, favoured round rather than square or oblong houses.*

through southern Gaul and across the Alps. Ever since the establishment of Massalia *c.* 600 BC, the land link between Italy and Iberia – regions later known as Provence and Languedoc – had been increasingly drawn into the orbit of classical civilization. Celtic tribes such as the Saluvii of the Rhône delta had been so Hellenized that Julius Caesar considered their settlements to be *civitates* rather than *oppida*. Around Toulouse, there are fields so cluttered with *amphora* shards that, even today, ploughing presents problems. (It is estimated that forty million *amphorae* were imported into Gaul in the century after 150 BC.) By the mid-second century, the southern coastlands of Gaul were becoming thoroughly integrated into the economy of the Roman world. In 123 BC, the threat to Roman convoys posed by inland tribes led Rome to establish the province of Transalpine Gaul and also to destroy Entremont, the *civitas* of the Saluvii. In 118, Narbo Martius (Narbonne), the first Roman colony in Gaul, was founded. Romanization of the new province proved rapid. Indeed, Provincia Narbonensis, or Provence, with great Roman cities such as Arles, Nîmes, Orange and Aix, was to become as redolent of Roman power as Rome itself. Until the second quarter of the first century BC, the Romans were content to confine their power in Gaul to the Mediterranean littoral, where the climate and the vegetation were familiar to them. They had no desire to be involved in what they saw as Gallia 'Comata' – the land of the long-haired Gauls. In 58 BC, however, Julius Caesar was appointed governor of Transalpine Gaul, and also of Cisalpine Gaul and Illyria, an appointment which opened a new chapter in the history of the Romanization of the Celts.

While it was annexing Iberia and Provence, Rome was also flexing its muscles further to the east. It became involved in Illyria in 228, when it sent an expedition to suppress piracy and established a protectorate over the Dalmatian coast. In Macedonia, as in Cisalpine Gaul and Iberia, the wars with Carthage brought about an extension of Roman power. The alliance of Philip V of Macedon with Hannibal led in 198 to the subjugation of his kingdom, and in 146 to its division into Roman provinces. Whatever Celtic inhabitants the region possessed – including those of the probably defunct enclave of Thylia – were Hellenized or Romanized, as were the Scordisci of the Belgrade region following Roman campaigns in the first century BC. The same century also saw Roman expansion into Rhaetia, Noricum and Pannonia, German migration to Bohemia and the eastern Rhineland and Dacian penetration into Transdanubia. These pressures effectively extinguished the Celtic presence east of the Alps and the Rhine, regions in which the Celts had, in any case, long been only one component in a rich ethnic mix. The Galatians too came under Roman rule, following the death in 133 BC of Attalus III of Pergamum, who bequeathed his kingdom to Rome, and the destruction in 66 BC of the kingdom of Pontus.

By then, the heartland of Celtic Europe was Gaul and the central drama in the history of the Celts of the first century BC was its conquest by the Romans. Thanks to the writings of Julius Caesar, it is a conquest that can be traced in detail. By any standards, it was an appalling catastrophe. In 60 BC, Gaul probably had some six and a half million inhabitants. Ten years later, one million had been killed and another million sold into slavery, a scale of oppression greater even than that suffered by the Poles in the Second World War. Caesar's main motivation in attacking Gallia 'Comata' was his desire to enhance his position in the

An inscription commemorating the Roman siege of Alesia. (Musée des Antiquités Nationales, St-Germain-en-Laye)

labyrinthine politics of the twilight years of the Roman Republic and to amass slaves whom he could sell in order to clear his enormous debts. It was, however, useful for him to argue that his main objective was to save the Celts of Gaul, barbaric though they were, from the greater barbarism of the Germans, a people whom he introduced to history. The argument had some substance. In about 120 BC, the Teutones and the Cimbri – German tribes, it is generally assumed – had rampaged through central and western Europe until they had been annihilated by Gaius Marius in 102–1, an annihilation still marked by the Provençal predilection for the name Marius. In 58 BC, pressure from Germans caused the Helvetii to migrate from the central Alps; Caesar's description of the migration is the first detailed account of a Celtic folk movement. The notion that the Romans saved Gaul from the Germans (a people who, according to classical writers of the first century BC, were remarkably similar to the Celts as described by authors two centuries earlier) struck deep roots. At Alesia, where the Gauls made their last stand against Rome, a monument, erected in 1949, celebrates the reconciliation between the victor and the vanquished, which had enabled Gaul to be defended against the Germans, to enjoy three centuries of peace and to be enriched by the enlightenment of Greece and Rome.

The governorships to which Julius Caesar was appointed in 59 BC meant that he had full command of the entire frontier between Rome and those Celtic peoples who were still independent. Year by year, Caesar undermined that independence. In 58, he frustrated the migration of the Helvetii and destroyed the army of the Germanic Suebi, the enemy of the Gallic Aedui, allies of Rome. In 57, he subdued the Belgae of north-east Gaul, a people which seemed to have contained Germanic as well as Celtic elements. In 56, he pulverized the Veneti of the north-west. In 55, he was again involved with the Belgae, made his first crossing of the Rhine and led a brief expedition to Britain. In 54, the Belgae, led by Ambiorix, once more claimed his attention, as did Britain, which he penetrated as far as Wheathampstead near St

The statue of Vercingetorix unveiled at Alesia by Emperor Napoleon III in 1865.

Albans. In 53, there were further campaigns against the Belgae and a second crossing of the Rhine. All Caesar's operations were conducted with a ferocity which he delighted in chronicling – the hundreds of thousands of deaths among the Helvetii, the massacre of all the elders of the Veneti, the virtual annihilation of the Nervi and the sale of the Atuatuci in a single auctioned lot of fifty-three thousand people.

Reaction came in 52 when the Gauls, meeting at Bibracte, accepted a supreme leader. He was Vercingetorix, a noble of the Arverni tribe of the Massif Central; his elevation represented a return to older traditions for, among the Arverni and others, the notion of a supreme leader belonged to the past; indeed, Vercingetorix's father had been executed for seeking such a position. By the spring of 52, most of the tribes of central Gaul were in revolt. Caesar proceeded to capture and destroy their *oppida* one by one; among the Boturiges who inhabited the region later known as Poitou, only eight hundred out of forty thousand survived the Roman assault on Avaricum, their capital. Frustrated in his attack on Gergovia, the *oppidum* of the Arverni, Caesar recruited German mercenaries and succeeded in boxing up Vercingetorix in the *oppidum* of Alesia, generally believed to be Alise, some fifty kilometres north-west of Dijon. A massive siege was launched, with the *oppidum*'s fortifications surrounded by trenches, walls, palisades and towers. Attempts by a quarter-of-a-million-strong relief force of Gauls failed to break through to the besieged. Vercingetorix surrendered and, after a six-year imprisonment in Rome, was strangled at Caesar's command. In 51, mopping up operations were undertaken in the north-east and south-west when the hands of the defenders of Uxellodunum were severed. Caesar returned to Rome where he was assassinated seven years later.

The Gauls had been subdued. There were still regions, in particular in the Pyrenees and the Alps, where Roman power had not penetrated, but during the reign of Augustus (17 BC to AD 14) these also came under Roman rule. The year 6 BC saw the inauguration of a memorial on the Via Julia – later the Grande Corniche – high above Monaco. Known as the Alpine Trophy, it commemorates the completion of the conquest of Gaul. Fifty metres high and bearing a tribute to Augustus and a list of the conquered peoples, it is the lengthiest Latin inscription to have survived from the classical world.

Despite Caesar's bloodbath, the inhabitants of Gaul were still essentially Gallic, and were to remain so until the present day. Much of the Celtic heritage survived. Roman administrative divisions respected pre-conquest boundaries, and by establishing *civitates* to replace

The broch at Carloway, Isle of Lewis, Scotland. Brochs were hollow round towers of dry stone masonry and were extensively built in Scotland between 200 BC and AD 400.

oppida – Autun, for example, took over the role of Bibracte – much of the tribal structure remained intact. Celtic cult centres such as Sequana continued to be venerated and, as late as the fourth century AD, there were savants who claimed druidic descent. Nevertheless, in religion as in other spheres, there was a growing tendency for Celtic traditions to be subsumed into those of Rome. A first-century AD stele or upright stone column at Reims depicts the heavily bearded Celtic god Cernunnos sitting between classical carved standing images of Apollo and Mercury. Sometimes statuary can suggest the subordination of the natives to their overlords: a funerary monument at Trier portrays clean-shaven figures in Roman dress receiving tribute from bearded Celtic peasants.

Nevertheless, despite considerable anti-provincial prejudice, the Roman élite was not exclusive; that it could assimilate the élites of conquered peoples is suggested by an inscription on the triumphal arch in the south-western *civitas* of Saintes. Dedicated in 18 BC, it mentions the Gaul, Caius Julius Rufus, his father and his grandfather, with the names less Celtic and more Roman as each generation passed. A major uprising in AD 20 notwithstanding, the Gauls were, by the mid-first century AD, considered to be loyal subjects of the Emperor; indeed, the Emperor Claudius suggested in AD 48 that leading members of the Aedui tribe should be allowed to sit in the Roman Senate itself.

Evidence of the survival of the Celtic language of Gaul is more difficult to assess. The country is still rich in Celtic place-names, and Latin borrowed from Gaulish words – such as *leuga* (league) – and a number of terms dealing with horsemanship, including the term *carrus*, the source of the modern word car. For Gaulish speakers to become fluent in Latin was not dificult, for the Celtic family of languages is closer to the Italic family than it is to any other branch of Indo-European, and the similarities were far greater two thousand years ago. Celtic names have been found on Gallic pottery of the first century, when lead plaques inscribed with Gaulish curses were thrown into springs at Amélie-les-Bains and elsewhere. If St Jerome's comment is to be believed, Celtic was still a living language in north-east Gaul in the fourth century AD, and if theories concerning the twin origins of Breton are correct, it was spoken in north-west Gaul after the fall of the empire. Nevertheless, it is likely that Latin had supplanted Gaulish as the dominant language of the core areas of Gaul within a century or so of the conquest. By then, the people continuing to be Celtic-speaking and having meaningful Celtic characteristics were those inhabiting regions where Roman rule was either absent or incomplete. By the early centuries of the Christian era, such regions only existed in the remoter regions of Gaul, in Ireland and in the Highland Zone of Britain. Thus, during the last two thousand years, the history of the Celts is the history of peoples living in sea-girt lands on the furthest reaches of Atlantic Europe.

chapter three

Sacred Groves

'Flow of the Sacred Waters' (The Stock Market)

IN 1974, attendants at the Cannes Film Festival were treated to the sight of a huge man-shaped wooden image burning fiercely on the Boulevard de la Croisette. It was there to advertise the film *The Wickerman*, a reworking of a theme touched upon by Caesar and Strabo — that the Celts conducted human sacrifices by immolating live victims in enormous mannequins of woven timber. The film's denouement is one of the most horrific in the history of the cinema. Thus was Celtic religious ritual pressed into service to create gruesome barbarity. Yet, such is the versatility of Celtic religious traditions that they can be presented in far more elevating ways. Books on the spiritual wisdom of the Celts rarely fail to find enthusiastic buyers. Earnest neo-pagans are thereby assisted in finding kinship with nature and love for the Mother Goddess, enabling them to create for themselves an ecologically sound, non-sexist, politically correct body of doctrine, all inspired by the Celtic predilection for sacred groves.

The ability of Celtic religion to be used for both horrific and constructive ends is evidence of what the distinguished Irish scholar Proinsias Mac Cana identified as its 'fertile chaos'. Mac Cana was writing specifically about the religion of the insular Celts, but the comment is equally relevant to the Celtic world as a whole. Yet, if chaos is one of the defining features of Celtic religion, this can be a barrier to any intelligible analysis of its nature. Was there, indeed, such a thing as Celtic religion – that is, a body of beliefs and practices common to those communities believed to be Celtic-speaking? If there were, is it possible to discern whether it contained those elements generally considered to be the characteristics of a religion: concepts of the nature of a supreme being or beings; ways of worshipping or propitiating

Dawn in the upper reaches of the Seine Valley, not far from the cult centre of Sequana.

such a being or beings; patterns of ritual with holy days and festivals; veneration of sacred places and objects; principles of ethical living; belief in the existence of the soul and notions of its destiny after death; a priesthood or a class of interpreters of the divine purpose and will.

The nature of the evidence concerning the religion of the Celts makes it difficult to offer any definitive answers to these questions. In the record of the Celtic world provided by archaeology and by written sources, it is religion which looms largest. Thus, it is not the paucity of evidence which presents problems, but rather its lack of clarity and precision. The classical authors, who were fascinated by Celtic religious practices, offer evidence that is seriously flawed. They were particularly concerned to describe the more ghoulish aspects, especially those relating to human sacrifice. Like imperialists in every age, the Romans sought to demonstrate that the inhabitants of the lands they were invading, conquering and colonizing were so barbarous that Roman imperialism was justified. Furthermore, there is much self-righteousness in what they wrote, for the rituals of the Celts, rooted as they were in a common Indo-European tradition, were not unlike those of the Romans themselves a few centuries earlier, when human sacrifice had been widely practised in Rome. Indeed, Julius Caesar, the fullest chronicler of the religion of the Gauls, assumed when describing their gods that he was dealing with a debased version of the Roman pantheon. Rather than recording the Gaulish names of deities, he referred to Mercury, Mars and so on, thus depriving his readers of a wealth of information. His work is an example of what Tacitus called interpretatio romana, the Roman habit of conflating what they studied with what they knew. Furthermore, there is little written evidence of Celtic religion in the era when it was in full vigour. Classical sources do not become extensive until the first century BC, when, in Gaul at least, traditional practices were in decline; this was particularly true of the country's southern coastlands, where Celtic culture had long been subject to classical influences. Evidence from the following century, provided by writers such as Pliny the Elder, Tacitus and Lucan, can be valuable, although those writers do not present a coherent account, preferring instead to stress the bizarre and malign. Later writers, especially the Alexandrines, are more sympathetic but the information they offer is slight.

The early literature of the insular Celts is an even more opaque source of information. Irish began to be written down — in Latin script — in the seventh century AD, but surviving documents which throw light upon traditional beliefs belong at the earliest to the eleventh and twelfth centuries. Much of the contents of those documents, in particular the corpus of Irish law and the large collection of stories and sagas, clearly belongs to far earlier centuries — so much so that Kenneth Jackson called his study of early Irish literature *A Window on the Iron Age*. There is a fond belief in Ireland that the island has been Christian since the time of St Patrick and, indeed, evidence from the sixth and seventh centuries suggests a country wholly Christianized. Yet, as Michael Richter has commented, it is unlikely that earlier traditions had vanished, and these traditions percolated through in the manuscripts of later centuries. Those manuscripts were written by devout Christians, monks who seem to have retained considerable affection for their country's pre-Christian past, perhaps because Ireland, unlike other regions of Christendom, did not experience any memorable struggles between the old religion and the new. Thus, although archaeological evidence for religious activities is considerably less in pre-Christian Ireland than it is in Britain, Gaul and elsewhere, Irish literary evidence can make a unique contribution to an understanding of the religion of the ancient Celts.

Yet it must always be remembered that the literary evidence does not consist of an unvarnished account of pre-Christian religion, but rather of material which Christian monks in later centuries deemed to be worthy of preservation. In the process of preservation, that material was subject to much redaction and filtration. As the monastic scribes rejected any notion that the supernatural beings in the stories they were recounting were worthy of worship, they euhemerized the gods into heroes of the past, heroes whose magical powers were an echo of their one-time divinity. Thus, the Irish sources, while offering a wealth of myth, provide no

direct evidence of religion. In one version of the text of *Táin Bó Cúailgne* (The Cattle Raid of Cuailgne), the scribe expressed his desire to distance himself from what he was writing: 'I, who have written out this history, or more properly fiction, do not accept as a matter of belief certain things in this history, or rather fiction; for some things are diabolical impositions, some are poetical inventions, some have a semblance of truth, and some are meant to be the entertainment of fools.'

Such considerations are even more apposite when considering the literary evidence from Wales, a country in which there seems to have been less affection for the pre-Christian past than there was in Ireland. What survives in Welsh was written down at a later date than was the case with the earliest Irish material, and most of it has a less archaic character. Nevertheless, *Pedair Cainc y Mabinogi*, four tales likely to have been composed in the eleventh century but drawing upon a long tradition of oral storytelling, contains elements which belong to ancient mythology, especially those relating to the transmogrification of gods into heroes. Other tales, too — *Culhwch ac Olwen* in particular — are rich storehouses of legendary lore. Early Welsh verse offers valuable insights; for example, the *Gododdin* of Aneirin, 1480 lines of poetry, probably written in the ninth century, but apparently based upon a nucleus of verses composed two hundred years earlier, provides evidence of the values of Celtic warriors who were only superficially Christianized.

The unwillingness of the upholders of Celtic religion to commit to writing anything relating to their rites and beliefs means there is a total absence of the litanies, incantations and supplications used by them. This lack, together with the lacunae in the writings that do exist, is partly compensated for by archaeology, which can provide evidence of cult centres, sacred images, ritual offerings and liturgical regalia, along with inscriptions revealing the names of deities. What it cannot provide is a systematic account of the nature of the ceremonies conducted at cult centres, the meaning a worshipper attached to a sacred image, the intention of the bestower of a ritual offering and the context in which liturgical regalia were used. Yet, despite its limitations, archaeological evidence is of central importance, and, in the case of the Celts, as in that of most other ancient peoples, artefacts and sites relating to religion are far more abundant than those relating to any other aspect of their lives. This evidence is invaluable when assessing the reliability of the accounts of the classical authors. For example, it is the relative paucity of archaeological evidence for human sacrifice which permits scholars to argue that the Latin authors in particular greatly exaggerated the popularity of the practice.

Furthermore, it is archaeological discoveries, above all, which permit the statement — to quote Nora Chadwick — that 'it might be assumed that a certain unity of belief ... prevailed throughout the Celtic world'. One aspect of Celtic ritual practice may be cited in support of that statement. That is the prevalence of

Detail from The Book of Aneirin. *The line 'Gwyr a aeth Gatraeth' (Men went to Catraeth) is clearly visible.*

Groups of carved severed heads which adorned shrines at Entremont near Marseille. The shrines were sacked by the Romans in the late second century BC. (Musée Granet, Aix-en-Provence)

A stone double head joined in the centre by the beak of bird of prey. It originally adorned the entrance to a shrine at Roquepertuse near Marseille and dates from about 300 BC. (Musée d'Archéologie Méditerranéenne, Marseille)

images of the human head at cult sites in virtually all the regions believed to have been inhabited by Celts. The lower Rhône valley can offer the astounding skulls and heads found at Entremont and Roquepertuse. From elsewhere in Gaul come the bronze heads of Tarbes and Lezoux and the triple-headed god of Bavay. Corleck in County Cavan in Ireland has another triple head. In Bath in England there is a splendidly rococo face, while Caerwent in Wales has yielded a rather more morose visage. Manerbio in Italy offers a *phalera* bearing nine heads and another bearing eighteen. At Heidelberg in Germany there is a fabulous crowned head of a deity, an artefact only surpassed in its exoticism by the astonishing face from Mšecke Žehrovice in Bohemia. Such an obsession surely justifies Paul Jacobsthal's comment that 'amongst the Celts, the human head was venerated above all else, since the head was to the Celts the soul, centre of the emotions as well as of life itself, a symbol of divinity and of the powers of the other-world'.

Other features indicating 'a certain unity of belief' could be cited: the belief in the efficacy of propitiating the gods by depositing votive offerings in lakes and rivers, for example, or the delight in the lore of the places sacred to the gods, as described in the Irish manuscript the *Dindshenchas*. Their links with water, trees and groves suggest that the gods were viewed as chthonic, that is earth gods, as opposed to the sky gods of the Greeks and Romans. Indeed, as has already been noted, the Pergame monument at Athens celebrating the defeat of the Galatians makes explicit the link between the Celts and the Titans, the chthonic deities, children of Gaia, defeated by Zeus. Caesar recorded that the Gauls believed that they were descended from Dis Pater, the god of the underworld and of the night, and that they reckoned periods of time not in days but in nights – a reckoning preserved in the Welsh words for week and fortnight (*wythnos* and *pythefnos*). Earlier peoples, such as the builders of megalithic monuments, seem to have thought in terms of solar and lunar gods, but the Celtic predilection for depositing items of value in the earth suggests an abandonment of such beliefs, and that is perhaps corroborated by the apparent lack of interest shown by the Celts in such cult sites as Stonehenge.

Yet to consider Celtic gods as exclusively chthonic is perhaps to do an injustice to the fertility of the Celtic religious imagination. The names of some four hundred Celtic gods are known, three hundred of which only occur once. Many of those may well have been gods with only a very local following. The Irish affirmation 'I swear by the gods by whom my people swear' seems indicative of this, and the prominence of some gods may well reflect the power of the tribe whose gods they originally were; after all, there are many examples, in the Old Testament and elsewhere, of a conquering people imposing its gods on the conquered. The knowledge that classical gods had specific attributes may give rise to the expectation that this was also the case with the Celtic pantheon, but it seems that the Celts did not visualize gods with exclusive functions. Not only were they adept at all things – and therefore polyvalent – they were also able to appear in many guises – and therefore polymorphic. A god with many guises is presumably a god with many names – a key, perhaps, to the copiousness of divine nomenclature among the Celts. It has been suggested that the many guises represented the multifarious aspects of a single god, and that the Celts were in fact groping towards monotheism; yet, as Mac Cana put it: 'If the Celts were monotheists at heart, then they were very successful in disguising this.'

When discussing the religion of the Gauls, Caesar noted that 'the god they worship most is Mercury, and they have very many images of him'. Writing a century after Caesar, Lucan gave particular prominence to the names of three gods: Teutates, Taranis and Esus. Early annotators equated Mercury with Teutates, but as it is a name which rarely features on Gaulish inscriptions, it is difficult to believe that he was the god about whom Caesar was writing. Teutates may be a general epithet for the god of the tribe, for the word is cognate with the Irish *tuath* (province or kingdom) and the Welsh *tudri* or *tudur* (the king of a province). The annotators equated Taranis with Jupiter – a reasonable supposition, for the name survives in the Welsh *taran* and the Irish *torann* (thunder). Esus was considered to be equivalent to Mars; he was popular among the Celts judging by the number of Celtic god-names joined to his – Mars-Oculus at Caerwent, for example, or Mars-Lenus at

This head, the most remarkable surviving portrayal of a Celtic deity, was found in a sacred enclosure at Mšecke Žehrovice in Bohemia. Carved in ragstone, it is 23.5 centimetres (9.25 inches) high and dates from about 250 BC. (Národní Muzeum, Prague)

The Cerne Giant carved in outline in chalkland near Cerne Abbas, Dorset. It is fifty-five metres (180 foot) high. Although there is no agreement about its origins, it may represent a portrayal of the Celtic god Lug, or perhaps the classical god, Hercules. Visits to it by women hoping to become pregnant occurred until very recently.

Trier and Mars-Corotiacus in Suffolk. Like Teutates, Taranis and Esus are poorly represented on inscriptions and therefore they also may be general epithets rather than the names of specific gods.

The god who can most convincingly be equated with Caesar's Mercury is Lug – the Irish Lugh and the Welsh Lleu. Although not widely attested in inscriptions, the fifteen and more places whose names are based on his – towns stretching from Carlisle to Leignitz – mean that Lug's influence upon the toponomy of Europe is greater than that of any other Celtic god. His name may have given rise to a word for oath – *lugae* in Old Irish and *llw* in Welsh. In Irish mythology, he is given the epithets *lamfhada* (of the long arm) and *samildanach* (skilled in many arts); in the *Mabinogi* he appears as Lleu llaw gyffes (Lleu of the skilful hand). These are attributes consistent with Caesar's description of the chief god of the Gauls as a deity who was the inventor of all the arts. Yet, there are elements in Lug's character which suggest similarities with Jupiter, Mars and Hercules, and even with Savitar of the Rigveda of India. The *Lughnasa* – the festival of the games of Lug – was celebrated on the first of August, a date whose ritual importance is stressed by the Coligny Calendar. A major celebration of the festival was held at Lug's fort – Lugudunum, or Lyon – a festival which was superceded in 12 BC by that in honour of the Emperor Augustus. Irish mythology is rich in references to the *Lughnasa*; the god honoured in the festival seems to be rather less archaic than other gods of ancient Ireland, indicating perhaps that the cult was imported from Gaul in the closing years of the pre-Christian era. Indeed, the Dagda, a deity who was good at everything and who dwelt in the great Neolithic monument of New Grange, seems to have been a more primitive version of the many-skilled Lug. Portrayed as armed with a great club, he may be the giant in the chalk-cut image at Cerne Abbas in Dorset, although it has been argued that the image is that of Hercules. Another name for Lug appears to have been Vin, commemorated in Vindobana or Vienna; Vin is the Irish Finn, the central figure in the Irish Fenian Cycle, and the Welsh Gwyn, sometimes portrayed as the king of the other-world.

Some of the gods prominent in insular sources seem to have no equivalents in mainland Europe. The largest temple in Roman Britain dedicated to a Celtic god was the late fourth-century sanctuary at Lydney in Gloucestershire, built in honour of Nodens, a god apparently unknown outside Britain and Ireland. In Irish mythology he appears as Nuada Argetlám. A central figure in the *Leabhar Gabhála* (The Book of Conquests), he received his epithet – of the silver hand – because of the metal limb made for him to replace the arm he had lost in the battle of Moytura. In Welsh tradition, he is apparently Nudd, the father of Gwyn in *Culhwch ac Olwen*. In that story, Gwyn ap Nudd seeks the hand of Creiddylad, the daughter of Lludd Llawereint (Lludd of the silver hand). In view of Nuada's identical epithet, Lludd must surely be the Welsh equivalent of Nuada and Nodens. Yet, as Nodens is generally identified with Nudd, it would seem that, in *Culhwch ac Olwen*, the son of Nodens is seeking the hand of the daughter of Nodens. This suggests that, by the eleventh century, story-tellers were groping with material related to a Celtic pantheon which was by then collapsing into chaos.

Culhwch ac Olwen also features Mabon, a name derived from Maponus, a god worshipped along Hadrian's Wall, in Scotland and at several springs in Gaul. The son of Modron – Matrona, the divine mother – he has been equated with Apollo, as has also the god Belenus. To judge from inscriptions, Belenus was the most widely venerated of the gods of the Celts. There is evidence of his cult in Noricum, southern Gaul and northern Italy, and he may have given his name to *Beltane*, the Irish festival celebrated on the first of May. Worship of him proved enduring; Ausonius of Bordeaux, writing in the fourth century AD, mentioned a contemporary of his who was a grandson of Phoebicius, a temple priest of Belenus, and whose family bore names associated with the great Apollonian shrine at Delphi.

Of the gods recorded on inscriptions, the most popular – at least among today's neo-pagans – is the antler-god, an image of whom was discovered beneath Notre Dame Cathedral in Paris. The inscription associated with the image mentions the word Cernunnos. This is the only example of the antler-god being given a name; as it merely means horned god, it may be a description rather than his title. Cernunnos

The horned god as portrayed on the Gundestrup Cauldron.

was perhaps the patron of the chase and the lord of the forest; splendidly portrayed on the Gundestrup Cauldron, he is also delineated on a potsherd from Numantia and a stone relief in Reims. Holed antlers discovered in Hertfordshire appear to have been used as a human headdress, a practice widely present in ancient cultures. The mythical significance of the antlered stag may be reflected in the deer-priests mentioned in the *Táin Bó Cúailgne*, and in the hunting scene with which the *Mabinogi* opens. As well as stags, horned gods were associated with bulls, such as the Deiotorus of Galatia, the Tavros Trigaranus (the bull with three cranes or herons) discovered in Paris, and the remarkable Lucifer-like head from Lezoux.

Cernunnos was one of many zoomorphic gods. The most widely attested – indeed one of the rare examples of a Celtic deity with occurrences exceeding a score – was Epona. She was the goddess-mare – indicative, surely, of the Celts' high regard for the horse, a devotion which dates back to their very origins as a recognizable ethnic group. The word is cognate with the modern Welsh *eboles* (filly); it is instructive to compare *epona* with the Latin *equus*, proof that Latin, like Irish, preferred its *q*s to its *p*s. Monuments to Epona may be found in Wales, England, Iberia, Transalpine Gaul, Cisalpine Gaul, the Rhineland, Pannonia, Transdanubia and Thrace. Symbolic of the horse – the reason for her popularity among Roman cavalrymen – Epona seems also to have represented fertility and to have been the epitome of the mother goddess. In studies of Welsh mythology, she has been equated with Rhiannon – Rigantone, the divine queen – and in Irish studies with Medb or Maeve, queen of Connacht, and Macha of Ulster. Emain Macha or Navan Fort, a place central to the largest body of Irish epic literature, acknowledged her as patroness; so did Alesia, a factor perhaps in Vercingetorix's choice of the place as the site of the last stand of the Celts of Gaul.

Other zoomorphic deities included Artio, the bear-goddess, with a dedication at Muri in Switzerland – a name not without significance, perhaps, when considering the supernatural reverberations in stories of the great Celtic hero, Arthur. There was also Arduinna, the boar-goddess commemorated in the Ardennes, a figure who may have echoes in the story of the hunt of the boar in the Welsh Arthurian tale, *Culhwch ac Olwen*. Yet, perhaps too much should not be read into zoomorphic gods. As Stuart Piggott commented, Christian iconography illustrating the lion of St Mark or the winged ox of St Luke could, in the absence of a knowledge of the hagiography involved, give rise to many weird theories.

The prominence of Epona is an indication of the role played by goddesses in the Celtic pantheon. Female deities may originally have been paramount. The remarkable funerary cart of the seventh century BC found at Strettweg in Austria is dominated by a bronze female figure at least three times larger than the mostly male figures which surround her. Although it would seem that goddesses were generally more benign than gods, some received very bloodthirsty offerings. Dio Cassius, describing the revolt of Boudicca, wrote of the murder and mutilation of Roman women in the grove of the goddess Andraste; she was, he noted, the goddess of victory, and the impalings and other horrors were,

The bronze cult wagon found in a warrior's grave at Strettweg, Austria. It dates from the seventh century BC and depicts a goddess holding up a sacred cauldron. Below her is a group of mainly male figures who are believed to be engaged in a ritual stag hunt. (Steiermärkisches Landesmuseum Joanneum, Graz)

The White Horse at Uffington, Oxfordshire. It is believed to have been carved in the chalkland during the Iron Age and almost certainly had ritual significance.

presumably, in her honour. Others were more benevolent. The Irish goddess Brigit, also attested in Wales and in Gaul, seems to have been the patroness of *Imbolc*, the festival held on the first of February to celebrate the lactation of the ewes. In the Christian calendar, the day became the feast of St Brigit, which suggests that the transmogrified goddess could convincingly be presented as a Christian saint.

Consistent with the Celtic delight in triadism, goddesses, even more than gods, are frequently portrayed in triplicate. There are the three cloaked figures from Housesteads on Hadrian's Wall, the three mothers on the stone relief from Vertillum in Burgundy and the triad of deities on a plaque found at Bath. In Irish literature, the story of Cú Chulainn features the three mother goddesses, Morrigan, Mache and Bodh, battle furies with an uncanny resemblance to Macbeth's three witches. It is unlikely that these triadic sculptures carried with them a suggestion of a trinity; more convincing is the theory that the multiplying of images emphasized the extreme potency of the deity. Some of the earth goddesses or *Deae Matres* seem generic, with epithets derived from the towns in which they enjoyed particular veneration – the Matres Nemausicae of Nîmes, for example, or the Matres Glanicae of Glenum; a comparison with the later cult of the Blessed Virgin Mary seems inescapable. Irish mythology suggests a dualism between the male deities of the tribe and the female deities of the land. Assuming that the Celtic pantheon is susceptible of coherent interpretation, perhaps the most convincing is Cunliffe's suggestion that gods represented war, the sky and the tribe and that goddesses represented fertility, the earth and the locality, and that it was the constructive tension between them which produced balance, harmony and productivity.

In any consideration of the ways in which the deities were worshipped or propitiated, written and archaeological sources again present difficulties. As has already been noted, the Latin authors delighted in gory details. Lucan described a

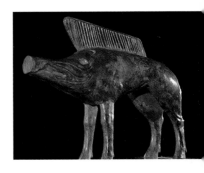

An almost life-size statue of a boar found at Neuvy-en-Sullias near Orléans, dating from the first century BC. (Musée Historique et Archéologique de l'Orléanais, Orléans)

A close-up of the ritual drowning portrayed on the Gundestrup Cauldron.

The face of Tollund Man, whose body was found in a bog in Denmark. He was a victim of the threefold ritual killing – the smashing of the skull, the garotting of the neck and the cutting of the throat – characteristic of Celtic tradition. That these practices were carried out in Denmark indicates that such traditions were not confined to Celtic-speaking peoples. (Silkeborgmuseet, Silkeborg)

grove near Massalia where 'altars are heaped with hideous offerings and every tree is sprinkled with human blood', and Tacitus wrote of altars in Anglesey 'drenched in the blood of prisoners'. Dio Cassius's account of the sacrifices to Andraste includes a description of severed breasts stuffed into the mouths of murdered Roman matrons, and Strabo's portrayal of the wicker man is particularly ghoulish. Diodorus Siculus describes killings conducted in the interests of divination: 'They stab [the victim] … and foretell the future from his fall … from the convulsions of his limbs and from the spurting of the blood.' Lucan states that those sacrificed to Teutates were drowned, those to Taranis burnt and those to Esus hanged. The archaeological record confirms that human sacrifice did indeed occur. On the Gundestrup Cauldron there is a figure held upside-down over what appears to be a pail of water – the portrayal perhaps of a sacrifice to Teutates. The man whose body was recovered from Lindow Moss in Cheshire in 1984 had had his skull smashed, his neck garotted and his throat cut – possibly another example of triadism. A bog victim in Gallagh in County Galway had been killed with a garotte

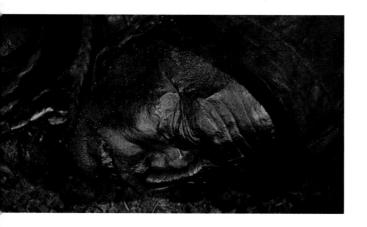

made of hazel rods, and the stomach of another victim at Lindow was full of hazel nuts – hazel had strong symbolic significance in Celtic mythology. A body found at Danebury in Hampshire may represent a sacrifical victim, as may that excavated in a ritual enclosure at Libenice in Bohemia. Some double burials – that at Hohmichele, for example – have been cited as possible examples of the suttee version of ritual murder.

Yet, despite these examples and others, wholly persuasive evidence of human sacrifice is rare, surprisingly so in view of the emphasis placed upon it by classical authors. A close reading of their work suggests that the practice was largely obsolete by their time. The writings of 50 BC to AD 100 – the most prolific period – were much indebted to the work of Posidonius, who gave an account of what he heard and saw *c.* 100 BC, and they also drew on that of Timaeus which were composed *c.* 300 BC. Strabo was careful to use the past tense when describing the wicker man, and Caesar acknowledged that nothing resembling suttee was practised in the Gaul of his time. It is possible that human sacrifice took place only at times of tension and danger; Lindow Man was perhaps murdered at the time of the Roman attack upon the druidical centre of Anglesey, and may have represented an attempt to persuade supernatural forces to circumvent the enemies of Celtic religion. Furthermore, the archaeological record shows that animal sacrifice was replacing human sacrifice – exactly the process which had occurred among the Israelites in Abraham's time. At Soissons, bulls, horses, goats, rams, pigs and dogs accompanied a warrior to his grave; oxen were sacrificed at Gournay, an *oppidum* of the Bellovaci in Picardy, and a ritual burial of a horse and a dog was found at Danebury. A statue from Le Touget, west of Toulouse, depicts a hunter carrying a hare which he is perhaps about to sacrifice, an act performed by Boudica during her revolt. Hares enjoyed particular sanctity in Celtic tradition; Caesar stated that there was a taboo against eating them.

Sacrifice, human and animal, was part of a body of ritual which it was believed necessary to perform in order to ensure the smooth running of the universe, the renewal of fecundity, the rising of the sun and the return of the spring. It was the study of the prescribed methods of ritual which presumably consitituted the greater part of the twenty-year training undertaken by apprentice druids. As in most traditional communities, all learning was considered to be sacred, and, as writing was not sanctioned by ancient tradition, learning was passed on orally. Seeking to explain the Celts' opposition to the commitment of their doctrines to writing, Caesar wrote: 'I suppose this practice began originally for two reasons: they did not want their doctrines to be accessible to ordinary people and they did not want their pupils to rely on the written word and so neglect to train their memories. For it does usually happen that if people have the help of written documents, they do not pay as much attention to learning by heart, and so let their memories become less efficient.' A rigid adherence to prescribed rituals was deemed to be essential, as indeed it was among the Romans. Those flouting the rituals were the

A close-up of the garotte used in the killing of Tollund Man. (Silkeborgmuseet, Silkeborg)

equivalent of the damned – 'the sacrilegious criminals', as Caesar called them. 'No one would go near or speak to them for fear of being contaminated in some way by contact with them.' It was believed that ritual, correctly conducted, necessarily led to the result which was sought – a successful harvest, for example. Ceremonies were held before rather than after the desired event, and therefore there was nothing in Celtic rites resembling the Christian tradition of thanksgiving.

Ritual was woven into all aspects of life, for there was an everyday need to propitiate the deities. There were, however, several major annual ceremonies. Caesar wrote of the yearly gathering of all the Gauls held in the territory of the Carnutes – the region around Chartres – at which legal as well as religious issues were discussed and settled. Irish sources mention the great assembly at Tara, the probable occasion of the ritual mating between the ruler and the territorial goddess, a practice described by Gerald of Wales in his *Topographica Hiberna* of 1185. The Coligny Calendar, in noting which periods of the year were auspicious or inauspicious, attaches particular significance to the first of May and the first of August, dates identifiable from Irish sources as the festivals of *Beltane* and *Lughnasa*. Those sources provide fuller information about the ritual year. As has already been mentioned, *Imbolc* – the first of February – was linked with the lactation of ewes and was the feast of Brigit. *Beltane* marked the beginning of summer when stock was driven to graze in the high pastures and when ceremonies related to fire were held. Indeed, the *Dindshenchas* mentions a *Beltane* fire lit at Tara which consumed the whole of Ireland. Some echo of the significance of *Beltane* may be present in the Welsh tale *Cyfranc Lludd a Llefelys* in which the cries of dragons on May Eve produce infertility. *Lughnasa* seems to have been the time of rites aimed at ensuring good harvests and thus, unlike the other major festivals, it was concerned with the crop-raising rather than the stock-raising aspect of agriculture. The fourth festival, *Samain*, was held on the first of November and may have had associations with the early winter cull of stock. *Samain* was a time of elaborate ceremonies when, according to the more archaic sources, the Dagda mated with the goddess, usually identified as Morrigan – the intercourse ensuring the well-being of the tribe. The date represented the break between the old year and the new, when the world was overrun by the forces of magic. This provided an opportunity for the spirits of the dead to mingle with the living, a tradition which survives in Hallowe'en.

The Stone of Destiny on the Hill of Tara, County Meath, Ireland.

A scene from the Beltane Fire Festival which is re-enacted on May Day on Calton Hill, Edinburgh. (Graham Burns/Collections)

Sunset on the Hill of Tara.

The emphasis of the Irish sources upon the importance of the ritual site at Tara is evidence that the Celts considered some places to be of particular sanctity. Yet, as Miranda Green put it: 'Every mountain, spring, marsh, tree and outcrop was endowed with divinity.' Thus, ritual enactments could take place anywhere. Lakes, rivers and springs had a special appeal, as can be seen from the votive deposits in Lake Neuchâtel and Lake Geneva in Switzerland, Sequana in France, Duchov in Bohemia, Llyn Cerrig Bach in Wales and Flag Fen and the rivers Thames and Witham in England. At some of the sites, a timber pier was built to serve as a platform from which objects could be thrown into the waters; elsewhere – at Llyn Cerrig Bach, for example – rocky outcrops were pressed into service. Groves, especially the dark and mysterious, were held in high regard. Tacitus wrote of the groves of Anglesey and Lucan described a sacred wood near Massalia which was destroyed by Caesar's soldiers. It was in such groves that white-robed priests cut mistletoe from oak trees with golden pruning hooks. Although the ceremony is vouched for only

Llyn Cerrig Bach, Anglesey, Wales. When the War Office was constructing an airfield on adjoining land in 1943, a large body of metalwork – some 144 pieces in all – was recovered from the lake. It is believed that the lake was the site for ritual deposition over the two hundred years preceding the Roman invasion of Anglesey in AD 61. Most of the Llyn Cerrig Bach artefacts are in the National Museum of Wales, Cardiff.

by Pliny the Elder, it is perhaps the best known of all the rituals of the Celts. Other suggestions of the sanctity of mistletoe have been discerned: the mistletoe-leaf shaped crowns on a pillar from Pfalzfeld in the Rhineland, for example, or the mistletoe pollen found in the stomach of Lindow Man. The evergreen mistletoe is considered to have represented the winter spirit of the leafless oak, and the oak enjoyed great esteem; indeed, there is a belief that the word druid means knowledge of the oak. (Oak in Welsh is *derw*; druid is *derwydd*.) It is curious therefore that Ireland and the Isle of Anglesey, high places in druidical lore, are wholly bereft of mistletoe.

Votive offerings found in places lacking watery contexts may have been deposited in what were originally groves. The most remarkable of such deposits – indeed the largest Iron Age hoard found in Europe – is that at Snettisham in Norfolk, where excavation has yielded seventy-five complete torcs, fragments of a hundred others, the remains of over a hundred pieces of jewellery and a hundred and seventy coins. Among other rich hoards is that from Tayac near Bordeaux, consisting of torcs, coins and ingots amounting to almost four kilograms of gold. Niederzier in the Rhineland has also yielded a wealth of gold, while at Gournay more than two thousand weapons, presumably seized from defeated enemies, were ritually deposited. The Latin for a sacred grove is *nemus*, and the Celts had a similar word, *nemeton*. The Galatians held their tribal meetings at their *drunemeton*, and the word appears in a number of place-names, among them Nemetobrigo in Iberia, Aquae Arnemetae in Derbyshire, Medionemeton in southern Scotland and Nemetodurum – the modern Nanterre – near Paris.

In most cases, the *nemeton* probably consisted of nothing more than a clearing in the woods. However, the Mediterranean practice of enclosing a sacred site and raising a sacred building within it did spread to the lands of the Celts, the fifth-century BC enclosure at Závist in Bohemia being perhaps the earliest example north

The Great Torque of Snettisham, from Norfolk, England. The Snettisham site has yielded fourteen hoards including objects containing fifteen kilograms (thirty-three pounds) of gold and twenty kilograms (forty-four pounds) of silver. The Great Torque consists of a hoop made of eight strands of gold wire twisted together and terminals of great sophistication. It dates from the early first century AD and is one of Britain's finest antiquities. It may have been worn by Queen Boudica. (British Museum, London)

A typical scene in the Forest of Brocéliande. The forest occupies much of central Brittany and is the archetypal landscape of Arthurian romance.

of the Alps. Strabo wrote of the sanctuary built in the third century BC at Entremont near Aix-en-Provence, which had a monumental portico although its roof consisted of branches covered with clay. In regions less influenced by the classical world, the building of temples was rare, at least until those regions were absorbed into the Roman Empire. Central and northern Gaul had a number of crude versions of the Entremont temple, among them that at Gournay. The Gournay sanctuary was originally established in the fourth century as a ditch-surrounded enclosure and did not contain a roofed structure until the first century BC. Southern Britain had some earlier structures; a crude rectangular building lying to the west of Heathrow's Terminal Four has been interpreted as a wooden temple built in the third century BC. Similar structures have come to light on Hayling Island in Hampshire, at Lancing Down in Sussex and in the hillforts of Danebury (Hampshire) and South Cadbury (Somerset). Mortar came with the Romans, and in the late first century AD temples such as that at Hayling Island were rebuilt in masonry. The most elaborate Celtic sanctuary in Britain was that at Lydney, dedicated to the god Nodens. Basilican in shape and completed in the fourth century, it was a kind of Celtic Lourdes, complete with offices, visitors' quarters and even the equivalent of a souvenir shop. There is a paucity of archaeological evidence of early Celtic ritual sites in Ireland – a marked contrast with the richness of the literary evidence. Two sites, however, were on a scale unique in the prehistory of the Celts. At Emain Macha in County Antrim, a massive circular structure forty metres in diameter was built around an oak trunk felled in 94 BC. The entire edifice was embedded in stone, set on fire and then covered with turf. A series of structures at Dun Ailinne in County Kildare, dating from the third century BC to the third century AD, had not dissimilar proportions and there also fire seems to have played a central role.

For the Celts, the sacredness of objects was an extension of their belief in the sacredness of places. It has already been suggested that La Tène art was infused with a sense of the divine. Thus all artefacts could have a ritual significance. The possessions of a dead person were sacred to the departed, which explains the multiplicity of grave goods deliberately broken. The design of a torc gave magical powers to its wearer and the motifs on swords and shields gave potency to their users. Music must have played a role in ritual, and the extraordinary craftsmanship employed in the construction of musical instruments – the thousand rivets in the trumpet found at Ardbrinn in County Down, for example – suggests that they were held to be sacred.

Among the most highly venerated objects were cauldrons, symbols not only of abundance but also of regeneration and rebirth. Of all the artefacts relating to the prehistoric Celts, the most remarkable is the Gundestrup Cauldron. Found in Denmark and using a technique – silver embossed in high relief and partially gilded – which was the speciality of regions to the east of the Celtic world, it is generally

A general view of the Gundestrup Cauldron. (Nationalmuseet, Copenhagen)

believed to be of Thracian origin. Yet, although its imagery is eclectic, Celtic motifs predominate and there is a growing willingness to accept that it was made by Celts, possibly in the Titelburg area now in Luxembourg, and was part of the booty gathered by the Teutonic raiders of the first century BC. According to Strabo, the raiders used cauldrons to hold the sacrificial blood of the victims of their rituals. Veneration of cauldrons had deep roots. The goddess on the seventh-century Strettweg wagon holds a cauldron above her head, and a vast bronze cauldron was one of the main features of the sixth-century tomb at Hochdorf. The discoveries at La Tène include a fine cauldron which hung from chains, and in Scotland the counties of Berwick and Kirkcudbright have yielded cauldron deposits. In Irish mythology, the Dagda's cauldron provided sustenance for the tribe and enabled warriors to return from the dead. The cauldron's ability to restore life also features in Welsh literature, particularly in the second branch of the *Mabinogi*. In addition, stories and poems associated with Taliesin describe the cauldron of knowledge which made all-knowing those who tasted the magic potion boiled in it, and Arthur's quest for the cauldron of the lord of the other-world which was heated by the breath of nine maidens.

A head, presumed to be that of a Celtic deity, portrayed on the Gundestrup Cauldron. (Nationalmuseet, Copenhagen)

Information from Celtic sources concerning another aspect considered to be a characteristic of religion – the teaching of the principles of ethical living – is sparse. Almost by definition, this is a subject on which archaeological evidence can offer little, although what evidence there is, with its weapons, its slave-chains and its hints of human sacrifice and head-hunting, does not suggest that Celtic religion gave priority to compassion and philanthropy. Neither does the evidence provided by the classical authors, although they do mention traditions of conviviality and hospitality. The insular sources stress the virtues of open-handedness. One of the objections to Bres, king of the Fomoiri, was that, after visiting him, the breath of his guests 'did not smell of ale' nor had 'their knives been greased'. As Celtic religion was above all concerned to constrain the powers of magic and to know the will of the gods, it is vain to seek in it anything which can be interpreted as constituting a moral theology. Admittedly, Diogenes Laertes, writing in the second century AD, claimed that the druids taught their pupils the triad: 'Honour the gods, do no evil and practise bravery.' Yet there is nothing in early Irish and Welsh literature defining evil or suggesting the concept of sin and of punishment for committing it. The first and the third elements of Diogenes's triad were certainly deeply rooted. Indeed, the practise of bravery is the chief earthly virtue extolled in the insular literature. It was a virtue unaccompanied by compassion. When Aneirin in the *Gododdin* described the widows and the orphans created by the valour of his heroes, that was a matter to exult in rather than to lament as a sad consequence of war. It may therefore be unwise to apply developed concepts of religion to the beliefs of the Celts. As T. G. E. Powell put it: 'It is well to stress the word magic, for of religion, except in the modern anthropological sense of primitive religion, it cannot be said that the Celts were at all conscious.'

According to Caesar, the bravery of the Celts sprang from their lack of fear of death, the result of their belief that the soul does not die. Certainly, the abundant evidence of grave goods is ample proof of faith in the existence of an afterlife. What the Celts considered to be the form in which that afterlife manifested itself is a matter of uncertainty. The classical authors, Caesar, Lucan and Diodorus Siculus in particular, emphasize belief in metempsychosis – that after death the soul passes from one body to another. This could well have been the doctrine held in southern Gaul, where Hellenistic influences may have introduced Pythagorean ideas of the transmigration of souls. Perhaps such notions were being accepted in other parts of the Celtic world. Indeed, it has been argued that the adoption of cremation in much of that world in the second and first centuries BC was a consequence of such an acceptance. Cremation, leading to the presumed releasing of the soul into the air, seems appropriate for believers in metempsychosis, while inhumation seems appropriate for believers in a bodily afterlife.

During most of Celtic prehistory, inhumation was preferred to cremation, and the lavish goods deposited in aristocratic tombs were presumably intended to ensure that aristocrats were equipped with the means of reclaiming their privileges in the other-world. Furthermore, the notion that belief in metempsychosis was unusual in regions beyond those which had experienced strong classical influences seems to be confirmed by the virtual absence of that doctrine in the literature of the insular Celts. Irish and Welsh mythologies have much to say about the other-world; indeed, one of their dominant themes is the easy passage to and fro from the one world to the other. The other-world as conceived of by the insular sources resembles an

A bronze head adorning a chariot found at Dejbjerg, Denmark. It dates from the first century BC and was probably made in Jutland. The arched moustache and the geometric character of the face are typical of Celtic art, suggesting that Celtic influences, particularly where ritual objects were concerned, became dominant in regions beyond those inhabited by speakers of Celtic languages. (Nationalmuseet, Copenhagen)

Modern druids celebrating the summer solstice at Stonehenge in 1999.

improved version of this one. It was like Tennyson's description of Arthur's final resting-place, 'Where falls not hail, nor rain, or any snow / Nor ever wind blows loudly'. It was the Island of Avalon, Lyonesse, the Tir Na n-Og of the Irish and the Annwfn of the Welsh. Magic apart, however, the eschatalogical processes whereby mortals reach such a paradise were not even sketchily outlined.

A further aspect characteristic of a religion is the existence of a priesthood or a class of interpreters of the divine purpose and will. On that aspect, the classical writers are more vocal than they are on any other. In particular, the druids fascinated them, as they continue to fascinate two thousand years later. Caesar provides a succinct account of their functions: 'They officiate at the worship of the gods, regulate public and private sacrifices, and give rulings on all religious questions … They act as judges in practically all disputes between tribes or between individuals.' He also stresses their role as teachers with 'young men flocking to them for education'. This emphasis on law and education, together with the references in the work of Pliny and others to the office of the *sacerdos* (priest) as well as to that of the druid, has given rise to the notion that the druid's role was political rather than priestly.

That druids had a political role is undeniable. The Gaulish rising of 53 BC began among the Carnutes, in whose lands the druids held the annual pan-Gaulish assembly, and Boudicca's revolt may have been a reaction to the Roman attack on the druidical centre of Anglesey. The Romans, generally tolerant of the religious practices of the people they conquered, were determined to stamp out druidism, presumably because they saw it as central to Celtic resistance to their rule. In early Irish literature, Cathbadh, the druid of Conochbar, king of Ulster, is portrayed as the king's adviser and prophet – a role, as Green argues, not dissimilar to that of

Samuel at the court of King David. In the *Táin*, the king was forbidden to speak until his druid had expressed himself. The notion of the priest as a political figure would have been familiar to Caesar. He became *pontifex maximus* in 63 BC, a position he held for twenty years and one which gave him control of the city's temples, its expiatory ceremonies and the regulation of the calendar, thus making him Rome's equivalent of an archdruid.

As Caesar is unambiguous about the druids officiating at worship, and as he emphasizes that their strongest sanction was their power to exclude those disobedient to them from attendance at rituals, attempts to distinguish druids from priests seem unjustifiable. Several classical sources do, however, mention other callings of a quasi-sacred character; for example, Strabo writes of druids, bards and *vates*. This threefold division of the sacral office is also present in Irish sources which mention druids, bards and *fili*. The *vates* or *fili* were the seers, while the bards sang the praises of men, just as the druids sang the praises of the gods. Central to the powers of all three was the gift of eloquence, a characteristic of the Celts noted by Cato and Diodorus Siculus. The significance of eloquence is illustrated by an anecdote told by Lucian, a Greek writer of the second century AD. He described an old man he had met in Gaul whose followers' ears were attached to his tongue by delicate gold chains. Such was the power of words that Irish mythology recounts an occasion when Queen Medb sent bards to kill an enemy with satire. It may be significant that a Welsh word cognate with *fili* is *gwawd*, which originally meant praise, but came to mean satire or derision.

Caesar stated that druidical doctrines originated in Britain, a statement of doubtful accuracy. By his day, the Celtic religion of Gaul was disintegrating under the impact of classical influences and the dislocation caused by invasion; in the Britain of the first century BC, that religion was still intact and Caesar probably assumed that the doctrines originated in that part of the world where they were still held in the highest regard. It is likely that the doctrines and the roles of the druids, bards and *vates* had been inherited from a body of beliefs once current throughout the Indo-European world. Indeed, some practices – the bull sacrifice among the Irish, for example – are reminiscent of the rites of the shamans of Siberia and may represent practices once prevalent among all manner of peoples. Posidonius, who subscribed to the belief that classical civilization represented a fall from some golden age, viewed druids as 'the most just of men, the moral philosophers and men of science' who had survived from the bright

A further view of the druidical ceremonies at Stonehenge.

morning of the world. Some of the Alexandrine commentators, admittedly relying on sources which were second if not third hand, compared the druids with the *magi* of Iran, while modern scholars have stressed their similarity to the brahmins of ancient Hindu culture – another example, they argue, of the congruences between the westernmost and the easternmost members of the Indo-European family.

Unlike the brahmins, who became a hereditary caste, druids were recruited from the sons of free-born warriors. It would appear that the daughters as well as the sons of such warriors could have ritual functions. Strabo described women living on an island at the mouth of the Loire who, on the occasion of the annual reroofing of their temple, chose one of their number for sacrifice. Pomponius Mela also mentioned an island – perhaps one of the Scilly Isles – inhabited by nine virgin priestesses, and Tacitus wrote of the weird black-robed women 'with dishevelled hair like furies' who greeted the Roman invasion of Anglesey in AD 61. The archaeological sources, rich in evidence of goddesses, also suggest the existence of priestesses; as has been seen, the 'princess' of Vix may well have been some kind of shaman. In the insular sources, druidesses make fleeting appearances in the Fenian Cycle, and the nine virgins of Welsh tradition, who heated the cauldron of the lord of the otherworld, presumably had some sacral role.

Written evidence of Celtic religion is at its richest in the Gaul of the first century BC, with Caesar providing the fullest information. The military campaigns he undertook while describing that religion helped to ensure its demise. His immense depredations in the fifties dislocated Gaulish society to such an extent that the old order – already in decline – was dealt a devastating blow. Subsequent Roman activities, such as the moving of the centre of the Aeduian tribe from the hilltop stronghold of Bibracte to the lowland Roman-style city of Augustodunum (Autun), meant further disruption, as did the introduction of Latin education and Roman social habits. In addition, there were deliberate attempts to stamp out at least some aspects of Celtic religion. Suetonius noted that Augustus prohibited Roman citizens from involving themselves in the *religio druidorum,* and there were further prohibitions under Tiberius, Claudius and Nero. In the first century AD, Britain underwent experiences similar to those of Gaul a century earlier, experiences which included the destruction of the ritual centres of Anglesey and the massacre of their devotees. The process which Caesar believed was already extant in the Gaul of his day – the identification of Celtic with classical gods – proceeded apace and led to the further attenuation of the distinctiveness of Celtic religion. In addition, some Celtic practices may have been absorbed into the rituals of the eastern cults which were winning increasing acceptance, especially among those serving in the imperial armies. For example, the Mithraic cult of Iran, with its

The May Queen at the Beltane Fire Festival at Calton Hill, Edinburgh, in 1998.

god of light identified with the sun, who had slain a primordial bull and had fertilized the world with its blood, offered doctrines not worlds away from those of the Celts.

Nevertheless some vestiges did survive and, indeed, there seems to have been a revival in respect for Celtic traditions in the last centuries of the Empire. Pseudo chronicles of the fourth century state that the emperors Alexander Severus, Diocletian and Aurelian had dealings with druidesses. The temple to Nodens at Lydney attained its most elaborate form in the 360s.

Phoebicius, the temple priest of Belenus referred to by Ausonius of Bordeaux (died *c.* 392), has already been mentioned. He had 'sprung from the druids of Bayeux' and his son and grandson became distinguished professors of rhetoric at the University of Bordeaux. They could 'compose an epic in verse more readily than another could compose one in prose' and were thus continuing the traditions of eloquence characteristic of the druids. The abiding delight in eloquence is also suggested by Symmacus (died *c.* 402), the greatest Roman orator of his day, who was proud to state that he had been trained by a Gaulish rhetorician.

Carved severed heads from Entremont, near Marseille, France. (Musée Granet, Aix-en-Provence)

Phoebicius's descendants included Hedibia, who became a Christian and one of the correspondents of St Jerome (died 420). In a letter to her, the saint acknowledged her family's 'mastery of eloquence and of secular knowledge, [but] deservedly I shall deny them knowledge of the Law of God.' Jerome's insistence that Christianity represented a complete break with the religion of the Celts is less evident in insular sources, for among the Britons and the Gaels the interplay between the old religion and the new is a fascinating theme. In a fourteenth-century manuscript recounting the life of the Welsh saint Beuno (died *c.* 642), the saint, on his arrival in heaven, was greeted by St Peter accompanied by the other apostles and the druids. According to Irish tradition, St Brigit was brought up in a druidical household; Brucher, the Leinster druid, was aware of the significance of the cosmic happenings he witnessed at the hour of the crucifixion, for, as Yeats suggests, the Celtic sages were at Golgotha in spirit. In Muirchú's *Life of St Patrick*, the saint is portrayed not as the bringer of a new religion but as one who excels in the practices of the old. As commander of the elements and the performer of the most fantastic miracles, he was, as Michael Richter put it, 'the supreme druid'. There was thus a melding of the old traditions with the far higher moral teaching of Christianity. It is that melding which causes the spirituality of the Celtic Church to be so captivating in its appeal.

The Atlantic Celts

Llyn Padarn, Snowdon and the Llanberis Pass,
Gwynedd, Wales. (Mick Sharp)

At the end of the first century AD, Publius Tacitus wrote a biography of his father-in-law, Agricola, governor from AD 77 to 84 of the Roman province of Britannia. In it he described how the Britons 'were gradually led on to the amenities which make vice agreeable – arcades, baths and sumptuous banquets. They spoke of such novelties as civilization, when really they were only a feature of enslavement.' His comments indicate that, within a generation of the Roman conquest of Britain, the island's upper classes were embracing a Roman lifestyle. He noted that 'in place of a distaste for the Latin language, there was a passion to command it'. 'Our native dress came into favour, and the toga is everywhere to be seen.' The Roman authorities were assisting in the 'building of temples, public squares and private mansions', training 'the sons of chiefs in the liberal arts' and much appreciating 'the natural ability' displayed by the Britons.

In the mid-first century BC, Gaul, the heartland of Celtic power in mainland Europe, was conquered and its inhabitants were progressively Romanized. Tacitus's comments are proof that, a century and a half later, the same processes were under way among the insular Celts. Admittedly, Agricola had not succeeded in bringing the whole of Britain under Roman rule, and Ireland remained inviolate. Nevertheless, when Agricola gave up the governorship, the Empire had not yet attained its fullest extent. In AD 84, Roman rule hardly reached beyond the Pennines and, in Wales, structures of control were only just being put in place. In the 120s, the decade of the building of Hadrian's Wall, Rome seemed content not to venture beyond the foothills of the Cheviot Range; in the 140s, however, the legions advanced to the Antonine Wall built across the narrow waist of Scotland, suggesting that the conquest of the entire island was still a possibility. Had not Roman intrigue led to the recall of Agricola, he might well have sought to annex Ireland. 'I have often heard Agricola say', wrote Tacitus, 'that Ireland could be reduced and held by

Tre'r Ceiri, the dramatically sited fortified Iron-Age settlement on the slopes of Yr Eifl, Gwynedd, Wales. The walls enclose some one hundred and fifty round houses and the site was occupied from the second century BC well into the period of the Roman occupation of Wales.

a single legion … and that it would be easier to hold Britain if it were completely surrounded by Roman armies so that liberty was banished from its sight.'

Thus, when Tacitus was writing, the extinction of Celtic polities in their entirety seemed a likely prospect. This, however, did not happen, for in the mid-second century, the Empire reached its furthest limits, and, thereafter, outlying lands were progressively abandoned. Thus, southern Scotland had only a partial experience of Roman power, and northern Scoland and Ireland none at all. Even within the imperial province of Britannia, the impact of Rome varied greatly from region to region. The north, Wales and the far south-west only received the lightest veneer of Latin culture. Tacitus's comments undoubtedly referred to the fertile lands of the south and east – the regions defined by Cyril Fox as Britain's Lowland Zone. That zone had long had close links with Gaul. Hengistbury on the Dorset coast, the source of Britain's largest collection of Roman and Celtic coins, was, in the first century BC, the chief entrepôt of cross-channel trade and has been described as the island's first urban community. The Atrebates had a homeland in Gaul as well as in Britain; Caesar is specific about Belgae settlements in the south-east and argued that his invasions of Britain were necessary in order to punish the inhabitants for their support of their kinsfolk in Gaul.

This remote loch region of the Isle of Mull, Scotland, typifies the highland landscape which proved so effective a barrier to Roman ambitions to subdue the whole of Britain.

Indeed, all the evidence suggests that south-eastern Britain was a somewhat paler replica of Gaul. It would therefore be reasonable to assume that its Romanization – or deCelticization – was a process similar to that which took place in Gaul. There were modifying factors, however: Britain – even its quasi-Gaulish regions – was geographically more remote; its Romanizing agencies were smaller in size and number, and Britannia adjoined independent Celtic-speaking polities. Furthermore, the time-scale was different: the Roman presence in southern Gaul lasted for almost five and a half centuries, in central and northern Gaul for four and a half centuries and in Britain for three and a half centuries.

But for the great Gaulish revolt of 52 BC, Caesar's expeditions to Britain in 55 and 54 could well have been the prelude to his conquest of the island. His account of the expeditions provides the name of the first Briton known to history. He was Cassivellaunus, king of the Catuvellauni, whose main centre of power lay immediately to the north of the Thames. In Welsh tradition, he appears in the *Mabinogi* as Caswallon and is presented in the context of transmogrified gods. He was the son of Beli – possibly the euhemerized god Belenus – and cousin of Bendigeidfran and Manawydan fab Llyr – versions perhaps of the Irish gods Bran and

Manannán mac Lir. He is described as the conqueror of Britain, and there have been suggestions that, like Ireland, pre-Roman Britain recognized a high king. Cassivellaunus led the British resistance to Caesar, and, after he submitted, the Trinovantes of Essex, freed of his overlordship, seem to have enjoyed the patronage of Rome. Indeed, the quantity of Roman luxury goods found in Essex suggests that they had a monopoly of trade with Roman-held territory in the decades following Caesar's invasion. Eventually, however, the Catuvellauni regained their superiority. Cassivellaunus's son, Tasciovanus, issued a coin bearing the Celtic inscription TASCIO RIGON – the great king – and Tasciovanus's son, Cunobelinus – Shakespeare's Cymbeline and the Cynfelin of Welsh tradition – was described by Tacitus as 'the great king of Britain'. Coins of Cunobelinus have been found in a wide swathe of southern and eastern England, from Kent to the Wash and across to the upper Thames. The heartland of his kingdom is rich in evidence of what is known as the Aylesford-Swayling Culture, a culture characterized by wheel-made pottery and artefacts in the most developed form of the La Tène style.

Cunobelinus's death *c.* AD 42 may have provided the occasion for the sustained Roman invasion of Britain which began in 43. However, while Rome might well have been concerned by the growth of the power of the Catuvellauni, the invasion was probably motivated more by knowledge of Britain's wealth in corn and other resources, and by the Emperor Claudius's desire to have the right to celebrate the conquest of what his triumphal arch would call *Gentes Barbaras Trans Oceanus*. By 47, Aulus Plautius, the first governor of Britannia, was master of the south-east of the island; a road, the Fosse Way stretching from Lincoln to Exeter, was built to mark the frontier of the conquered territories. Released from the power of the Catuvellauni, rulers of polities previously threatened by them hastened to embrace imperial authority. Cogidubnus of Sussex became a Roman citizen, took the title *Rex et legatus Augusti in Britannia*, adopted the names Tiberius Claudius and built a temple to the Roman gods in a wholly classical style.

The Fosse Way proved to be an unstable frontier, for the lands it demarcated were open to invasion by tribes living beyond it. In 47 and 48, the new province was attacked by the Silures of south-east Wales. They were led by Caratacus, the Caradog of Welsh tradition and the exiled son of Cunobelinus; the readiness of a westerly people to accept the leadership of the heir of an easterly dynasty would seem to be an indication of the essential unity of the inhabitants of southern Britain. Caratacus was captured in 52 and was sent to Rome where, according to Tacitus, he expressed astonishment that 'you who possess so many palaces, covet our poor tents'.

The defeat of Caratacus did not end the resistance of the tribes of Wales. In 52, the Silures defeated a Roman legion and some five years later the Emperor Nero decided upon a more thorough conquest. In 61, the druids of Anglesey were

The statue of Boudica, queen of the Iceni, erected on the Victoria Embankment, London, in 1902. Its inscription boasts that the empire of her descendants – the British Empire – was far more extensive than that of Boudica's persecutor – the Roman Empire.

PICTLAND

Iona

DALRIADA

LORN

St. Vigeans

ISLAY

KINTYRE

Antonine Wall

Traprain Law

GODODDIN

STRATHCLYDE

Lindisfarne

DÁL
RIATA

RHEGED

BERNICIA
NORTHUMBRIA

Hadrian's Wall

ULSTER

Armagh

MAN

DEIRA

CONNACHT

MEATH

Tara

Doolin

GWYNEDD

Ennis

LEINSTER

MERCIA

CEREDIGION

POWYS

EAST ANGLIA

MUNSTER

BRYCHEINIOG

St. Davids

DYFED

ERGING
GWENT

GLYWYSING

Llanilltud
Fawr

WESSEX

KENT

DEVON

SUSSEX

Tintagel

CORNWALL

Britain, Ireland and Brittany

AD 400–700

CORIOSOLITAE

OSISMII

Forest of Brocéliande

REDONES

DYFED   Celtic Kingdoms

VENETI

MERCIA   Anglo Saxon Kingdoms

VENETI   Armorican Tribal Groupings

NAMNATES

Tours

Folk Movements

The hillfort on the summit of the Malvern Hills, England. Its massive ramparts are typical of the great hillforts of the Welsh borderland. Situated at 430 metres (1400 foot) above sea level, it offers superb views in all directions. Tradition suggests that Vortigern was a native of the Welsh borderland.

massacred, and in the same year the governor, Suetonius Paulinus, defeated the great rising of the Iceni of Norfolk led by their queen, Boudicca. Even Caesar's slaughter in Gaul seems to have been mild compared with Suetonius's massacres in East Anglia, a factor perhaps in the subsequent paucity of evidence of Brythonic culture there. Agricola, in his turn, was equally ferocious in dealing with the Ordovices of north-west and central Wales. It is small wonder that his son-in-law, Tacitus, recorded the Highland chief, Calgacus, when offering a British view of Roman agression, as speaking of 'looting, killing and raping ... By twisting their words they call it "empire" and, wherever they have created a wilderness, they call it "peace"'.

By the 80s, the conquest of what would be England and Wales was virtually complete. As Gibbon put it: 'After a war of about forty years, undertaken by the most stupid [Claudius], maintained by the most dissolute [Nero] and terminated by the most timid [Domitian] of all the emperors, the greater part of the island submitted to the Roman yoke.' The structure of Roman control was, by then, becoming apparent. London, seriously mauled by Boudicca's forces, was emerging as the *de facto,* if not the *de jure,* capital of Britannia. It was the hub of the province's roads and would become the seat of the governor and of the provincial treasury. Its walls, first built *c.* 140, enclosed 135 hectars, giving it an area one and a half times larger than Cirencester, its nearest rival. The province's leading port, it attracted merchants not only from Italy and Gaul but also from Iberia, Greece and the Levant. It contained the chief mint, which provided the Roman coinage essential in ensuring that the core region of the province was a single economic unit.

Unlike most of the urban centres of Britannia, the precise status of Roman London is uncertain. Of the others, at least three, Colchester, Lincoln and Gloucester, were *colonae,* that is settlements for the veterans of the legions. In addition, there were *municipia*, of which only one – Verulam (St Albans) – is known in Britain. Far more numerous were the *civitates*, Roman-style towns established as the capitals of those tribal units considered loyal by the imperial authorities. Cirencester (Corinium) was the centre of the Dobuni of the Cotswolds, Dorchester (Durnovaria) that of the Durotriges of Dorset, and Wroxeter (Viroconium) that of the Cornovii of Shropshire and the Welsh border. As the years passed, even previously hostile tribes were granted *civitates*. Thus, the Iceni came to enjoy a measure of self-government at Caistor-next-Norwich (Venta Icenorum) and the Silures at Caerwent (Venta Silurum).

With the exception of the doubtful *civitas* of Maridunum (Carmarthen), all the *civitates* were situated in the region south and east of a line from the mouth of the Tamar to the mouth of the Tees, with those of the Dumnonii and the Brigantes – Isca Dumnoniorum (Exeter) and Isurium (Aldborough) – the westernmost and the northernmost of them. That region was the Lowland Zone of Britain and the civil zone of Britannia. It was also the region of the *villae*, the country houses, Roman in style and comfort, which were the centres of landed estates practising capitalist agriculture. At their most numerous in the third and fourth centuries, when the province had several hundred of them, they existed in large clusters, especially in Kent, Hampshire, Dorset and the Cotswolds.

All these developments were forces for Romanization and deCelticization. The establishment of the *colonae*, settlements of Roman citizens fluent and literate in Latin, cannot but have meant the creation of localities in which the Brythonic language had no place. London was, no doubt, a polyglot city, but Latin would have enjoyed a status denied to other languages. The *civitates*, while permitting the survival of tribal structures, were intended to impress upon the natives the superiority of Roman ways. While the fields of the *villae* were undoubtedly worked by local Celts, it would be apparent to them that power, wealth and comfort belonged to those who embraced *Romanitas*. As Tacitus's comments prove, this the British ruling class was eager to do, for Tiberius Claudius Cogidubnus had numerous imitators. In the Lowland Zone, many members of that class adopted not only the language of the conquerors but also their lifestyle, art and religion. They came to consider themselves to be Roman, particularly after 214, when the Emperor Caracalla granted Roman citizenship to all free men throughout the Empire. Rome was their country, and the memory of that self-identification remained for centuries after its substance had vanished.

In Gaul, such processes led to almost total deCelticization. It would appear that this did not happen in the civil zone of Britannia. As has already been suggested, distance, scale, time and the proximity of independent Celtic-speaking polities ensured that this zone did not experience Romanization with the intensity which

The Forum in Rome near the modern mosaic map outlining the extent of the Roman Empire.

characterized Gaul. Apart from London, one of the largest cities north of the Alps, urban centres were smaller and *villae* were less numerous. It has been estimated that in the third century, when Britannia was at its most prosperous, its civil zone contained at least two million of the three million people believed to have inhabited the province. Of these, perhaps two hundred thousand were urban dwellers, and a further fifty thousand constituted the Romano-British element of the *villae*. While these figures are very tentative, they suggest that the Romanized population represented only a small proportion of the total inhabitants. Given time, that minority, with its higher status, would probably have ensured that its language, values and culture became those of society as a whole. Time, however, was precisely what it was not granted.

It is suppositions such as these which permit the belief that the bulk of the population of Britannia's civil zone remained Celtic-speaking throughout the centuries of Roman occupation. Precise evidence is less forthcoming. Urban Roman Britain has yielded a wealth of graffiti, much of it in working-class contexts. It is all in Latin, suggesting that literacy in that language was widespread in the towns. However, the lack of Brythonic graffiti is not conclusive evidence that Brythonic was not spoken; rather does it indicate that it was not a written language. In his influential study, *Language and History in Early Britain*, Kenneth Jackson argued that the Celtic river names abundant in lowland Britain were passed on directly to the Anglo-Saxons by Celtic-speakers, which would suggest that, in the fifth and sixth centuries, the rural inhabitants of regions such as Hampshire and Berkshire were Celtic-speaking. The absorption by Brythonic of Latin words, those for the days of the week, for example — words which were inherited by Welsh — must, he maintained, have occurred in the bilingual setting of the Lowland Zone. Jackson also argued that the Latin spoken, even among Romano-British *villa* owners, was a language learnt at school rather than the mother tongue, an argument which would seem to be confirmed by a comment in the *Confessio* of St Patrick and by the stilted character of the Latin from which many of the loan words in Welsh were borrowed. Some authorities, D. Ellis Evans in particular, believe that too much has been made of this, and point to loan words from Vulgar Latin. Yet even if Latin were widely in use as a vernacular in Roman Britain, this does not imply the extinction of Brythonic, even in the civil zone. Sources such as the *Life of St Guthlac* indicate that there were speakers of Welsh in eastern England as late as the year 700. But perhaps the most telling argument arises from a comparison between the

The great pool at Bath, England, which is still fed through Roman plumbing from the natural hot springs of the Avon Valley. It was in such luxurious surroundings that the British aristocracy came to adopt a Roman lifestyle.

The footings of the barracks at the Roman legionary fortress at Caerleon, Wales. The only legionary barracks visible in Europe, they were built in the mid-second century AD. The fortress could accommodate about 5,500 heavily-armed infantrymen.

experience of Gaul and that of Britain. The descendants of the Germanic-speaking Franks, Goths and Burgundians who conquered Gaul came eventually to adopt the language and culture of the Gallo-Romans. The descendants of the Germanic-speaking Angles, Saxons and Jutes who conquered most of Britannia did not come to adopt those of the Romano-British. Their language and culture were clearly not as widespread and as rooted as were those of the Gallo-Romans.

It is possible that too much attention is given to Britannia's civil zone. After all, it constituted a mere 30 per cent of the total surface area of the homeland of the insular Celts – although it undoubtedly contained a higher proportion of that homeland's population. West and north of the Tamar–Tees line lay Cornwall, Wales and most of the north of England. While the Romanized urban settlements lay south and east of that line, the garrisoned forts lay to its west and north – at least until the building of coastal defences in the fourth century. Thus, the Highland Zone of Britannia was its military zone, where Romanization through urbanity and urbanization did not occur. This did not imply a complete absence of deCelticizing agencies there, for the garrisons were numerous and heavily manned. Aulus Plautius led forty thousand men to Britain in AD 43 and, at least until the mid-second century, 15 per cent of Rome's entire armed forces were stationed in Britannia, although the province hardly constituted 3 per cent of the surface area of the Empire. After the mid-first century, few of them were to be found in the civil zone, although the presence in the province of so large a body of troops had repercussions in that zone also; there was the need to make provision for veterans, for example, and to supply wheat to the garrisons – the key to the prosperity of the *villa* economy.

In the military zone, there were the legionary fortresses of Caerleon (Isca), Chester (Deva) and York (Eboracum), each capable of housing a legion of 5,500 men. Furthermore, Wales and its borderland had some thirty-five auxiliary forts,

Hadrian's Wall as it swings across the hills of Northumberland. Begun in the 120s AD, it was completed by the end of the second century. It extends for 117 kilometres (seventy-three miles) across northern England.

and there were at least as many in northern England, apart from the sixteen forts of Hadrian's Wall. In addition, the Highland Zone contained major industrial centres, inhabited no doubt by Latin-speaking overseers and Celtic-speaking workers – the goldmines at Dolaucothi near Carmarthen, for example, and the tileworks at Holt near Chester. Associated with each fortress was a *vicus*, a civil settlement whose inhabitants provided services for the garrison. The Empire did not permit recruits to serve in the provinces in which they were raised, and thus it would be rare for soldiers to speak the language of the local inhabitants. Some of the troops may have gone native; there were shrines to Celtic gods on Hadrian's Wall and soldiers certainly married women from the *vici* – gravestones at Caerleon offer examples of men with Latin names married to women with Celtic ones. While an agent of deCeltization, the army was not always a force for Romanization; the heavy recruitment among Germans in the later centuries of the Empire could well have caused Germanic languages to be as widely spoken in military encampments as Latin. There were limiting factors, however. In some parts of the Highland Zone – Cornwall, for example, or south-west Wales – there is very little evidence of

Another view of Hadrian's Wall.

military occupation. In others, such as the territory of the Ordovices, hostility to Rome was so great that there was probably only minimal contact between the conquerors and the conquered. Indeed, it can be claimed that the Ordovices were never really brought under Roman authority; their territory is specifically excluded on the modern map of the Empire displayed in mosaic at the Forum in Rome. In addition, Rome's formidable array of fortifications

was not fully garrisoned throughout the centuries of Roman occupation; in the 120s, members of the Second Legion based at Caerleon and the Twentieth based at Chester were involved in the building of Hadrian's Wall, and, by the late second century, most of the auxiliary forts had been abandoned. Thus, although there were areas in which the military presence was substantial and long-lasting enough to undermine native traditions, it is likely that, in most of the military zone, Celtic culture remained largely intact throughout the Roman era.

That was even more true of the region between the Hadrianic and Antonine Walls. Agricola built a number of forts in southern Scotland, including a pivotal one at Newstead (Trimontium) in the Tweed valley. The building of the Antonine Wall in the 140s indicates the intention of annexing the region, but that was a policy which was quickly abandoned. In the late second and early third centuries and again in the early fourth century, imperial forces invaded Scotland on several occasions, but these seem to have been punitive expeditions rather than attempts at conquest. Roman influence in the region may well have been considerable; some farming settlements appear to have been organized to serve the Roman economy and southern Scotland provided recruits for the Roman army. Eventually, however, the Empire seems to have been content to accept that the region's inhabitants were allies or client peoples of Rome rather than its subjects. Chief among them were the Selgovae and Votadini tribes. The hillforts of the Selgovae, such as Bonchester and North Eildon, have yielded few objects of Roman provenance, suggesting that the culture of the tribe experienced little Romanization. Traprain Law near Edinburgh, the probable capital of the Votadini, has yielded a spectacular collection of late-Roman silverware — the Traprain Law Treasure which is one of the glories of the Museum of Scotland. It has been interpreted as a bribe paid to the tribe to keep the

The ditch and ramparts of the Antonine Wall. The wall was begun in the 140s AD, but had been abandoned by the end of the second century. Unlike the stone-built Hadrian's Wall, it was constructed of clay and turf. It stretched for sixty kilometres (thirty-seven miles) across the narrowest part of Scotland.

peace or as the loot of a raiding expedition. It would appear that tribal structures beyond Hadrian's Wall proved more enduring than those in territories directly subject to the Empire; this may explain why that region is the source of Britain's earliest surviving literature in a Celtic language. The territory of the Selgovae and their neighbours, the Damnoni and the Novantae, came to form Strathclyde, a particularly tenacious Brythonic kingdom. The Votadini were to play a fascinating role in the political, military and literary history of the Brythonic Celts in the post-Roman years.

In Scotland, north of the Antonine Wall, the impact of Rome was minimal. In 83, Agricola's victory in the battle of Mons Graupius – presumed to be near Montrose – resulted in much slaughter. It also led to the building of a fort at Inchtutill in the Tay valley, capable of housing an entire legion. It was, however, garrisoned very briefly; its builders, on leaving it, abandoned a million unused nails. During Septimus Severus's invasion of 309, an extensive fort was built at Carpow on the Tay estuary, but that was also short lived. The Highlanders could sustain quasi-urban centres, such as the hillfort at Tap o'Noth in Aberdeenshire with its two hundred round houses. Ptolemy noted that Scotland beyond the Antonine Wall was inhabited by ten tribes, and Dio Cassius reported in 197 that they consisted of two groupings, the Caledonians and the Maeatae; comments in 297 and 310 indicate that they were known collectively as Picts, a name which may have its origins in a Latin slang word for painted peoples. Apart from those found at Roman-built sites, Roman artefacts are sparsely represented in Pictland and are very rare indeed beyond the Great Glen, indicating that the Picts experienced virtually no Romanization. As has been noted, they are generally believed to have been speakers of P-Celtic, although one form of Pictish may represent a pre-Indo-European survival.

The western coastlands of Scotland may also have had Q-Celtic-speaking inhabitants, for the narrow sea between those coastlands and Ireland was a highway rather than a barrier. Of all the lands of the Celts, Ireland was alone in having no experience of Roman invasion. That did not mean that the island was unaffected by the Empire. At Loughshinny near Skerries in County Dublin, the excavation of a structure not unlike a Roman fort created a frisson among Celtic scholars, who, for a time, believed that history would have to be rewritten. However, the structure proved to be a large trading post, and indicates that there was much to-ing and fro-ing between Ireland and Roman Britain. The royal capital at Tara has yielded some Roman artefacts, and hoards of Roman coins at

Iron-Age round houses reconstructed at the National Museum of Welsh Life, St. Fagans.

The statue of Cú Chulainn at the General Post Office in Dublin, Ireland, It commemorates the Irish insurrectionists of Easter 1916 who chose the Post Office as their headquarters.

Limerick, Antrim, Derry and elsewhere are proof of trade, or loot or payments to mercenaries. During the imperial era, some of the Irish may well have learnt Latin, but Roman influences did not disrupt the development of the Celtic culture of Ireland. Some suggestion of the nature of that culture may be gleaned from the *Táin Bó Cúailgne*, an epic which is believed to be set in the fourth century. With Cú Chulainn as its hero, it deals with the struggle between the men of Connacht and the men of Ulster. Rich on matters such as the status of the warrior, the practice of fosterage, the ritual of banquets and the role of the poets, its contents accord remarkably with the accounts of the Celts given by such classical writers as Posidonious and Caesar.

Thus in Ireland, circumstances were favourable to the durability of Celtic culture, as they were in much of Britain. That was not the case in mainland Europe. As has been seen, St Jerome's comment suggests that Celtic was still a living language in the Mosel valley in the fourth century; if so, it was soon to be obliterated by German-speaking incomers, as it had already been in the heartlands of the Hallstatt and the La Tène cultures. Comments by Sidonius Apollinaris, Gregory of Tours and Venantius Fortunatus indicate that Gaulish was still being spoken in the fifth and sixth centuries, even as far south as the Auvergne. The existence of such pockets of survival is not incredible; Gothic, carried to the Crimea by sixth-century raiders, was still spoken there in the sixteenth century.

But where the mainland Celts are concerned, the chief centre of interest is Armorica or Brittany, a country which has continued to be a major centre of Celtic language and culture until the present day. On the eve of Caesar's invasion, Armorica, like the rest of Gaul, had a Celtic-speaking population. Of its five polities, the names of three – the Namnates, the Veneti and the Redones – survive in those of three of its major cities – Nantes (Naoned), Vannes (Gwened) and Rennes

(Roazhon) – and the two others, the Osismii and the Coriosolitae, are remembered at Carhaix (Karaez) and Corseul. There are historians who believe that Armorica, like the rest of Gaul, wholly abandoned Gaulish, and that Breton Celticity owes everything to migrants from Britain. Yet since the eighteenth century, there have been advocates of the view that Brittany's Celticity is indebted, at least in part, to the survival of Gaulish. The great Celticist Joseph Loth, writing in 1883, rejected this view. From the early 1950s onwards, however, François Falc'hun argued insistently that, while the Breton of Finisterre and Côte du Nord is largely British in origin, that of the Vannes region is essentially Gaulish. In 1980, Leon Fleuriot's magisterial if flawed study, *Les Origines de la Bretagne*, was published, a book destined to become the starting-point for all subsequent discussions of Breton Celticity. Fleuriot placed the history of Brittany in the context of millennia of contact between Armorica and Britain. He maintained that Breton is fundamentally a language which sprang from that of migrants from Britain, but was influenced by the Gaulish substratum, in the north and west of Armorica as much as, if not more, than in the Vannes region. If Fleuriot's thesis is accepted, it is only in Armorica that any significant elements of the original Celticity of mainland Europe survive.

This survey of the lands wholly or partially Celtic-speaking in the last centuries of the Roman Empire indicates that Celticity was secure in Ireland, tenacious in much of northern and western Britain, and challenged in the east and the south of the island and in Armorica. In the history of Celtic culture, the most significant change in the immediate post-Roman centuries was the disappearance of that culture in most of southern and central Britain, and the triumph there of the culture of the Anglo-Saxons. So inadequately documented is that change that it is the subject of much controversy and of even more implausible theorizing. To leading nineteenth-century English historians, the story was simple. Following the fall of the Empire, the Romano-British, helpless in the face of the attacks of the Picts and Scots, called in Teutonic warriors. Led by Hengist and Horsa, the warriors sailed across the North Sea and landed at Ebbsfleet on the Isle of Thanet. J. R. Green, the nineteenth century's most popular chronicler of the history of the English, wrote of Ebbsfleet: 'No spot can be so sacred to the English as the spot which first felt the tread of English feet.' After a long struggle, the invaders and their descendants established their English kingdoms and killed or drove out all the previous inhabitants. 'Not a Briton', wrote Green, 'remained as subject or slave on English ground.' For the English, the portrayal was attractive. In accord with the rampant racism of the period, the Celts – the Irish in particular – were seen as unenterprising, treacherous and fanatical, and thus wholly different from the practical, trustworthy and enlightened English. It was comforting therefore to believe in the extinction of the Celts of England, for that meant that the English had no Celtic ancestry.

The story is now believed to be more complex. Green's portrayal of Thanet feeling 'the tread of English feet' is anachronistic to say the least. As Norman Davies put it, the English did not land 'pre-mixed, pre-cooked and pre-packaged ... [and] no one uttered the word England until at least three hundred years after Hengist's death'. There were numerous Teutonic speakers in Britain before the fall of the Empire, for the imperial forces were becoming armies of Germans recruited to defend the Empire from Germans. Cemeteries with German characteristics have been found near all the Roman cities of eastern Britain, and the Anglian kingdom of Deira may owe its origins to the German veterans of York. Britannia did indeed slip from the grasp of the Empire, although any sudden 'withdrawal of the legions' would be far from the mark. The province had been progressively denuded of its garrisons, particularly by Magnus Maximus – the Macsen Wledig of Welsh tradition – who in 383 sought to dethrone the Emperor Gratian. In 409, the Romano-British, deprived of the protection of imperial troops, seized power for themselves. The following year, the Emperor Honorius, writing at a time when Rome itself was falling into the hands of the Gothic forces of Alaric, recognized their action and advised them to defend themselves. For a generation or so, the Romano-British, presumably the leading men of the *civitates*, had a measure of success. Although the *villa* economy collapsed, possibly because of the disappearance of the market represented by the Roman army, the cities continued to function. When Germanus of Auxerre visited one of them in 429 – Verulam, probably – the civic officials were still fulfilling their duties.

Within a further generation, however, power had passed to leaders from the less Romanized parts of Britain, presumably because military skills were more widespread there. Chief among them was Vortigern – the Gwrtheyrn of Welsh tradition – a Brythonic chieftain from the borders of Wales. He defeated Ambrosius Aurelianus – the Emrys Wledig of Welsh tradition – who is portrayed as an aristocratic if not an imperial Roman, and his defeat is considered to be evidence of a 'Celtic revival'. According to the ninth-century Welsh chronicler Nennius, it was Vortigern who invited Hengist and Horsa to Britain, apparently sometime in the 440s. It is possible too that it was he who invited Cunedda of the Votadini people to lead a force to drive out the Irish who had colonized north-west Wales, an enterprise which led to the establishment of the kingdom of Gwynedd. The Irish were also colonizing south Wales, where the kingdoms of Dyfed and Brycheiniog were long to be ruled by dynasties of Irish descent. In addition, Armorica was experiencing large-scale migration from Britain. At the same time, there was a major incursion of migrants from northern Ireland into the islands and peninsulas of Dalriada in western Scotland. These were the Scotti, who would eventually give their name to Scotland.

Germanic incomers to Britain should therefore be seen in the context of large-scale wanderings of people. Indeed – natives as they were of the Netherlands and the lower neck of Denmark – they were responding to a chain of pressures extending from the depths of Asia to the North Sea, the *Völkerwanderung* which escorted the western Roman Empire to its grave. This, no doubt, was the context of the appeal of the Britons to Aetius, who upheld some remnants of the power of the western Roman Empire in the 440s and the 450s, an appeal recorded by the Welsh monk Gildas in about 540: 'The barbarians push us back to the sea, and the sea pushes us back to the barbarians; between these two kinds of death, we are either drowned or slaughtered.' That statement and others in Gildas's work provided the basis for the belief in the genocide of the Britons. The reality is more prosaic. By *c.* 500, the Saxons had established kingdoms in Kent, Sussex and East Anglia; some of the previous inhabitants were no doubt killed and others migrated, but the vast majority were eventually assimilated by their conquerors, for the notion that the Celtic west could have accommodated hundreds of thousands of refugees beggars belief. Clauses in the laws of Aethelbert of Kent, drawn up in about 602, refer to his Brythonic subjects, thus indicating that even the earliest of the conquered regions had a significant British population. Furthermore, during the whole of the fifth century and much of the sixth, the territories held by German rulers constituted only a small part of Britain. That, as Nora Chadwick put it, was a period when it was possible to travel from Edinburgh to Cornwall in the assurance that Brythonic would be understood along the whole of the journey and when Brythonic kingdoms were paramount in the island.

According to Gildas, the containment of the Germanic kingdoms was the result of the Britons' victory at Badon Hill, presumed to have been fought either in Sussex or near Bath and to have occurred around 496. Nennius attributed the victory to the figure who was to become central to the mythology of the Brythonic Celts. 'The twelfth battle', he wrote, 'was on Badon Hill and in it nine hundred and sixty men fell in one day from a single charge of Arthur's, and no one laid them low save he alone; and he was victorious in all his campaigns.' Nennius's comments, two entries in the Welsh Annals, some scattered allusions in Welsh poetry and the early tale *Culhwch ac Olwen* are the sole surviving references to Arthur which predate 1100. Then in the 1130s came Geoffrey of Monmouth's *Historia Regum Britanniae*, and thereafter a vast literature was written in almost all the languages of western Europe. Arthur continues to fascinate: the number of scholarly books, articles and reviews concerning him now exceeds twenty thousand. He has come to epitomize all that is appealing in Celticity. Camelot, his mythical court, is the symbol of a myriad hopes – from the vibrancy of J. F. Kennedy's White House to a host of novels, plays and films.

Again, the reality is more prosaic. Assuming that Arthur was indeed a historic figure, he can plausibly be portrayed in the context of the survival of at least some elements of Roman Britain. His name is Latin in origin, and the list of his battles suggests that he fought in southern Scotland as well as in eastern, southern and south-western England. Nennius stated that he had links with eastern Wales and Herefordshire, and traditions associating him with Cornwall and Somerset may not be without substance. His wide-ranging geographical connections are consistent with the notion that he was the leader of mobile cavalrymen, perhaps on the model of the *Dux Britanniarum*, an office first established by the Roman authorities in about 300. Despite the paucity of references to Arthur predating the publication of *Historia Regum Britanniae*, Geoffrey undoubtedly drew upon a mass of traditions which had survived among the Brythonic Celts. Why Arthur should apparently have figured more largely in their memory than anyone else is not wholly clear. The answer may lie in their spirited resistance to invaders from beyond the frontiers of the Roman Empire. In Italy, Gaul and Iberia, the Romanized inhabitants rapidly submitted to the invaders, but in Britain there was a three-hundred-year struggle for control of the former Roman province. In establishing that province, the Romans had created an image of authority – the image of Britannia under a single government, the image of the Crown of the Kingdom. The natural inheritors of that authority were the Romano-British, but by the end of the long struggle the crown had passed to others. The anguish of that loss became the motive force of much of Welsh mythology. There was one period when the Brythonic Celts looked as if they were winning; that was the age of Arthur. Thus, his fame can be seen as the desire of the Welsh – indeed, the desire of all those who had been touched by *Romanitas* – to pay tribute to the last of the heirs of Rome to make a successful stand against the 'barbarians'.

A glimpse of the waters of the great pool of Roman Bath.

Gildas stated that, following Badon Hill, there was a generation of peace. According to Frankish sources, some of the Germanic invaders returned to mainland Europe, a migration seemingly confirmed by excavations in the Low Countries. In the middle decades of the sixth century, however, the woes of the Brythonic Celts returned. There is growing evidence that the period suffered much dislocation, caused by debris thrown into the atmosphere by a vast volcanic eruption in south-east Asia, and also, perhaps, by a close brush with a comet. In addition, there was the plague, which in 549 carried off Cunedda's descendant, Maelgwn, king of Gwynedd. It would seem that the plague was less virulent among Germanic peoples than among the British; the latter, unlike the former, had at least vestigial contacts with the Mediterranean lands to which the disease had been brought from southern Asia.

The Germanic advance resumed. In 577, the men of Wessex won the battle of Dyrham near the Severn estuary in a campaign which led to the capture of

Gloucester, Cirencester and Bath. Further north, the threat came from Bernicia and Deira, settlements which eventually coalesced to create the kingdom of Northumbria. Some time around the 570s, Urien of the Brythonic kingdom of Rheged – the region around the Solway Firth – besieged the Bernician stronghold of Lindisfarne, but was killed during the seige. A decade or two later, the Gododdin or Votadini of the Edinburgh region attacked Deira but were decisively defeated at Catraeth or Catterick. Praise of Urien is the main theme of the poems of Taliesin, and the attack upon Catraeth is the subject of the *Gododdin* of Aneirin, two of the poets hailed by Nennius as 'famed in British verse'. In 616, the Northumbrians defeated the British in the battle of Chester. In *c.* 635, Rheged fell to the Northumbrians, as did the territory of the Votadini *c.* 638. In the 640s, Mercia expanded into the upper Severn valley, giving rise to the greatest glory of early Welsh poetry, the lament of Heledd, princess of Powys. At the same time, the kingdom of Wessex was expanding towards the borders of Devon. In the entry for 682, the Welsh Annals contains a bald statement of the death from plague of Cadwaladr, king of Gwynedd. Centuries later, a scribe felt the need to embellish the entry; he added: 'And from that time onward, the Britons lost the crown of the kingdom and the Saxons won it.' A little over a century after the death of Cadwaladr, the reality of that loss was made manifest when Offa, king of Mercia, ordered, as Alfred's biographer put it, 'a great *vallum* to be made from sea to sea *inter Britanniam atque Merciam*'. To quote J. E. Lloyd, it was an act which marked 'a deliberate closing of the era of conquest'.

The chapel of St Gofan which nestles in a coign in the cliffs west of Tenby, Wales. It is an example of the remote sanctuaries sought by the 'saints' of the Celtic Church.

Thus was control of most of southern Britain lost by the Brythonic Celts. That loss did not mean their extinction. As has been seen, Aethelbert of Kent was obliged to take account of them in 602, as was Ine of Wessex *c.* 710. Yet, despite the doggedness of their resistance to Germanic advance, once conquered they seem to have been assimilated fairly rapidly. The process was a matter of the absorption of the majority by the minority, and central to it was the nature of Germanic rural colonization. The incomers settled in nucleated villages on the heaviest soils, living alongside rather than among the natives. Rather than being destroyed, the natives were surrounded and subsequently engulfed, a process greatly assisted by the fact that it was the newcomers who wielded political power. Although Wessex made legal provision for its British inhabitants, they could not but have been aware of their inferior status. A West Saxon noble had a wergild of 1200 shillings (the payment due to his family as satisfaction from his killer), a British noble one of 600 shillings. The Franks drew a similar distinction between themselves and the Gallo-Romans, but in Gaul there was a vital difference. The years of Roman occupation had ensured that the language of the Britons was low in status. The Germanic-speaking invaders of Gaul, on encountering natives who spoke high-status Latin, abandoned their own language, whereas the Germanic-speaking invaders of Britain, on encountering natives who spoke low-status Brythonic, did not abandon theirs. As a result, the Brythonic language, to quote Thomas Charles-Edwards, lost 'speakers in the post-Roman period on a scale not to be matched until the twentieth century. ... [In] lowland Britain [the language] disappeared almost without trace.' In addition, Charles-Edwards argued that the unity of the English language resulted, not from an amalgamation of the different dialects of the Saxons, Angles, Jutes and Frisians, but from the lingua franca created as the British under English rule sought to interpret the language of their conquerors. Thus, the Brythonic Celts not only invented Welsh, Cornish and Breton; they also invented English.

During the Germanic advance, the language of the Brythonic Celts underwent major change. It lost its inflections – its Latin-like endings – and thus a name like Maglocunus became Maelgwn. Two broad dialects can be dimly perceived – that of the west which gave rise to Welsh and that of the south-west which gave rise to Cornish and, in the main, to Breton. Speakers of the western dialect devised a name for themselves; it was *Cymry*, rooted in the Brythonic word *Combrogi*, or fellow-countrymen, and, as the name Cumbria indicates, it applied to the Britons of the north as well as to those of Wales. The *Cymry* were those who spoke *Cymraeg*, suggesting that their sense of nationality – if that is not an anachronistic term in this context – was rooted in language; this meant that, when they abandoned their language, they abandoned their nationality. The earliest surviving example of the use of the word comes in a poem of about 633, but it did not wholly oust the word *Brython* for at least a thousand years. The *Cymry* also devised a word for the Germanic invaders. Although their worst woes came at the hands of the Northumbrians, who are presumed to be Angles – or English – the *Cymry* chose to consider the invaders, in their totality, as Saxons; borrowing from the Latin *Saxones*, they called them *Saeson*. The *Saeson*, in turn, devised a name for their Brythonic-speaking neighbours. They called them *Welisc* or Welsh, a word usually interpreted as meaning strangers or foreigners. It did not mean any foreigner, however, for it applied only to those who had been Romanized. Other versions of the word may be found along the borders of the Empire – the Walloons of Belgium, the Welsch of the Italian Tyrol and the Vlachs of Romania – and the *welschnuss*, the walnut, was the nut of the Roman lands. As foreigners, they had a lower status; thus *Welisc* also suggested servility, much as the foreigners of eastern Europe came to be known as Slavs.

Of only one region of Britain can it be convincingly argued that the advance of the English led to large-scale migration. That region is the south-west. From there, so great was the outward movement to Armorica that it has been suggested that, when Devon was annexed by Wessex early in the eighth century, it was very thinly populated. As has been seen, the impact of the migration from Britain upon the Celticity of Brittany is a matter of controversy. So are the date and the causes of the migration. While Fleuriot saw it in the context of at least half a millennium of contact, others have stressed Nennius's comment about the settlement in Armorica of the followers of Magnus Maximus in the 380s; indeed, in 1983, there were festivities in Brittany to celebrate the country's sixteen-hundredth anniversary. Much has been made of the reference in the 470s to the twelve thousand Britanni who had settled north of the Loire. They were followers of Riothamus, who had answered Emperor Anthemius's appeal for help against the Goths, and memories of Riothamus's enterprise may have provided the basis for legends concerning Arthur's conquests in mainland Europe. There is some basis for believing that the first major wave of migration occurred between *c.* 440 and 480, when migrants from Britain may have settled in many parts of coastal northern Gaul; Normandy has about twenty places called Bretteville – the settlement of the Britons. If they were fleeing from Germanic invaders, they would have been Britons from south-eastern Britain, for the south-west was then a long way from any Germanic threat. Yet, as linguistic research is unanimous that the Brythonic carried to Armorica was that of the south-west, it has been argued that any fifth-century migration from south-eastern Britain was swamped by a later, far greater, one from the south-west. An alternative argument posits that the fifth-century migrants were indeed from the south-west and that they were fleeing, not from Germanic invaders, but from invaders from Ireland. On the other hand, there are some scholars who doubt whether fifth-century Armorica experienced any considerable influx of people from Britain.

Evidence from the sixth century is more substantial, and is specifically in the context of migrants displaced by Saxon advance. Wessex's victory at the battle of Dyrham in 577 may have been a trigger. Yet, some thirty years before that battle, Gregory of Tours referred to the country and its people, not as Armorica and Armorici but as Britannia and Britanni, and slightly later sources suggest that Armorica had come to be divided between a western Britannia and an eastern Romania. This fits in with place-name and other evidence which indicates that the region west of a line from St-Nazaire to St-Brieuc became thoroughly Celtic in speech, and that, between that line and one extending from Mont-St-Michel and the estuary of the Loire, Celtic-speakers became numerous if not dominant. Migration continued for another two centuries, and, at least until the tenth century, Cornwall and Brittany were a single cultural zone. So much so that the successor of south-western Brythonic was for long a single language; it is not easy to determine whether some of the marginal notes on ninth-century manuscripts in Brittany are in Cornish or in Breton. While the great majority of the migrants came from south-western Britain, Breton traditions indicate that their leaders were members of the royal houses of Wales. Thus, the colonization of Brittany appears to have been the joint enterprise of the Brythonic Celts as a whole.

Evidence of the way the settlement was carried out is scanty. There are advocates of the view that much of Armorica was deserted, and certainly a great deal of the country lay within the Forest of Brocéliande, the archetypal forest of Celtic legend. Fleuriot dismissed the notion of an uninhabited Armorica, and notes both evidence that the colonists were kindly received by the Gallo-Romans and that which suggests that there was conflict. The Merovingian dynasty of the Franks sought to bring Brittany under its control, and the Bretons were obliged, in theory at least, to accept the overlordship of the descendants of Clovis. In the ninth century, however, Nominoë, count of Vannes (died 851), won virtual independence. He conquered the Breton March and expanded his territory to include all the land later organized into the departments of Finistère, Morbihan, Ile-et-Vilaine, Loire-Atlantique and Côtes-du-Nord (renamed Côtes-d'Armor in 1989). The ninth century, in which the Celtic kingdom of Cornwall – the mother country, it could be claimed, of Celtic Brittany – was extinguished, saw Brittany becoming the most powerful of all the Celtic realms.

While migration by P-Celtic-speakers was giving rise to a new Celtic polity, so also was migration by Q-Celtic-speakers. The twenty-kilometre channel between Ulster and Kintyre had always been a major thoroughfare, but voyages across it seem to have increased in the late fifth century. Inhabitants of the Irish kingdom of Dál Riata in Antrim, under pressure perhaps from expansionist neighbours, began establishing colonies in Kintyre, Islay and Lorn, a region which came to be known as eastern Gael – Ar Gael, or Argyll. The three sons of Erc of Dál Riata settled in Argyll in about 500. The descendants of Gabhráin (died 557), the grandson of Fergus mac Erc, seem to have exercised sovereignty over the small kingdoms of Dalriada, the new Dál Riata in Argyll. The colonists were called Scotti, a name which may have its origins in an Irish word for raiders or plunderers. It was used by the Romans to describe all transmaritime Irish migrants and would, in later centuries, be applied to the Irish monastic communities of Germany, Switzerland and Italy; the great monastery at St Gallen near Lake Constance is rich in *libri scottice scripti*.

Initially, the Scotti of Dalriada were a small offshoot from Ireland, vastly overshadowed by the kingdoms of the Picts to the north and those of the Britons to the south of the Antonine Wall. However, they proved to be energetic and aggressive. Gabhráin's son, Áedhán (died 608), sent expeditions to Orkney and the

The cross on the Hill of Slane, County Meath, Ireland. It was erected on the hill on which, on Easter Eve, St Patrick defied the druids who were conducting their ceremonies on the nearby Hill of Tara.

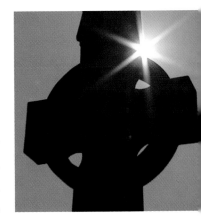

Isle of Man, and led his army in battles against the Picts and the Northumbrians. The unusual dynastic practices of the Picts made their kingdoms vulnerable to infiltration. Kingship passed among the Picts, not from father to son, but from the king to his sister's son, a matrilinear system unique in Europe and confirmation, perhaps, of the belief that some at least of the Picts belonged to a pre-Indo-European ethnic group. (Names of some of the legendary Pictish kings – Bliesblituth, for example, or Uipoigamet – reinforce such a belief.) The sisters married foreigners, usually Scots, thus ensuring that there was Dalriadan influence at the heart of Pictish kingdoms. The penetration of Pictland by such influences eventually brought about the amalgamation of the two peoples. In 839, Gabhráin's descendant, Kenneth mac Alpin, became king of both the Picts and the Scots. That led to the spread throughout Pictland of the Gaelic language of the Scots, which in its literary form was indistinguishable from Irish. Thus did the Picts abandon their P-Celtic language – and possibly a non-Celtic language also – and adopt the Q-Celtic of the Scots.

A similar process occurred in south-west Scotland, following the absorption by the kingdom of Scotland of P-Celtic-speaking Strathclyde in 1018. That year also saw the kingdom's annexation of the ancient territory of the Votadini or the Gododdin, but the language its Anglian colonizers had planted there – a northern dialect of the English of Northumbria – proved both durable and penetrative. Therefore, unlike most of the rest of Scotland, the inhabitants of Lothian and the south-east did not adopt Gaelic on coming under the rule of the descendants of Gabhráin. As Lothian eventually became the core of the kingdom, its deCelticization had a profound impact upon the history of Scotland. Although their roots were in Dalriada, the Scottish kings came to view Lothian as their homeland and the Highlands as an outlying and even a disdained and alienated part of their realm. Rather than being another name for the Gaelic of the original Scotti, the word Scots, when applied to language, became the word for the speech that developed from the Anglian dialect of Lothian, which was originally called Englis. As a consequence, citizens of Edinburgh consider that they are Angles rather than Celts, although – jocularly – in order to distinguish themselves from the English, they insist that they are descendants of the northern, 'acute', Angles rather than the southern, 'obtuse', ones.

Irish migration led to the evolution, not only of Scottish Gaelic, but also of Manx. Located as it was in the centre of what can be considered the 'Mediterranean' Sea of the Celts, the Isle of Man lay at the intersection of many sea routes. It is believed that in the early centuries of the Christian era, Brythonic was the main language of its inhabitants. From the fifth century onwards, however, Irish migration caused the island to be progressively Q-Celticized. Through the aggressive activity of Áedhán mac Gabhráin, Man was drawn into the orbit of Dalriada and, with the Gaelicization of Galloway, its links with Scotland were strengthened. The Manx language evolved to be closer to the Gaelic of Scotland than to Irish, a fact obscured by the phonetic conventions used in writing it.

Irish colonization of Man and Argyll coincided with a considerable influx from Ireland to Wales and south-west Britain. Indeed, as the Irish lexicographer Cormac wrote in the ninth century: 'The power of the Irish over the British was great … and the Irish lived as much east of the sea as they did [to the west].' The chief evidence of that influx consists of inscriptions in ogam, an alphabet of twenty letters written through carving grooves on a stone slab. They represent an attempt to adapt the Latin alphabet to the writing of Irish. Some three hundred ogam inscriptions have been found in Ireland, the great majority in the south. Argyll has yielded two, the Isle of

The sixth-century memorial stone in the churchyard at Cilgerran, Pembrokeshire, Wales. On the right angle of the face, an ogam inscription has been incised. Reading upwards, the letters are TRENAGUSU MAQI MAQITRENI. ([The stone of] Trenagusus, son of Maquitrenus.) The Latin inscription reads: TRENEGUSSI FILI MACUTRENI HIC IACET. ([The stone of] Trenegussus, son of Macutrenus. He lies here.) The memorial is one of the forty bilingual – Latin and Irish – inscribed stones known in Wales.

Man six, Cornwall and Devon eight and Wales forty; in addition, a stray ogam inscription was discovered in the Roman town of Silchester in Hampshire. Irish settlement in Cornwall may well have been considerable; as has been noted already, it was perhaps a factor in the British migration to Armorica. Cormac mentions the building of an Irish fortress in Cornwall; Irish pottery and tools have parallels in Cornwall and there are traditions that Irish rulers exercised overlordship in south-west Britain in the fourth and fifth centuries. The fate of these Irish settlements is unknown, but Jackson suggested that Irish was spoken in Cornwall as late as the seventh century.

Evidence of Irish settlement in Wales is more substantial. Of the forty ogam inscriptions found there, the largest number are in what became the kingdom of Dyfed (essentially Pembrokeshire and west Carmarthenshire), a region where Irish loan-words feature in place-names. The early Irish epic, *The Expulsion of the Deisi*, records the migration of the Deisi of south-east Ireland to Wales under their king Eochaid Allmuir (Eochaid over-the-sea). Welsh and Irish genealogies indicate that his descendants ruled in Dyfed until the ninth century. The regnal lists include the name Voteporix, a ruler mentioned by Gildas and commemorated in a bilingual Latin and ogam tombstone found a few kilometres west of Carmarthen. Details in the lists suggest that the earliest kings of Dyfed had Roman associations, and it is not impossible that the migration occurred under Roman auspices, possibly in the 380s when Magnus Maximus denuded Britannia of troops. The main Roman road through south Wales linked Dyfed with the Usk valley, where the kingdom of Brycheiniog was established, also under an Irish dynasty. Its first ruler was the eponymous Brychan, the father of twenty-six children who loom large in Celtic hagiography. Yet, unlike Scotland and the Isle of Man, the descendants of the Irish of Brycheiniog and Dyfed were eventually absorbed by the P-Celtic-speaking natives and adopted Welsh as their language.

There were also Irish colonists in north-west Wales, a region which has yielded three ogam inscriptions, together with hut circles known locally as *cytiau'r Gwyddelod* or the cots of the Gaels. Nennius recorded that 'Cunedda with his sons ... [came] down from the north, from the country called Manaw Gododdin ... and expelled the *Scottus* from [Gwynedd] with immense slaughter, so that they never again returned to dwell there'. Manaw Gododdin was that part of the territory of the Votadini lying around the head of the Firth of Forth, and the link between Wales and the 'Men of the North' would be significant in Welsh literary and dynastic history. If Nennius's account is to be believed, Cunedda's migration could have occurred in the 380s and may, like that of the Deisi, have been associated with the career of Magnus

The 'Island' at Tintagel, the reputed site of the court of King Arthur, in Cornwall.

Maximus. However, a more convincing suggestion is that it occurred under the aegis of Vortigern around the 440s. Some evidence of the Irish colonists survives in place-names; Llŷn and Dinllaen, for example, are forms of *Lagan* or Leinstermen. Nennius seems to have been correct about the effectiveness of Cunedda's slaughter, for there is a determinedly Brythonic, and indeed Roman, swagger to Gwynedd, the kingdom which would be ruled by his descendants for the next four hundred years.

The extensive migration from Ireland indicates that, in the fourth and fifth centuries, the island had a vigorous and enterprising population. Indeed, it was at the dawn of its golden age. Although more influenced by the Roman Empire than was once believed, the language, society and legal systems of the Irish Celts preserved more of an older world than did those of the Brythonic Celts, upon whom the impact of Rome had been direct and often ruthless. More documents have survived in Archaic Old Irish (*c.* 350–750) and Old Irish (750–900) than in any other western European language of that period with the exception of Latin. Partly because of abundant documentation, knowledge of the culture of the Irish in the second half of the first Christian millennium greatly exceeds that of the cultures of the other Celtic-speaking peoples. As a result, the achievements of the Irish of that era seem – perhaps unjustifiably – to be greater than those of their fellow Celts. Among the documentation, the law-codes are a particularly rich source. They portray Ireland as divided into small kingdoms, *tuatha*, perhaps as many as a hundred and fifty in all. The king, the *ri* of the *tuath*, was a warrior rather than a law-giver and the ambition of a vigorous *ri* was to make himself a *ruiri* – the overlord of many *tuatha*. In consequence, a new dynastic kingship came to eclipse the old tribal kingship, with the emergence of powerful families such as the Uí Néill, and the creation of the five provinces of Ulster, Connacht, Meath, Leinster and Munster.

Although sharing an astonishingly unified literary language and a broadly similar culture and social organization, it is unlikely that the Irish of the fourth and fifth centuries saw themselves as a single people. It would appear that they had no name for the inhabitants of the island in their entirety until they heard the Brythonic-speaking Celts refer to them as *Guoidel* (later *Gwyddel*, the Welsh word for the Irish). The word was adopted in Old Irish as *Gaidel* or *Goidel* (Modern Irish, *Gaedheal*). This was only the beginning of the debt of the Celts of Ireland to those of Britain. Many of the Latin words borrowed by Old Irish came through the medium of Brythonic, or from Latin spoken as if it were Brythonic. The way the Irish language came to be spelled owed much to Brythonic interpretations of the spelling conventions of the Romans. Above all, it was in the context of the interrelationships between Britain and Ireland that the Irish were Christianized. That Christianization ushered in the golden age of Ireland and gave the Celtic-speaking peoples as a whole a renewed splendour and a renewed unity.

chapter five

Saints and Kingdoms

Ogwen Falls and Foel Goch, Snowdonia, Gwynedd.
(Jean Williamson / Mick Sharp)

O N the coast of south-east Wales lies a little inlet where Afon Col-huw flows into the sea. It is perhaps the most significant place in the history of the spread of Christianity among Celtic-speaking peoples, for it was there in the late fifth century that pilgrims landed on their way to Illtud's monastery two kilometres inland. The monastery of Llanilltud Fawr (Llantwit Major) can be considered the axis of early Celtic Christianity, for it had contacts, not only within Wales and with Cornwall and Brittany, but also with the world of the Gaelic-speaking Christians. It was located in south-east Wales, a region unique in western Europe, for it was the only part of the Western Roman Empire not to be overrun by invaders from beyond the Empire's frontiers. Such was the fate of Italy, Gaul and Iberia; in Britannia, it was the fate of England, and also – of those parts of Wales which can in any meaningful sense be considered to have been within the Empire – of Dyfed, Brycheiniog and Gwynedd. The exception is the land of the Silures – the later kingdoms of Glywysing, Gwent and Erging. Siluria was the cradle of Christianity among speakers of Celtic languages, or, to use a more concise term, the cradle of the Celtic Church.

The ruins of the monastery at Clonmacnois situated on the banks of the River Shannon, near Athlone, Ireland. Founded by St Kieran in 545, it was the burial place of the kings of Connacht. The ruins are those of a church begun in the tenth century and completed in the fifteenth. Two high crosses – the South Cross of about 830 and the Cross of the Scripture of about 920 – adorn the site.

The term 'Celtic Church' can be misleading, for it suggests a structured religious institution detached from the rest of Christendom. There are no grounds for such a suggestion. As John T. McNeill put it: 'In religious and cultural life, the Celtic churches experienced a large measure of unity, but they never sought a mutual coordination in structure that could have made of their various parts one externally visible church.' While lacking the preoccupation with doctrinal issues which split the Eastern Church, Celtic Christians were impeccably orthodox. Although unwilling to submit to the inept demands of papal representatives, they did not reject the claims of the Popes, claims which, in any case, had not yet been fully

SAINTS AND KINGDOMS

The church of Llanilltud Fawr (Llantwit Major) in the Vale of Glamorgan, Wales. It was the site of probably the earliest monastery of the Celtic Church — that founded by St Illtud in about 500. The present church dates from the twelfth to the fifteenth centuries.

developed. Certainly, there is no substance to the arguments of sixteenth-century reformers that Celtic Christians were proto-Protestants. Yet, despite the ambiguities of the term Celtic Church, it may usefully be employed collectively to describe the churches of Celtic-speaking countries in the immediate post-Roman centuries.

While the Celtic churches would eventually be absorbed into the hierarchical system centred upon the papacy, those churches had, from the fifth to the eighth century, an untrammelled energy which, to quote Nora Chadwick, expressed 'the Christian ideal with a sanctity and a sweetness which have never been surpassed'. The origins of Christianity among the Celts are a matter of debate. The religion had taken root in Britain long before the fall of the Empire. Tertullian of Carthage (died *c.* 220) reported that even in 'regions of the Britons beyond the sway of Rome … the name of Christ now reigns'. Alban was martyred at Verulam *c.* 220, and Julius and Aaron at Caerleon in perhaps 303. Three bishops from Britain attended the Council of Arles in 324 and a larger but unspecified number that of Rimini in 359. The theologian and heresiarch Pelagius left Britain in the late fourth century after having received a thorough grounding in Christian theology. St Patrick, born into a family of Brythonic Celts, probably some time in the early fifth century, claimed that his family had been Christian for at least three generations. The Christianity of Britain during the imperial era was undoubtedly Roman in structure, headed by urban-based bishops and having adherents in the cities and among *villa* dwellers; the word pagan has its roots in the Latin for an inhabitant of the *pagus*, the countryside.

Bede, writing in 731, depicted England in the period between the fall of the Empire and the coming of Augustus to Canterbury in 597 as a country in which Christianity had become extinct as the result of conquest by the pagan Anglo-Saxons. His portrait

The annual Croagh Patrick pilgrimage in Ireland. A celebration of Celtic christianity which involves a strenuous ascent of Ireland's holy mountain.

may be overdrawn, but there can be little doubt that, in England, the episcopate collapsed. It seems to have survived in south-east Wales, for Dubricius or Dyfrig (*fl. c.* 475) can convincingly be portrayed as a bishop, based probably in the Roman settlement of Ariconium in Erging or Archenfield. He is reputed to have been ordained by Germanus of Auxerre, an indication of the links with Gaul which were central to the early history of Celtic Christianity. Dyfrig's successor as the leading figure among the Christians of Wales was Illtud. He was an abbot rather than a bishop, proof that the monastic tradition established by Anthony in Egypt and upheld in Gaul by Martin of Tours had struck roots among the Celts. Illtud, as the biographer of his disciple Samson put it, was 'the renowned master of the Britons, learned in the teachings of the Church, in the culture of the Latins and in the traditions of his own people'. To quote Gildas, he was 'the refined master of nearly all Britain'. Illtud's monastery was the university of the saints of the early Celtic Church – saints in the sense that they were men and women of holiness rather than that they had formally been canonized. Samson was a student at Llanilltud, leaving for Dol in about 520 to become the father of Breton monasticism. Other students included Paul Aurelian, a prominent figure in the traditions of Cornwall, and Gildas, considered by the Irish to be the pre-eminent authority on ritual and discipline.

Like the career of Dyfrig, that of Patrick, the first major figure of Irish Christianity, was Roman in its episcopal setting and Gaulish in its associations. Like Dyfrig also, Patrick was, as a Briton, an inheritor of the Christianity of the Romanized Brythonic Celts. His work in Ireland was undoubtedly built upon evangelization already undertaken there by missionaries from Britain, and possibly from Gaul. If the traditional dates for Patrick's work in Ireland – that is, 432 to 61 – are accepted, his career predates that of Dyfrig; modern scholars, however, prefer rather later dates. The dates of Ninian, the first major figure in the Christianity of Scotland, are even more imprecise, but he too may have been a contemporary of Dyfrig. Like Dyfrig and Patrick, Ninian owed his Christianity to the Romanized Brythonic Celts, laboured in an episcopal Roman setting and had associations with Gaul. The links with Gaul were maintained by voyagers using the western seaways, seaways which had been of central importance since remote antiquity.

The development of what are considered to be the distinctive characteristics of Celtic Christianity belongs to the century after Dyfrig, Patrick and Ninian. As that Christianity was operating in a wholly rural environment, the Roman model, with its urban-based bishops, proved unsuitable. In Ireland, the Roman-style episcopacy established by Patrick was abandoned, and, until the appearance of the work of seventh-century hagiographers, Patrick himself seems to have been largely forgotten. While the episcopate continued to exist, the emphasis moved from the bishop to the abbot and the monastery. Illtud appears to have been the pioneer of Celtic monasticism for, judging by death dates, all the leading founders of

The Ardagh chalice. Ireland's finest ecclesiastical altar vessel, it dates from about 700. It was discovered in a rath in Ardagh, County Limerick, and is of silver, decorated with gold, gilded bronze and enamel. (National Museum of Ireland, Dublin)

Detail of the Ardagh chalice, indicating the continuing use of La Tène curvilinear designs.

Part of the so-called Monogram Page of The Book of Kells. *The page has been described as the most elaborate specimen of calligraphy ever executed. (Trinity College Library, Dublin)*

monasteries in the Irish tradition belong to an era later than his. He is believed to have died *c.* 525; while Finnian, founder of Clonard, died *c.* 549; Brendan, founder of Clonfert, *c.* 580; Colum Cille or Columba, founder of Derry, Durrow and Iona, in 597; Comgall, founder of Bangor and Tiree, in 603; Columbanus, founder of Luxeuil and Bobbio, in 615; Gallus, founder of St Gallen, *c.* 645 and Aidan, founder of Lindisfarne, in 651.

Illtud's tradition stressed learning, but the later generation of abbots considered ascetic practices directed towards the goal of spiritual contemplation to be a greater priority. Asceticism loomed large in the life of David (died *c.* 589), Wales's patron saint, and his vegetarianism, teetotalism and emphasis on hard physical labour aroused the scorn of the more worldly Gildas. In seeking remote places for their devotions, Celtic ascetics could establish themselves in the most astonishing locations – the coign in a Dyfed cliff which housed St Gofan, for example, or a hermit cell on the bleak sea-girt rock of Sceilg Mhichíl. The concept of spiritual exile – *peregrinatio pro Christo* – was another aspect of asceticism. It was the motive for settlements by Irish hermits in places around the Alps, such as Luxeuil, St Gallen and Bobbio, settlements which were, according to Thomas Cahill, an episode in the story of *How the Irish Saved Civilization.* Celtic pilgrims also made their way to Iceland, which may have been settled by Irish monks before the ninth-century colonization of the

Two adjoining pages of The Book of Kells. *That on the left portrays Christ and the Virgin Mary; that on the right bears the opening words of the summary of the Gospel of St Matthew. It reads:* Natiuitas XPI in bethlem judeae. Magi munera offerunt infantes interficiuntur *(The birth of Christ in Bethlehem, Judea. The Magi bestowed gifts and children were slaughtered). (Trinity College Library, Dublin)*

island by the Vikings. The Brythonic Celts preferred warmer climes. Not only was there the migration to Armorica, there were also spiritual exiles from Britain in Galicia where, in 572, a *Britaniensis ecclesia* was headed by Bishop Mailoc.

Ascetic practices, the appeal of desert places and *peregrinatio pro Christo* were in part the result of disdain for secular life, life which the future abbots would have known at its highest levels, for most of them seem to have been of royal stock. There were also influences from the Eastern Church which came in the main through Gaul. Some, however, came directly from the east, for pottery shards found at Tintagel, Dinas Powys and elsewhere prove that, in the fifth and sixth centuries, there were trade contacts between the Levant and the Celtic-speaking countries. The history of the desert fathers written by Theodoret of Antioch (died 458) was read among the Celts, and Theodoret noted that the fame of ascetics such as Simeon Stylites (died 459) 'was circulated everywhere … even among the Britons'. The seventh-century antiphony of the monks of Bangor (County Down) praised their monastery as 'the true vine transplanted out of Egypt', and Alcuin, Charlemagne's English adviser, described Celtic monks as *pueri egyptiaci*. The *martyrion* of the east, the place where the saint was witness to his faith, was carried westwards, as Welsh place-names containing the element *merthyr* testify. Some of the best-known features of the Celtic Church, such as the frontal tonsure, the hand bells and the wheeled cross, appear to have been derived from eastern prototypes. So did some elements of the greatest achievement of Celtic monasticism – the superb illuminated manuscripts. In the earliest of the great manuscripts of the Hibernian school, *The Book of Durrow* of c. 675, the portraits are iconically identical with those in early eastern gospel books. The art of illumination culminated in *The Book of Kells* of c. 800, 'the chief treasure of the western world' as an Ulster annalist described it. The 'carpet pages' in that and other manuscripts have a distinctly eastern orthodox character, but some features – the closely wound spirals, for example, or the fantastical animal forms – hark back to the traditions of La Tène art.

As William Dalrymple notes in his splendid evocation of the present day monks of Egypt and the Levant, the eastern monastic tradition delighted in the association between the saints and the natural world. This was also a major theme in Celtic monasticism for, as the distinguished Celticist Kuno Meyer put it: 'To seek out and love nature was given to no people so early and so fully as to the Celts.' St Brigit hung her mantle to dry on a sunbeam, St Brynach's tame wolf herded his cows, St

An example of the interlacing and fantastical figures characteristic of Celtic illuminated manuscripts.

Mocholmoc charmed the bees and an Irishman near Lake Constance, seeking relief from copying notes on Greek declensions, wrote a poem expressing his delight in the companionship of his cat, Pangar Ban. When he was engrossed in prayer, a blackbird laid its eggs on the hands of St Kevin of Glendalough; in order that they should not be disturbed, the saint remained on his knees until the eggs had hatched. St Francis of Assisi's love of the natural world – a love which led in 1980 to his designation as the patron saint of ecology – was an ever-present feature of the Celtic Church six hundred years before the establishment of the Franciscan Order. To quote H. J. Massingham, had the Celtic Church survived, 'it is possible that the fissure between Christianity and nature, widening through the centuries, would not have cracked the unity of western man's attitude to the universe'.

So rich is the evidence from Ireland – written material such as saints' lives, penitentiary works, letters, account of visions, tales of pilgrimages and the great illuminated manuscripts, and superb artefacts such as the Ardagh Chalice and the carved high crosses – that the Celtic Church can appear to be the Church of the Irish with a few appendages. Yet, while lacking the Irish splendours, all the constituent parts of the Celtic Church produced material in the same tradition as that of Ireland. A copyist at Llandeilo in Wales produced *Llyfr Teilo* or The Book of St Chad, containing the text of the gospels of St Matthew, St Mark and part of that of St Luke. (It is gratifying to note that it is in Wales that the first handwritten illuminated bible since the invention of printing is being produced; the distinguished Welsh calligrapher, Donald Jackson, under the patronage of the Benedictine monks of Collegeville, Minnesota, is hard at work in Monmouth embellishing calf skin using a goose quill.) Wales also has carved high crosses and monuments with superb interlacing. Some of the most fascinating early Christian stone carvings are those of the Picts – that at St Vigeans near Dundee, for example. The Bretons also created high crosses, such as the Christianized menhir at Rungleo, and so great was the work of their copyists that McNeill claimed that 'no estimate can be placed on the value of the numerous writings saved [by them] for posterity'. Cornwall too has its stone monuments – the five crosses at Sancreed, for example. In offering evidence of Celtic piety, the Isle of Man is pre-eminent, for its two hundred and more *keeills* or oratories represent a unique concentration of early Christian remains.

Even more indicative of the essential unity of the Celtic Church were the myriad linkages between its saints. The central role of Illtud and his disciples has already been stressed. David was perhaps the key figure in the development of Celtic asceticism, and, in his monastery of Menevia, Irish was perhaps more widely spoken than Welsh. In addition to those in Wales, he has dedications in Ireland, Cornwall and Brittany, as do the numerous children of Brychan. Among the chief monasteries of Brittany was the one founded by St Meen, a member of the royal house of Powys,

An example of the fine script employed by the scribes of Celtic illuminated manuscripts.

One of the most elaborate pages of The Book of Kells. *It is believed to be the portrait of either St Mark or St Luke. (Trinity College Library, Dublin)*

The ruins of Lindisfarne Priory on Holy Island, Northumberland, England. Begun in 1093, the priory occupies the site of the monastery founded in 634 by St Aidan and destroyed in Viking raids.

and Wales in its turn has dedications to Breton saints such as Tydecho. The cult of St Kentigern links Strathclyde, Cumbria and Wales, and the greatest female saint of Ireland, St Brigit, is commemorated throughout the Celtic world.

As the institutions of Celtic monasticism matured, they proved capable of export. The chief Celtic mission to a non-Celtic-speaking people was that of Aidan, who left Iona in 634 to establish the monastery of Lindisfarne in the Anglian kingdom of Northumbria. Over the following thirty years, two Irish monks, Finan and Colman, followed Aidan as abbot-bishops of Northumbria. So great was Irish influence there that the early Christian culture of the kingdom – the culture which produced masterpieces such as *The Lindisfarne Gospels* – is known as Hiberno-Northumbrian. The evangelization of Mercia and Essex was launched from Lindisfarne, and thus, over most of England, the roots of Christianity are Celtic – a fact played down in later centuries in order to give pride of place to Augustine, whose mission to England in 597 was initiated by Pope Gregory the Great.

The extension of Celtic Christianity, not only to England but also to places in the very heart of mainland Europe, meant the spread of practices which differed from those of churches in the Roman tradition. Adherence to such practices sprang not from separatism but from a desire to abide by the traditions of the Celtic fathers. Chief among them was the date of Easter, the Celtic Church adhering to a system devised by the Western Church in 314 and Rome adopting a different system in 457. In Brittany, there was early pressure to conform to Roman practice. Imperial structures had not collapsed in Gaul as they had in Britain, and therefore the framework of the imperial provinces survived there. Under the Empire, Brittany had been situated in the province which had its capital at Tours, and the city became the seat of the metropolitan of the archdiocese of Tours, which included Brittany.

Thus, in theory at least, the Celtic Church in Brittany was, from the beginning, subject to a senior Roman prelate.

Among the insular Celts, the impact of Roman ecclesiastical strictures came to be felt following the establishment of Augustine at Canterbury in 597. Gregory had granted Augustine authority over all the Christians of Britain, but the contrast between the suave religious diplomat from Rome and the unworldly leaders of the Celtic Church was great. Tradition maintains that Augustine greeted the British bishops with arrogance, and, in addition, submission to Canterbury, whose archbishop could not but be under the influence of his patron, the powerful king of the Germanic kingdom of Kent, was a step fraught with danger for Celtic polities.

Yet the loosely structured Celtic Church was ill-placed to resist the strong centralizing authority of Rome, especially as Rome's pontiff was successor to St Peter, the holder of the keys of heaven. One by one, the Celtic churches accepted the Roman Easter. Southern Ireland, which had close contacts with Gaul, did so in 630. Northumbria followed in 664, as the result of the celebrated Synod of Whitby. Then came northern Ireland *c.* 697, and the Ionian Church of the Scots and the Picts in 716. In the early eighth century, Brittany and the Irish missions in central Europe also seem to have conformed to the Roman Easter. When Bede was writing his *Ecclesiastical History of the English People* in 731, Wales was the most substantial of the territories resisting Rome, which explains his hostility to that *perfida gens*, the Welsh. It was not until 768 that the Roman Easter was celebrated in Wales, initially, it would seem, in the north, and perhaps a generation later in the south.

There is some evidence that, by the eighth century, the vitality of the Celtic churches was ebbing. Towards the end of that century, they began suffering the devastation brought about by the raids of the Northmen. The efflux from Scandinavia was caused by overpopulation and by the pressures created by centralizing rulers, and was vastly facilitated by growing seamanship skills. The homeland of the chief attackers of Scotland, Ireland and Wales seems to have been Rogaland – the region around Stavanger Fjord in Norway – the name which apparently gave rise to *Lochlann* and *Llychlyn*, the Irish and Welsh words for Scandinavia. The first recorded attacks on a region with Celtic connections took place in 793 when the monastery at Lindisfarne was sacked. That attack initiated the Viking aggression against Northumbria which led in the 870s to the collapse of the kingdom. The collapse permitted the expansion of the kingdom of the Picts and Scots into Lothian and the Tweed valley, a fateful development in the history of that realm's Celticity. It also enabled the kingdom of Strathclyde to annex Cumbria – the explanation for the numerous settlements with Brythonic, indeed Welsh names, established there in the ninth and tenth centuries.

The lone cross on Holy Island.

A reconstruction of a Viking long ship, exhibited at Roskilde, Denmark.

Although the attack upon Lindisfarne was among the first recorded Viking attacks upon Britain, Norse infiltration into the islands of Scotland had probably begun much earlier, for Scottish Gaelic had, by 800, absorbed many words of Scandinavian origin. By the mid-ninth century, Sultreyjar – Sodor, the Southern Isles – was a Norse polity extending from the Hebrides to the Isle of Man. It provided the base for the establishment at Dublin, Cork, Limerick and elsewhere, of Norse seaport towns which became miniature kingdoms actively participating in Irish power struggles. In addition, the Scottish islands and the Isle of Man were springboards for Viking attacks upon Iona and the island and coastal monasteries of Ireland. By sailing up the Shannon, the Northmen could also sack inland monasteries such as Clonfert, and even centres inaccessible by water – Armagh, for example – proved vulnerable. So great were the depredations of the Northmen that they gave rise to the last wave of *peregrini* – the Irish monks who established *Schottenkloester* at Regensburg, Wurzburg, and even in Kiev. The Irish Sea, once the 'Mediterranean' of the Celts, became that of the Northmen, causing an Irish poet to welcome the storms at sea, which meant that the Irish did not have to fear 'the fierce warriors of Norway / Coming over the smooth sea'.

Wales also suffered maraudings, with Anglesey a favourite target. In 987, the Northmen carried off two thousand of the island's inhabitants to sell as slaves and, in the following year, they plundered most of Wales's coastal monasteries. In 999, they attacked St David's, killing Morgenau, the bishop. Direct evidence of Norse settlement in Wales is absent; however, the numerous citizens of Viking Dublin with Cardiff as their surname, and the possibility that both Fishguard and Swansea have Norse names, suggest that the country may have had such settlements. Despite the depredations, there were those in Wales who saw the Vikings as potential allies in the age-old struggle against the English. *Armes Prydein*, a poem of about 929, probably written at St David's, called upon the Welsh and the men of Cornwall, Strathclyde and Dublin to unite to drive the English out of Britain.

Cornwall suffered too, although, like the Welsh, the Cornish saw advantage in allying with the Vikings to resist English aggression. In Brittany, the Northmen sacked Nantes in 843, and shortly afterwards they established settlements on Brittany's coastal islands and at the mouth of the Loire. The monastery at Redon was attacked in 868 and that of Landevennec in 913, and a chronicler recorded in 920 that 'the Northmen devastated all Brittany'. Of course, it was not only the Celtic-speaking countries which suffered Viking attacks. By the 870s, most of England was under Danish control; although Alfred (died 899) succeeded in bringing the country under the rule of the royal house of Wessex, a Scandinavian dynasty was to occupy the English throne from 1016 to 1042. For long periods in the ninth century, the Low Countries were under Viking domination, and, in 911, Charles the Simple,

The statue of King Alfred at Winchester, the ancient capital of Wessex.

king of France, ceded the lower Seine valley to Norwegian colonists. The ceded lands became the duchy of Normandy; in subsequent centuries, the Normans would represent the greatest threat faced by Celtic polities.

The Viking attacks, although a devastating blow to the centres of Celtic Christianity, were not wholly negative in their effects. They led to the expansion of trade, the circulation of money and the establishment of urban centres. The threat they represented created the need for stronger polities, probably the chief factor in the urge for unity so apparent in Ireland, Scotland, Wales and Brittany from the ninth century onwards. The distress suffered by the Church can be exaggerated, for artefacts created in the era of Norse aggression are among the finest achievements of Celtic Christianity. Indeed, some of them may have been made as a reaction to that aggression; for example, the high crosses perhaps came to be favoured because they were less portable and therefore less lootable works of art than the fine metalwork of previous centuries.

Although the Celtic churches had, by the age of the Vikings, conformed to Rome in the matter of the dating of Easter, many peculiarities remained: the organization of cathedral chapters was not in accord with Roman practice; boundaries of dioceses were indeterminate; the ecclesiastical hierarchy was vague; monasteries obedient to the Rule of St Benedict – the most powerful influence giving unity to Latin Europe – were absent; there were no elaborate churches in the Romanesque style; priests were usually married; many ecclesiastical offices were hereditary – indeed, an entire monastery could be the property of a single family; women could have a quasi-sacerdotal role; divorce was recognized; cousins could marry, in defiance of Roman Canon Law.

Among the chief developments in the history of Celtic-speaking peoples from the ninth to the thirteenth centuries was the process whereby they became full members of Latin Europe, a process which ensured that the Celtic Church as an intelligible entity ceased to exist. Cornwall was brought fully into the *unitas catholica* following its annexation by Wessex in the tenth century. In 818, Emperor Louis the Pious instructed the abbot of Landevennec, one of Brittany's premier monasteries, to ensure that the Bretons abandoned Celtic practices and adopted the Roman tonsure and the Rule of St Benedict. The Bretons resisted and sought the recognition of Dol as an archiepiscopal see. Dol received brief elevation in the eleventh century, but in the twelfth conformity with Rome and submission to the metropolitan at Tours were insisted upon, especially

A Viking long house reconstructed at Trelleborg, a stronghold of the early medieval kings of Denmark.

Scone Palace near Perth, Scotland. In the mid-ninth century, Kenneth mac Alpin made Scone, the site of a Celtic monastic community, the capital of the united kingdom of the Picts and Scots. The monastery became an Augustinian priory in about 1120. The priory was suppressed in 1559 and eventually became the property of the Murray family, who built a neo-Gothic mansion on the site in the early nineteenth century.

after obedience to the decisions of the council of 1127 was secured. Even afterwards, the Bretons, with their *pardons*, their ossuaries and their holy springs, retained many of the features they had inherited from the era of the Celtic Church.

In Scotland, the deCelticization of the Church is usually associated with St Margaret (died 1093), the wife of King Malcolm III and the great-niece of Edward the Confessor, the last English king of the West Saxon dynasty. Yet although she introduced Benedictine monks and elevated the cult of St Andrew at the expense of that of St Columba, her role in this respect has probably been exaggerated. However, under the rule of her sons and great-grandsons (1097–1214), 'peculiar' practices came under increasing attack, initially in Fife and Lothian, and then throughout Scotland. Monastic orders of French origin, such as the Cistercians, displaced the ancient monasteries of the Celtic Church, and the centres of the *celi de* (the culdees, the servants of God) were reorganized as Augustinian priories. Nevertheless, the Scottish Church resisted all attempts to make it subject to English prelates – specifically the archbishops of York. Although not granted an archbishop until 1472, the *Scotiana ecclesia* came under the direct authority of the Pope, tentatively in 1176 and decisively in 1192.

In Wales, unlike Scotland, the deCelticization of the Church occurred under the direct auspices of the kingdom of England. In the mid-eleventh century, the Welsh Church, adorned by distinguished families such as the one associated with the church at Llanbadarn, did not lack scholarship, although hereditary churches of that kind were under sustained attack from Rome. The Norman invasions ushered in the total reconstruction of the Church in Wales. Its dioceses were given precise boundaries and its bishops made subject to the Archbishop of Canterbury. The *clas* churches of the Celtic tradition were either suppressed or turned into Augustinian priories, and much of the Church's income was syphoned off to abbeys in England

and Normandy. The Benedictine Order established houses, as did the newer orders of French origin, a development eventually supported by the native Welsh dynasties, as their patronage of the Cistercian Order testifies. There was some reaction, with the burgeoning of the cult of St David and the attempt to elevate David's Church to archiepiscopal status. Nevertheless, by the thirteenth century, the *ecclesia Wallensica* had, in organizational terms, become nothing more than four westerly dioceses of the archdiocese of Canterbury.

In Ireland, there was a fuller awareness of developments in the heartland of Latin Europe than there was in the other Celtic-speaking countries. The *peregrini* were in contact with their homeland, and Irish monks maintained a presence, the *Sancta Trinitas Scottorum*, in Rome itself. The island retained its reputation for learning, the reputation which made it a magnet for English students in the age of Bede, and which led Sulien of Llanbadarn (died 1091) 'eager for learning [to go] to the Irish, renowned for their marvellous wisdom'. Links with England were cultivated, especially by the Norse communities, some of whose bishops professed obedience to the archbishop of Canterbury. In 1111, an assembly reorganized the Irish Church on Roman lines, ruling that ecclesiastical government was the responsibility of bishops rather than abbots, and defining diocesan boundaries. In 1127, the Benedictines established a monastery in Ireland, and in 1142, Malachy, the first Irishman to be canonized by a pope, founded at Mellifont the first Irish Cistercian monastery. In 1151, Ireland's first papal legate was appointed, and in 1152, Pope Eugenius III recognized Armagh, Cashel, Dublin and Tuam as archiepiscopal sees. Yet traditional values and customary attitudes proved deep-seated. In 1156, Pope Adrian IV, the sole Englishman to occupy St Peter's chair, called on King Henry II of England to invade Ireland 'to correct evil habits and introduce virtue'. In 1167, the island was invaded by Cambro-Norman knights from south-west Wales, and in 1171 Henry II proclaimed himself Lord of Ireland, an action endorsed the following year by Pope Alexander III. Thereafter, under papal patronage, the Irish Church was progressively Romanized and Anglicized. Although Irish Christianity still retains highly distinctive features, it had, by the end of the twelfth century, ceased to be what it once had been – the heartland of the Celtic Church.

The eclipse of the Celtic Church deprived Celticity of one of its central features. Indeed, authors of some of the major studies of the Celts – Nora Chadwick, for example – tacitly assume that, with that eclipse, there is nothing more to say and they are therefore reluctant to venture much beyond the end of the first Christian millennium. That reluctance surely stems from the fear that, by presenting the medieval and post-medieval history of the countries containing Celtic-speaking populations as if it were primarily the history of societies sharing Celtic

The Rock of Cashel, County Tipperary, Ireland. The capital of the kings of Munster, the rock was crowned with a round tower, a castle and the Romanesque chapel of St Cormac. The main building on the rock was the thirteenth-century cathedral which was the seat of one of the four archbishops of Ireland.

characteristics, a writer imposes a false unity on countries whose experiences were becoming increasingly divergent. There is also the likelihood that giving primacy to the Celtic element may create the impression that it is the only genuinely native element, and that any others represent regrettable intrusions. Such an approach not only ignores the fact that the Celts themselves were originally intruders, it also does an injustice to the rich tapestry which is the inheritance of all the Celtic countries. In his book *The Irish*, published in 1947, Seán O'Faolain, while recognizing the centrality of the Celtic element, rejected the practice of writing of Viking invasions, Norman invasions, English colonization and Scottish Presbyterian plantations, choosing instead to write of the Viking, Norman, English and Scottish contributions to Irish society, an enlightened attitude not fully accepted over half a century later.

The shrine of St Patrick's bell. The shrine to contain the plain iron bell, purported to have been owned by St Patrick, was made in about AD 1100. Constructed of thick bronze plates, it is decorated with gold filigree. (National Museum of Ireland, Dublin)

In addition, anyone stressing the unity of Celtic lands is obliged to acknowledge that, by the Middle Ages, they consisted of six non-contiguous territories. The modern Celts may thus appear to represent the broken fragments of what was once Europe's most dominant and vigorous people, and their history over the last millennium may therefore be in danger of being dismissed as that of the remnant people of a one-time glory. The vocabulary of some distinguished Celticists tends to encourage such a view – T. G. E. Powell's chapter heading, 'The Celtic Survival', for example, or Kenneth Jackson's reference to 'the Celtic aftermath in the Islands'. Thus, stressing Celticity can inhibit appreciation of the peoples of Ireland, Scotland, the Isle of Man, Wales, Cornwall and Brittany as peoples in their own right. The consequence of the concept of the modern Celts as the debris of a largely defunct people can be seen in the writings of the great philosopher and statesman, Tomás Masaryk. He considered the 'Bretons, Welsh, Irish and Gaels' to be 'national splinters', unworthy of the consideration which should be shown to his nation, the Czechs.

Yet, that there were similarities between the experiences of the Celtic-speaking peoples in the Middle Ages is undeniable. Some of them arose from the fact that those peoples were broadly at the same stage of economic and social development, and parallels can be drawn between their shared characteristics and those of non-Celtic-speaking societies which were at a corresponding stage in their evolution. Furthermore, social traditions and economic and political development among the Celts were determined to a large degree by their location and their environment. It could therefore be argued that the similarities in the experiences of the Celtic peoples in the Middle Ages arose, not primarily because they shared a joint Celtic heritage, but because they all inhabited windswept islands and peninsulas on the western extremities of Europe, and, partly as a consequence of that, had a subservient relationship with stronger polities centred upon more favoured

territories. It was such considerations, no doubt, which caused Rees Davies rigorously to eschew the word *Celtic* in his admirable study of the experience of Ireland, Scotland and Wales from 1100 to 1300.

Yet, if the concept of some coherent *Celtia* should be rejected, the continuing significance of a shared Celtic inheritance has some substance. The fossilized nature of Irish law as described in the surviving law codes makes it difficult to compare it with the more dynamic portrait provided by the earliest Welsh law codes, for the Irish material refers to the seventh century, if not earlier, while the Welsh material refers, in part at least, to the twelfth century. Nevertheless, careful work by D. A. Binchy, Thomas Charles-Edwards and others suggests that, on central matters such as kinship and kingship, both legal systems drew on a common Celtic tradition. Moreover, both were evolving in the same direction, although that of Wales, having been more exposed to Roman, Anglo-Saxon and Norman influences, was evolving more rapidly. Such considerations permit Charles-Edwards to make at least the minimal claim that 'Ireland and Wales in the early Middle Ages ... were fairly Celtic societies'. In addition, the role of the poet in Ireland and Wales clearly had similar origins, and in both countries poetic conventions developed on broadly parallel lines. Gerald of Wales (died 1223), who wrote extensively on Wales and Ireland, noted the resemblances between Welsh and Irish musical instruments, and the semi-mythical world of the *Mabinogi* is replete with Cambro-Hibernian themes. The evidence, admittedly slighter, from Brittany, Cornwall and Gaelic Scotland seems to confirm that their inhabitants also shared a similar social and cultural milieu.

Furthermore, the experiences of the four major Celtic-speaking peoples had remarkable resemblances. There was the urge for unity which produced the Brittany of Nominoë, the Ireland of Brian Ború, the Wales of Rhodri, Hywel and Gruffudd ap Llywelyn and the united kingdom of the Picts and Scots. Following the Norman invasions – invasions which can be considered to be the last outpouring of Viking energies – Brittany, Wales and Ireland became subject to the overlordship of an Anglo-French monarchy. At the same time, the House of Canmore made the Celtic-speakers of Scotland subject to a dynasty which, despite its Scottish roots, was also Anglo-French in its ethos. In all four countries, progressive forces, particularly those represented by trade and urbanization, came under the control of non-Celtic-speaking elements. Following the Norman invasions of Wales and Ireland, the native population became subject to different inheritance traditions, tenurial practices, taxation systems and legal codes from those of the *adventi*, causing both countries to experience profound ethnic division.

Kingship in Wales and Ireland failed to achieve the 'regnal solidarity' achieved in Scotland, and more so in England. While the English form of that stability was used against the Celtic-speakers of Wales and Ireland, that of Scotland was used against

The nineteenth-century chapel on Moot Hill near the Palace of Scone, Scotland. Moot Hill was the site of the coronation of the monarchs of Scotland.

SAINTS AND KINGDOMS

the Celtic-speakers of Scotland, as the Scottish kings campaigned to bring the Highlands under their control; these campaigns had, by 1266, brought about the extinction of Viking power in the northern and western isles. However, the Celtic-speakers of Scotland did not experience the institutional racism prevalent in Wales and Ireland, although readiness in the Lowlands to stigmatize Gaelic-speakers as 'savage and untamed' grew apace from the thirteenth century onwards. Indeed, the comments of Lowland Scots on Highland Gaels are considered to be early examples of the stereotyping of an aboriginal people. Such attitudes led in 1493 to the destruction by the Scottish monarchy of the Lordship of the Isles, an autonomous Celtic polity in which Gaelic was developing as a vigorous written vernacular.

In Brittany, as in Scotland, the ruling dynasty was progressively deCelticized. By skilfully using the rivalries between the French and English kings, the duchy continued as a powerful entity until Duchess Anne married King Charles VIII of France in 1491. Despite the strong particularist sentiments of medieval Bretons, ducal propaganda, as Michael Jones put it, 'did not exploit the Celtic element in defence of regional identity'. To the great Breton scholar, Abelard, Breton-speakers were barbarous, and it would seem that, by the thirteenth century, the upper echelons of Breton society had become wholly French in culture and language, even in the west where the mass of the population remained monoglot Breton. Thus in Brittany, as in the rest of the countries with Celtic-speaking inhabitants, it was not the Celtic-speakers who wielded political power.

Not only did the history of the Celtic countries in the medieval period have remarkable resemblances, their histories were also closely intertwined. Indeed, in that period, they were almost as much entwined as they had been in the immediate post-Roman centuries, although links with the rising powers of England and France progressively became more significant than those between the Celtic countries themselves. The relationship between the Gaelic Irish and the Gaelic Scots remained intimate. Both peoples used the same language for formal purposes, although traces of vernacular usage in the notes in *The Book of Deer* suggest that, by the twelfth century, spoken Scots Gaelic was developing its own distinct characteristics. There was ceaseless to-ing and fro-ing across the narrow seas, with the Celtic lords of Ulster, for example, basing their power on the *galloglaigh* or galloglass – the mercenaries recruited among the Gaelic-Norse of the Hebrides.

The reconstruction on Moot Hill of the Stone of Destiny on which the kings of Scotland were crowned. The original stone, removed from Scotland by King Edward 1 of England in 1296, is now in Edinburgh.

When the original dynasty of Gwynedd, which had sprung from Cunedda, came to an end in 825, the kingdom came into the possession of Rhodri, whose father Gwriad is commemorated by a cross in the Isle of Man, and whose ancestors, like those of Cunedda, may have originated in Scotland. The connection with the north seems to have inspired considerable literary activity in Wales, for it has been claimed that it was in the ninth century that the poems of Taliesin and Aneirin were first written down and the history of the 'Men of the North' associated with Nennius composed. When Norman invasions devastated the Welsh kingdoms, it was to Ireland that their rulers fled. The Gwynedd claimant married the daughter of the Viking king of Dublin, and it was with Hiberno-Norse support that his son, Gruffudd ap Cynan, successfully claimed his kingdom in 1081. As has been seen, the invasion of Ireland in 1169 was launched from south-west Wales and was partly the result of the reaction of Norman knights to the revival of native Welsh power under Rhys ap Gruffudd. The invasion eventually led to English control of at least the eastern seaboard of Ireland, a central factor in the ultimate subjugation of Wales, for English armies in Gwynedd could be supplied from Dublin. Wales's subjugation was a factor in the history of Scotland, for Edward I's expenditure on his Welsh wars and castles deprived him of the resources necessary to conquer Scotland fully.

With the Norman Conquest, there was an extensive movement of Bretons to Britain – a kind of reversal of the sixth-century migration. By the time the Domesday Book was compiled in the 1080s, some 20 per cent of the land of the kingdom of England was held by Breton landowners, with significant concentrations of them in Cornwall and the Welsh borders. The Breton migration may have been the context of the work of Geoffrey of Monmouth. If, as is generally believed, Geoffrey was of Breton stock, his glamourization of the history of the Brythonic Celts brought credit to his ancestors as well as to those of the Welsh. Throughout the Middle Ages, there were close links between Brittany and Cornwall, with Breton merchants settling in Penzance and Truro, and Cornish merchants in St-Malo and Brest. During the fifteenth century, Brittany's golden age, the duchy was the hub of the trade of the western Atlantic, and its duke was wealthy enough to maintain the Welsh-born Henry Tudor in comfortable exile in the magnificent châteaux of Suscinio and Largoet.

Perhaps the most remarkable 'pan-Celtic' episode of the Middle Ages arose as a consequence of Edward I's campaigns to assert dominion over the whole of Britain, for which he found justification in the writings of Geoffrey of Monmouth. Edward succeeded in Wales, and, as he lay on his deathbed in 1307, success in Scotland seemed also assured, for then Robert Bruce was watching spiders on Rathlin Island off the northern coast of Ireland. Yet, before the king died, he heard that Bruce's supporters had found a prophecy of Merlin that 'after the death of *Le Roi Covetous*,

The equestrian statue of King Robert the Bruce, sculpted in 1964, marks the site of Bruce's command post on the eve of the Battle of Bannockburn, 24 June 1314. It stands near Stirling, Scotland.

the people of Scotland and the Britons [the Welsh] shall league together'. Following his victory over Edward II at Bannockburn in 1314, Bruce seems to have thought in terms of even wider 'pan-Celtic' operations. He seized the Isle of Man, and in 1315 his brother Edward invaded Ireland, in part – as the Scottish raid on Holyhead suggests – as a stepping stone to Wales. In Ireland, the invaders stressed that they were all one nation, bound together by a common culture and a common ancestry. Edward Bruce wrote to leading figures in Wales in the same vein, one of whom, Gruffudd Llwyd, answered his letter, declaring that the Scots and the Welsh had both been deprived of their rightful inheritance by the English. In the event, however, the whole venture collapsed. It coincided with the worst famine to strike medieval Europe, and, following the death of Edward Bruce in battle in 1318, the Scottish army abandoned Ireland. A pendant to the venture was the Declaration of Arbroath of 1329, with its remarkable echoes of the declaration of the chief vassals of Llywelyn, prince of Wales, in 1282.

Similar themes found expression some eighty years later during the rising of Owain Glyndŵr, with Glyndŵr's appeal for help from the Scottish king and the native lords of Ireland. Writing to the king of the Scots, he claimed consanguinity on the basis of Geoffrey of Monmouth's portrayal of the descendants of Brutus, the eponymous founder of monarchy in Britain. To the Irish, he stressed the ancient prophecies and argued that, if he were successful, Ireland would be free from English interference. Glyndŵr did not receive assistance from either country, but memories of his struggle were preserved in Scotland. A monk of Dunfermline, writing in 1442, noted that the campaigns of the English 'against the Scots, the Welsh, the French and the Irish prove that they are the cruellest nation in the

The statue of Owain Glyndŵr sculpted in 1916. Glyndŵr led one of the most sustained national revolts in the history of medieval Europe. (City Hall, Cardiff)

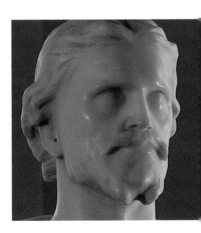

The castle at Chepstow, Wales. The castle's great tower, built in the 1070s, above the River Wye, was the first of the stone fortifications of the Norman conquerors of Wales.

world'. The fate of other small nations on the western periphery of Europe seems long to have reverberated in the consciousness of the Scots. In the sixteenth century, following the absorption of Brittany by France through dynastic marriage, Scots critics of close association with the French monarchy wrote of 'the warning of Brittany'. In the seventeenth century, when James VI and I sought closer union between Scotland and England, there were dire voices citing 'the warning of Wales'.

As the frequent references to Geoffrey of Monmouth indicate, his work was central to ethnic awareness among the Celts of the Middle Ages. In his *Historia Regum Britanniae* (c. 1138), he did not of course use the word 'Celt', and, admittedly, his 'history' was specific to the Brythonic branch, although the Irish were to develop a taste for stories in the Galfridian tradition. Working under the patronage of Robert, lord of Glamorgan and illegitimate son of King Henry I, he ended his life as bishop of St Asaph. Geoffrey wrote in the manner of the historians of the period, and provided details of his sources, including 'an old book' which Walter, archdeacon of Oxford, had brought *ex Britanniae* (probably from Brittany). All attempts to discover those sources have failed, and it seems that most of the *Historia* is the product of Geoffrey's own imagination. He claimed that he was giving an account of the history of Britain from its first colonization by human beings to the coming of the English. According to Geoffrey, the earliest of the Britons was Brutus, who fled from Troy after the Greeks had captured the city; thus the Britons shared their origins with the Romans, for it was claimed that Rome had been founded by Aeneas, who was also a Trojan. Brutus had three sons, Locrinus, Camber and Albanactus, and it was they who created the kingdoms of Lloegr (England), Cymru (Wales) and Alba (Scotland). The golden age of the Britons was the reign of Arthur, and almost a quarter of the book (pp. 176–230 of the 257 pages in the Thompson and Giles translation) is devoted to a description of its glories. The composition of the *Historia* coincided with a resurgence of Welsh native power, as the rulers of Gwynedd, Powys and Deheubarth strengthened their position and as Morgan ab Owain seized the lordship of Caerleon. Caerleon, wrote Geoffrey, was the seat of Britain's metropolitan see, and it was the archbishop of the city of the legions who consecrated Arthur as king of the Britons.

The Welsh became enamoured of Geoffrey's work, and, until the eighteenth century, there would be among them those prepared to defend its veracity. There are some eighty medieval manuscripts of *Brut y Brenhinedd*, the name given to the Welsh language version of the *Historia*, and the chief Welsh chronicle, *Brut y Tywysgyon*, was intended as its sequel. The Bretons were also delighted. Some ten years after the publication of Geoffrey's history, when Brittany's independence was threatened by France, a Breton rewrote the work in five thousand hexameters, linking the collapse of post-Arthurian Britain with the fate of its daughter. In particular, the Bretons warmed to the concept of the Trojan origins of their Brythonic ancestors, a story which Geoffrey no doubt borrowed from Nennius, who had given it an airing in his ninth-century *Historia Brittonum*. Such origins gave the Bretons parity with the French, who, as heirs of Rome, made similar claims. The Breton language, it was declared, was Trojan in its most pure and undefiled form. Arthur became one of the favoured names of the Breton ducal family, and the Forest of Brocéliande was chosen as the setting for a host of Arthurian legends.

As these stories developed, contributions from all the lands of the Brythonic Celts came to be woven together. Thus, in Tristan and Iseult, Iseult is the wife of King Mark of Cornwall, and Tristan, although sometimes referred to as Arthur's nephew, appears to have been based upon the Pictish hero Drystan. Arthur and his companion in arms, Hoel, king of Brittany, campaign in Strathclyde. Merlin, the subject of Geoffrey's poem *Vita Merlini*, had links with the Brythonic kingdom of Rheged, but he also prophesied the reclamation of sovereignty by the descendants of the Welsh Cadwaladr and the Breton Cynon. In the cycle of stories relating to Erec and Enid, there are scenes set in Ceredigion, Edinburgh and Tintagel, and the climax is the coronation of Arthur at Nantes. With Ireland such a strong influence upon the mythology of the Brythonic Celts, the Goidelic Celts were drawn into

The Pass of Glencoe, Scotland. The pass provides one of the routes between the lowlands and the highlands of Scotland. In 1692, it was the location of the massacre of forty members of the Macdonald clan by supporters of King William III.

The ruins of Glastonbury Abbey, Somerset, England. Legend claimed that it was the site of the first Christian church in Britain, founded in the first century by Joseph of Arimathea. Also according to legend, it was in the Island of Avalon or Glastonbury that the wounded King Arthur sought refuge after the Battle of Camlan.

the tradition. The notion of the Grail Bearer, featured in an eleventh-century Irish tale, may be the source of the concept of the Holy Grail, a central factor in the progressive Christianization of the Arthurian cycle. Myrddin or Merlin has parallels in the Irish story of Suibhne Geilt, and the story of Iseult, who sailed from Ireland to Cornwall, may be a version of the Irish tale of Diarmuit and Grainne. What basis these stories have, it is impossible to say. Yet, as Gwyn A. Williams put it: 'Any fool can demolish a legend; it takes a special kind of fool to try to answer the question of why a legend took the form it did; there is usually some ember under the smoke.'

A whole continent was bewitched by Geoffrey's portrait of Arthur – so much so, indeed, that the 'Matter of Britain', the legendary history of the Celts, became one of the central themes of the literature of medieval Europe. Almost three hundred Arthurian tales came to be in circulation, and they were used as the rail on which to hang Europe's aspirations to chivalry and gentility. The concept of the king as the first among equals found expression in the Round Table, grafted on to the Arthurian tradition by the Norman, Robert Wace (died *c.* 1183). Chrétien de Troyes (also died *c.* 1183), who has been described as 'the Ovid of a disintegrating Celtic mythology', introduced great tournaments and brought in Morgan le Fay, Camelot, Glastonbury, the Waste Land, the Fisher King, Lancelot with his love for Queen Guinevere, and Perceval and the quest for the Holy Grail. An anonymous writer of *c.* 1210 stressed the role of Glastonbury which he identified with the Isle of Avalon mentioned by Geoffrey, and linked the place with Joseph of Arimathea. Wolfram of Eschenbach (died *c.* 1220), the leading poet of medieval Germany, elaborated upon the story of Perceval, thus providing Wagner with the theme for

Parsifal. The Vulgate Cycle of *c.* 1230 told of the hurling of the sword Excalibur into the lake and described the departure by barge of the mortally wounded Arthur.

The Arthurian tradition found visual expression too. Within twenty years of the publication of Geoffrey's *Historia*, Rex Arturus was immortalized in mosaic on the floor of the cathedral at Otranto, on the furthest fringes of Latin Europe. Frescoes followed, as did tapestries, miniatures in illuminated manuscripts and carvings on ivory caskets. Both the literary and the visual celebrations of the Arthurian tradition reflected the values and the taste of the courtly class – that of northern France in particular – but some elements had deep Celtic roots. Arthur and his knights have their origins in the war bands of early Celtic society, and Merlin has his in the traditions of the druids; the hurling of Excalibur surely harks back to the cult site at La Tène, and many characters mentioned in the stories – Lear, Cymbeline, Lud and Cole among them – are the gods and heroes of the early Britons.

Although the outpouring inspired by the work of Geoffrey of Monmouth meant that Europe was immersed in traditions stemming from the Celts, Geoffrey's message to the Celts themselves was ambiguous. Central to the theme of the *Historia* was the unity of Britain under the Crown of London. It was stressed that Locrinus was Brutus's eldest son, thus indicating that Scotland and Wales, the territories of the younger sons, should be dependent upon that of the first-born. While the *Historia* eased the path for those Welshmen who sought to find a place for themselves within the hegemony represented by the Angevin kings of England, it proved a stumbling-block in the Scottish campaign to win full independence. Furthermore, the Arthurian legend underwent metamorphosis. In 1181, monks at Glastonbury discovered Arthur's grave; he was therefore a mortal man and was not sleeping in

The 'grave' of King Arthur, which the monks of Glastonbury claimed they discovered in 1191.

a cave awaiting the opportunity to rid Britain of the English, as Welsh tradition maintained. Instead, he was transformed from being the hero of the Britons into the glorious forerunner of the kings of England. Chrétien de Troyes, the key figure in the development of the Arthurian legend, enjoyed the patronage of the step-daughter of Henry II. Edward I celebrated his victory over the Welsh by holding an Arthurian Round Table. (It is gratifying to know that the revellers were injured when the floor collapsed beneath them.) On Emperor Maximilian's cenotaph at Innsbruck, Arthur's statue bears the legend *König von England*.

Yet although Arthur was taken into the Valhalla of his enemies, there remained a residue of myth which continued to inspire the Brythonic Celts. Geoffrey's *Historia* concludes with an adaptation of Gildas's fulminations, claiming that the Britons, because of their disharmony and sins, had been deprived of their right to rule Britain. But earlier in his work he quoted the prophecy of Merlin: 'At last the oppressed shall prevail and oppose the cruelty of foreigners. ... Menevia [St David's] shall put on the pall of the city of the legions. ... Then shall break forth the fountains of Armorica and they shall be crowned with the diadem of Brutus. Cambria shall be filled with joy and the oaks of Cornwall shall flourish. The island shall be called by the name of Brutus and the name given it by the foreigners shall be abolished.' Such prophecies became widely known. Two hundred years after the composition of the *Historia*, the biographer of Edward II of England wrote: 'At one time the Welsh were noble and had sovereignty over the whole of England ... and, according to the sayings of the prophet Merlin, they will one day repossess England. Thus the Welsh frequently revolt in the hope of fulfilling the prophecy; but, as they know not the hour, they are often deceived and their labour is in vain.'

In the opinion of many of the Welsh, the hour for the successful fulfilment of the prophecy did eventually come with the accession of Henry Tudor to the throne of England in 1485. Hailed as 'the long bulwark from Brutus' and from 'Cadwaladr's blood lineally descended', he married Elizabeth of York, whose descent from Llywelyn the Great gave her Welsh ancestry more exalted than his. The choice of Arthur for the name of their first-born indicates the conscious intention of using Celtic myth to buttress the Tudor dynasty.

Henry VII's successful bid for the English throne had repercussions for another Celtic people. During his thirteen-year exile in Brittany, Henry had lived on the bounty of Francis II, Brittany's last autonomous duke, and it was at Rennes, the duchy's capital, that Henry was recognized in 1483 as the rightful king of England. It was the politics of Brittany which motivated the king

The statue of St Patrick on the Hill of Slane, County Meath, Ireland.

The castle at Beaumaris, Anglesey, Wales. A superbly symmetrical construction, built between 1295 and 1306, it was one of a number of elaborate castles commissioned by King Edward I of England following the extinction of Welsh independence in 1282.

of France to give Henry the military, naval and financial assistance which ensured his success. The ailing Duke Francis lacked male heirs, and as the French state hoped to annex his duchy after his death, it would be useful for that state if England were ruled by a king so beholden to France that he would not oppose the annexation. Following Duke Francis's death in 1488, his heiress, Duchess Anne, married two French kings in succession. Brittany became a province of France, and, despite some threatening moves in 1492, it was a development in which Henry VII acquiesced. Thus the accession to the English throne of a dynasty of Welsh descent was a factor in the extinction of the autonomy of Brittany.

That extinction occurred phase by phase. Duchess Anne's marriage to her first husband, Charles VIII (died 1498) marked the end of Brittany as a virtual sovereign state. Her second husband, Louis XII (died 1515), permitted his queen's Breton Council to adminster the duchy as an autonomous unit, but the marriage of their daughter, Claude (died 1524) to Francis (died 1547), the heir presumptive to the French throne, led to increasing royal control. When Francis I succeeded to the throne in 1515, Claude made over her rights to her husband. Their son, another Francis, was invested with the title of duke of Brittany in an elaborate ceremony at Rennes in 1532. Thus, just as the heir to the English crown was prince of Wales, the heir to the French crown was duke of Brittany. Francis, however, died in 1536, and as the title was not formally granted to subsequent heirs, he was the last titular duke. The 1532 ceremony was accompanied by a contract which granted Breton institutions a significant degree of freedom of action. That freedom lasted until the French Revolution when the drive for centralization led to the abolition of all uniquely Breton legal and constitutional features and to the carving up of the

A portrait of Henry VIII. Henry's reign saw strenuous efforts to bring the whole of Britain and Ireland under the rule of the English monarch. (After Hans Holbein: National Portrait Gallery, London)

country into five departments. The contract proclaimed 'the perpetual union between the duchy of Brittany and the kingdom of France', a union commemorated by the statue at Rennes of the duchess of Brittany kneeling before the king of France, which was blown up by Breton patriots in 1932.

The 1530s also saw another union relating to a Celtic people. In 1536, the English parliament passed 'An Act for laws and justice to be administered in Wales in like form as it is in this realm'. Later known as 'the Act of Union', it was in fact an act of incorporation. It abolished the privileges of the lords of the Welsh March, divided the March into counties, laid down that English Law was to be the only law recognized by the courts of Wales, gave the Welsh representation in parliament and prohibited the use of the Welsh language in public affairs. The Anglo-Welsh 'union' was far more thoroughgoing than that between Brittany and France. Apart from the Council of Wales (abolished in 1689) and the Welsh Courts of Great Session (abolished in 1830), it gave Wales virtually the same administrative, constitutional and legal structures as those of England. That union was also incendiarily commemorated four hundred years later with the burning of the Bombing School in the Llŷn Peninsula by Welsh patriots in 1936.

Five years after he had secured the Welsh 'act of union', Henry VIII laid down that he was 'king of Ireland as united, annexed and knit forever to the imperial crown of the realm of England'. The origins of the proclamation lay in the decay of English lordship in Ireland. The original Norman and Cambro-Norman conquistadores had gone native, as the names given to them – Anglo-Hiberni, New Irish and Old Gaill – indicate. The colonists' descendants were viewed in England as the upholders of English power in Ireland, but legislative attempts to halt and reverse their

Celticization proved fruitless. The chief attempt was the Statute of Kilkenny of 1366, which forbade intermarriage between the English and the Irish, the speaking of Irish by those of English descent and their entertainment by Irish minstrels; it also barred the native Irish from the priesthood and from monastic life. Intended to ensure the perpetuation of the racial division of Ireland and the permanent subjugation of the native population, the Statute bore a strong resemblance to the Penal Code enacted against the Welsh during the revolt of Owain Glyndŵr.

The Statute of Kilkenny's failure is borne out by the English crown's enforced acceptance, from 1470 to 1534, of the fact that power in Ireland lay in the hands of the Fitz Gerald earls of Kildare, one of the most Gaelicized of the Anglo-Irish lineages with a tradition of intermarriage with the native Irish. In 1534, Henry VIII and his advisers felt they had sufficient resources to overthrow the Fitz Geralds. The ninth earl died in the Tower of London and in 1537 the tenth was executed, along with five of his uncles. Four years later came the proclamation of Henry as king of Ireland, and it is indicative of the Celticization of the Irish aristocracy that the upper house of the Irish parliament was informed of the proclamation solely in Irish. By establishing the kingdom of Ireland, Henry hoped to create a focus for loyalty and also to disabuse the Irish of the notion that he held the country as a lordship from the Pope. Although the full appurtenances of a kingdom were created, including a privy council and a great seal, nothing approaching autonomy for Ireland was intended. Power was confined to English-born officials and conciliation was replaced by a policy of conquest and plantation, a policy vastly complicated by deepening religious division.

Two years after Henry VIII became king of Ireland, he sought to ensure that his dynasty would also rule Scotland. James V of Scotland died in December 1542, six days after the birth of Mary, his daughter and heiress, and a fortnight after his defeat by the English at the battle of Solway Moss. Six months later, it was agreed that the infant queen should marry Edward, the six-year-old heir of Henry VIII. The Scottish parliament repudiated the agreement, causing Henry and, after his death, his son's regent, to undertake the seven-year harassment of Scotland known as the Rough Wooing. The Scots appealed to France, where Mary was sent in 1548. Ten years later she married Francis, the heir to

Edinburgh Castle, the chief seat of the monarchs of Scotland. The hall of Mynyddog Mwynfawr, chief of Y Gododdin, or the Votadini, was probably situated on the castle rock.

The Church of Ireland cathedral at Armagh, Ireland. Although it contains some medieval features, it dates in the main from 1765. It occupies the site of the monastery purported to have been founded by St Patrick.

the French crown, and it was the proviso that Scotland would become a French possession if Mary were to die without an heir which gave rise to dire warnings about the fate of Brittany. Francis died in 1560; by then, the dominant elements in Scotland, increasingly Protestantized, were seeing their future as inextricably linked with that of England. Mary, the great-grand-daughter of Henry VI, did eventually become the means whereby the crowns of England and Scotland were united. However, the half century between the Rough Wooing and the accession of her son, James VI and I, to the throne of England in 1603 saw Scotland experiencing so radical a religious revolution that full integration of the two kingdoms was to prove impossible.

The accession of James VII to the English throne meant that, by 1603, not one of the Celtic countries was a sovereign state with a ruler unique to itself. While the Isle of Man was a somewhat detached territory under the suzerainty of the Stanley family, Cornwall – apart from its status as a royal duchy – was, in legal terms, indistinguishable from an English county. Wales, it has been claimed, was an extinct palatinate with its administrative system largely absorbed into that of England. Ireland was a dependent kingdom; yet it took Henry VIII and his successors a century and a half to gain full control of it, a process which led to the uprooting or the exile of much of its native population and to its plantation by unassimilable colonists. Scotland was a quasi-independent kingdom whose Celtic-speaking

The Roman Catholic cathedral at Armagh, Ireland. It was built on a hill overlooking the city between 1840 and 1873.

inhabitants were becoming increasingly marginalized. Brittany was a province of France and there too Celticity was neither socially nor culturally dominant.

Thus, by the early modern period, the Celtic peoples came to be subject to increasingly divergent constitutional and political structures. Even more significant was their experience of increasingly divergent religious systems. While Brittany and most of Ireland came to be characterized by fervent Catholicism, Scotland adopted an advanced form of Protestantism. Cornwall, the Isle of Man and Wales initially accepted the Anglican compromise, although they all eventually came to be markedly Nonconformist. Such wide-ranging divergence can be taken to imply that, by the post-medieval centuries, Celticity had ceased to be a meaningful concept. Yet, there remain the Celtic languages, which – although they have also had divergent fortunes – give a fundamental meaning to the notion of Celtic countries. There is also the story of the discovery of the links between those languages and the significance with which Celtic-speakers and others have endowed those links. In the three-thousand-year history of Celticity, that is perhaps the most fascinating story of all.

A further view of the Roman Catholic cathedral. The statues in the niches represent the twelve apostles. The statue is that of Archbishop Crolly, who initiated the building of the cathedral.

Continuing

Legacy

Celtic crosses in the landscape, Llanddwyn, Angelsey.
(Jean Williamson / Mick Sharp)

The royal crown of Scotland, part of the so-called 'Honours of Scotland'. It was last used in the Scottish coronation of Charles I in 1633. Encrusted with pearls and other gems, it is Britain's only pre-Restoration crown to have escaped being melted down during the Cromwellian regime. (The Castle, Edinburgh)

The Stone of Destiny of the Kings of Scotland (The Castle, Edinburgh)

IN the sixteenth century, Scotland produced one of Europe's greatest scholars, a man of whom it has been said that he 'far excelled Erasmus in the originality and boldness of his thinking'. George Buchanan (1506–82) is now largely remembered for his role as tutor to James VI, when he poisoned his pupil's mind against his mother, Mary Queen of Scots, and for his contribution as moderator of the General Assembly of the Church of Scotland in the crucial year of 1567. Among students of Celtic, however, he is lauded as the first to realize that they had a field of study. In his *Rerum Scoticarum Historia* (1582) – hailed by Michael Lynch as the most influential book ever written on the history of Scotland – he declared: 'I endeavour in my researches to keep as free as possible from fable and from what is at variance with ancient writers.' In between ridiculing the stories of Geoffrey of Monmouth and lambasting the Welsh scholar Humphrey Llwyd, he argued that 'the Britons of Gallia Celtica, the ancient Scots in Ireland and Albion, the Welsh and the Cornish ... use the language of the Gauls'. Much impressed by classical references to the Celtiberians, he claimed that 'the Irish, having sprung from the Celtic inhabitants of Spain ... use the Celtic'. There had always been full awareness of the linguistic kinship between the Welsh, the Cornish and the Bretons, and also of that between the Irish, the Scots and the Manx. What was new in Buchanan's work was his assertion that the Brythonic and Goidelic languages belonged to the same linguistic family. Furthermore, through his lists of place-names containing elements such as *briga* and *dun*, he argued that languages belonging to that family had once been spoken across the breadth of Europe.

Over a century was to pass before any substantial scholarly work built upon Buchanan's perceptive comments, a period during which the subject material for such work – the Celtic languages themselves – experienced varying fortunes. In the early sixteenth century, probably the best placed among them was Irish. The decay

of English power had caused the Pale – the region under direct rule from London – to shrink until it consisted of little more than a band of land, thirty-five kilometres by twenty-five, lying between Dublin and Drogheda. Except in a few walled towns such as Waterford and Limerick, everyone beyond the Pale spoke Irish, and even within it communities were bilingual. To quote the prejudiced author of *The Penguin Atlas of Medieval History*, 'Ireland had drifted back to its aboriginally squalid freedom.' In the countryside, the old settler class had become *Hibernis ipsis Hiberniores* (more Irish than the Irish), with 'Silken' Thomas – soon to be the tenth earl of Kildare – moved to rebellion in 1534 by the chanting of his Irish harper, O'Keenan.

The attack on the great Hiberno-Norman families, initiated in the 1530s, was accompanied by an insistence upon the practice of surrendering and re-granting land, which enabled the English, or rather, after 1541, the Irish, crown greatly to expand the territory directly under its suzerainty. The plantation system adopted during the reign of Mary Tudor led in 1556 to English colonization of Offaly and Leix, regions renamed Queen's County and King's County. In the 1580s, the suppression of the rebellion of another branch of the Fitz Geralds – the earls of Desmond – resulted in massive land confiscation in Munster. The suppression was in part the work of the Welshman, Sir John Perrott, Lord Deputy of Ireland from 1584 to 1588, who assisted his fellow Welshmen to become owners of estates – a kind of re-enactment of the migration of the twelfth century which had brought the ancestors of the Fitz Geralds and others from Wales to Ireland. Thus, when George Buchanan was writing, only in Ulster and Connacht did an Irish-speaking landed class survive. At the same time, the forces of the Counter Reformation, led by Jesuit priests, were ensuring that the Irish would not conform to Elizabeth's Church settlement; indeed, the descendants of the Norman colonists proved even more zealous in adhering to Roman Catholicism than did the native Irish. With the new settlers representing Protestantism and English power, and with those resisting them representing Gaeldom and Catholicism, sectarian division reinforced ethnic division.

When O'Neill and O'Donnell of the ancient Celtic ruling class of Ulster, the chief stronghold of Gaeldom, rose in revolt in the 1590s, a Spanish army was sent to aid them. The defeat at Kinsale in 1601 and the submission of O'Neill in 1603 was followed in 1607 by the 'Flight of the Earls', when the O'Neill earl of Tyrone and the O'Donnell earl of Tyrconnel, together with a hundred chiefs of the north, migrated to Spain. Ulster was opened up to plantation. By 1620, some twenty thousand English colonists, generally Anglican in religion, had settled there, as had a considerably larger number of Presbyterian Scots – the latter representing a kind of reversal of the fifth-century migration of the Scotti. Further confiscations and plantations followed Cromwell's campaigns in the 1650s and the wars of

Sufferers from the Irish famine of 1847 as portrayed by The Illustrated London News.

William III in the 1690s. Catholics, who had owned 90 per cent of the land of Ireland in 1603, owned 10 per cent in 1703, when they represented 75 per cent of the population of the island. In addition to their disinheritance, they were subject to the Penal Laws, which banned Catholics from acquiring freehold land, excluded them from trades and professions, barred them from parliament and prohibited them from owning arms and horses.

The crushing of the Irish Catholics essentially meant the crushing of the Irish-speaking population. As the poet Edmund Spenser put it, in *A View of the Present State of Ireland*, written in 1596: 'It hath ever been the use of the conquerors to despise the language of the conquered and to force him by all means to learn his … The speech being Irish, the heart must needs be Irish.' In the Ireland of 1596, English was spoken by only a small minority, although it had high status as the language of administration, the urban élite and the growing number of Protestant landowners. By 1660, it was well established as the language of the plantation regions, especially in Ulster, and was increasingly dominant in Leinster and in the towns. It did not become the speech of half the inhabitants of Ireland until the end of the eighteenth century, when the two languages had some two million speakers apiece. By then, however, the Irish language was everywhere synonymous with poverty and illiteracy. The seizure by the conquerors of the most fertile land meant that knowledge of Irish was increasingly restricted to the inhabitants of the more barren lands of the west. The virtual extinction of the Irish-speaking landed class brought about an end to the patronage of poets in the classical tradition and the collapse of Gaelic scholarship. The standard literary language gave way to one which was simpler and more regionally diversified; indeed, Irish was in danger of degenerating into several mutually unintelligible dialects. It is little wonder therefore that, from the seventeenth century onwards, Irish poets, aware that they were heirs of a great tradition which had been cruelly brought down, lamented bitterly over the world they had lost.

There was worse to come. While Irish speakers increased markedly in number between the 1790s and the 1830s, the appalling famines of the 1840s affected them disproportionately. By 1851, the number fluent in the language – about a quarter of the island's inhabitants – was less than it had been in the 1790s. Of Ireland's thirty-two counties, only six – three in Munster and three in Connacht – had Irish-

The Irish Language

The area believed to be
Irish-speaking in 1800
(*after Reg. Hindley, 1990*)

The Gaeltacht as defined
in 1987

0   50   100 km

speaking majorities. Thus, by the middle of the nineteenth century, in the Celtic country *par excellence*, that primary marker of Celticity – fluency in a Celtic language – was outside the grasp of 75 per cent of the population.

Developments in Ireland had an impact upon Celtic Scotland. In the early sixteenth century, the territory of the Q-Celtic language extended from south-west Ireland to northern Scotland, with varieties of speech gradually shading into each other in a dialect continuum; within that territory, classical Irish was the recognized medium for writing. The decay of classical Irish weakened the literary links between Celtic Ireland and Celtic Scotland, as did the fact that the two countries came to follow different religious paths. Thus, John Carswell's 1567 translation of the prayer book of the Church of Scotland, the first published book in Q-Celtic, written in a Scots-modified classical Irish, received no welcome at all among the staunchly Catholic Gaelic-speakers of Ireland.

The need to translate the prayer book of the Church of Scotland underlines the

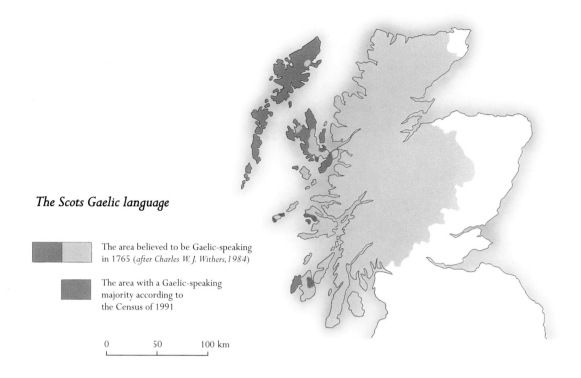

The Scots Gaelic language

The area believed to be Gaelic-speaking in 1765 (*after Charles W. J. Withers, 1984*)

The area with a Gaelic-speaking majority according to the Census of 1991

0   50   100 km

fact that the discussions which led to the compilation of the original were in English, or rather – in an example of the audacious purloining of an ethnic term – in Scots. As has been seen, Gaelic spread rapidly in early medieval Scotland at the expense of the languages of Pictland and the Welsh of Strathclyde, but failed to dislodge the English of Lothian. With the centre of the Scottish kingdom gravitating to Lothian, the language of that region came to be consciously fostered as the national tongue, initially under the sons and great-grandsons of Queen Margaret and later more blatantly under the basically Anglo-Norman dynasty founded by Robert Bruce. The east coast was deCelticized through trading contacts and migration, and Moray through ruthless displacement of the population. While Gaelic-speaking communities survived in Galloway and Ayrshire until the seventeenth century, in the Scotland of George Buchanan the Gaelic-speaking region was essentially that which lay beyond the Highland Line. Thus the region which was the heartland of the Scottish Reformation spoke English (or Scots), and the reformers gave scant attention to the needs of their Gaelic-speaking compatriots. After the publication of Carswell's work, over sixty years were to go by before another Gaelic book was published in Scotland. Buchanan, although fascinated by the Celtic languages, considered Gaelic to be a speech of 'barbarous sounds ... accrued to us by the infelicity of our birth'.

Yet despite the neglect, indeed the hostility, of the Scottish authorities, religious and secular, and the attenuation of Gaelic culture caused by the destruction of the

Lordship of the Isles and the weakening of the links with Ireland, the Gaelic-speaking community proved very resilient; as late as 1951, it was possible to gather examples of Gaelic speech in virtually every parish in the Highlands. Nevertheless, as Gaelic has been a minority language in Scotland for at least half a millennium, Scotland's claim to be a Celtic country can be considered to be somewhat flawed; indeed, many Scots would not wish to make such a claim.

The Celticity of the Isle of Man was bound up with that of Scotland. There are advocates of the view that Manx evolved, not from the Q-Celtic introduced by fifth-century Irish settlers, but from that brought to Man by post-Viking migrants from Galloway. That view is based upon the belief that the island's original Q-Celtic language was obliterated by Viking settlers; the paucity of Manx words of Norse origin, it is argued, indicates that Manx was a post-Viking introduction. Close links with Galloway distanced Manx from the conservative tradition of classical Irish, causing it to become the most evolved of the Q-Celtic languages. Its less archaic nature is highlighted by the fact that its spelling is based, not on the orthography of classical Irish, but – where consonants are concerned – upon that of the English of the early seventeenth century. This was the result of the work of John Phillips, bishop of Sodor and Man from 1605 to 1633, who in 1610 completed his Manx translation of the Book of Common Prayer. Phillips, a Welshman, followed Welsh conventions in his interpretation of Manx vowels. He failed to obtain a publisher for his translation, apparently because John Ireland, the governor of Man, believed that any work by a Welshman 'could never do any good'. However, manuscript copies of the prayer book seem to have been in circulation.

As the Isle of Man in the Early Modern period had no more than twelve thousand inhabitants, its population base would not have been large enough to sustain the Manx language had there not been constant contact with Galloway where a very similar Q-Celtic was spoken. At the beginning of the eighteenth century, Manx was the language of the mass of the island's inhabitants, and their religious needs were catered for by the publication of a Manx New Testament in 1767 and of the entire Bible in 1771–3. However, the decay of Galloway Gaelic boded ill for the future of Manx, as did the increasing links with Lancashire fostered by the Stanley family, who, until the resumption of sovereignty by the British monarch in 1765, were the overlords of the island. A century later, the language was becoming increasingly moribund. It had 4,657 speakers in 1901, and 529 in 1931. The last native speaker of Manx, Ned Maddrell, died on 27 December 1974, making Manx the only European language to become extinct in the twentieth century.

The history of the Celtic language of Cornwall has some similarities with that of the Celtic language of the Isle of Man. Both were long aided by contact with a closely related language – Galloway Gaelic in the case of Manx, and Breton in the

St Juliot's Well at Lateglos-by-Camelford, Cornwall. It is in an area rich in the centres of the Celtic Church, St Teath, St Breward, St Tudy, St Kew, St Endelion and St Mabyn among them. The roots of the veneration of wells lie deep in antiquity. They were held in high regard by the Celtic Church and traditions of honouring them have survived until today.

case of Cornish. In both countries it took about a century for the language to contract to a population base too small to be sustainable. The relevant dates, however, are different; the key period for the contraction of Manx was *c.* 1770 to 1870 while that for Cornish was *c.* 1550 to 1650. The difference is striking, especially when it is borne in mind that Cornwall is over six times larger than the Isle of Man. The explanation probably lies in the fact that Man is an island, whereas Cornwall is a peninsula into which the English language had been penetrating since at least the year 1000. It would appear that by 1200 the eastern half of Cornwall – the area beyond a line drawn through Bodmin – had been Anglicized. Three and a half centuries later, Anglicization had advanced towards Truro. Yet, in the 1540s, there were still monoglot Cornish communities. In the 'Prayer Book' rebellion of 1549, article eight of the demands of the insurgents declared: 'We, the Cornish

men, whereof certain of us understand no English, utterly refuse this new English [form of service].' A hundred years later, however, references to the enfeebled state of Cornish were multiplying. In 1768, Daines Barrington, a judge of the Welsh Courts of Great Sessions, tracked down at Mousehole, six kilometres south of Penzance, an old woman called Dolly Pentreath. She proved to be fluent in Cornish and claimed to have known no other language until she was twenty years old. A few Cornish speakers probably survived her, but her death in 1777 is generally considered to denote the demise of the Cornish language.

While Cornish was going to its death, its two fellow P-Celtic languages were growing markedly in terms of the number of their speakers. Admittedly, the boundary between the Celtic and the Romance speech areas of Brittany had retreated westwards, partly because there, as in Scotland, the centres of political power – Rennes and Nantes – were located in the least Celtic part of the country. In the ninth century, at the height of Breton power, the boundary had extended from St-Malo in the north to the mouth of the Loire in the south; by *c.* 1650, it was probably located between St-Brieuc and St-Nazaire. Thereafter, however, it remained remarkably stable for two hundred years and more, although the development of Brest as France's chief naval centre and of Lorient as the port for France's trade with the East meant the growth to the west of it of towns in which French was overwhelmingly dominant. Yet as the great mass of the inhabitants of western or Lower Brittany were rural dwellers living by an essentially subsistence agriculture, towns had only a marginal influence on their lives. The French state hardly impinged upon them, at least until the Revolution. The main force in their lives was the Church, whose chief concern was that its flock should not embrace heretical or secular ideas. To many priests, keeping that flock devout meant ensuring that its members continued to be illiterate and monoglot Breton. (It should be remembered that, while the sustaining of small ethnic groups is considered by modern radicals to be an act of liberation, if not of revolution, such an activity in the past has generally been inspired by conservatism.)

It has been estimated that in 1685 about 85 per cent of the inhabitants of Lower Brittany – some 660,000 people in all – were monoglot Breton and that they represented about a third of the population of Brittany as a whole. The numbers continued to rise until they peaked in 1905 when Breton had about 1.4 million speakers and was numerically the strongest of the Celtic languages. Yet, numerical strength was not accompanied by high status or by a rich literary culture. Although Breton was the first of the Celtic languages to be the medium of printed books, its history as a published language proved faltering, largely because there were few efforts to ensure the literacy of those who spoke it. When, in the wake of the French Revolution, schools were established on a large scale, they were concerned

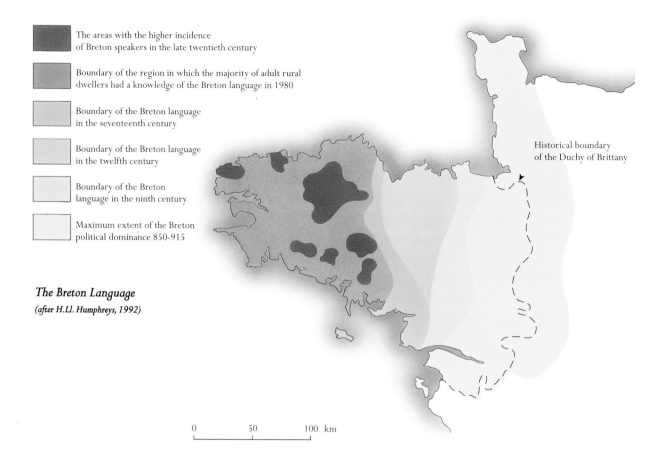

The areas with the higher incidence of Breton speakers in the late twentieth century

Boundary of the region in which the majority of adult rural dwellers had a knowledge of the Breton language in 1980

Boundary of the Breton language in the seventeenth century

Boundary of the Breton language in the twelfth century

Boundary of the Breton language in the ninth century

Maximum extent of the Breton political dominance 850-915

Historical boundary of the Duchy of Brittany

The Breton Language
(after H.Ll. Humphreys, 1992)

0   50   100 km

exclusively with literacy in French. In its initial phases under the Girondins, the Revolution proved sympathetic to federalist ideas, but with the victory of the Jacobins in 1793, at a time when the new republic faced dire dangers, centralism became the dominant ideology. The French language was elevated as a symbol, not only of the French nation, but also of an enlightened universalism. All manifestations of 'regional' particularism were branded as reactionary, dissident and dangerous. Yet as only 10 per cent of the inhabitants of France were well-versed in the standard form of French, Breton survived remarkably well as a spoken language, alongside the numerous other speech forms of the French state, for turning peasants into Frenchmen proved a protracted business.

Of the history of the Celtic languages since the Middle Ages, that of Welsh is perhaps the most fortunate. Although the 'language clause' of the Act of 'Union' of 1536 meant that, like all its Celtic fellows, it was barred from official life, the fact that the bulk of the population of Wales was monoglot Welsh obliged the authorities to grant the language some recognition. That they were prepared to do so is proof that the English state did not view the Welsh as a foreign, hostile people in the way that it viewed the Irish, and – to a lesser extent – as the Scottish state viewed the

Highland Gaels. Equally significant was the legislation authorizing the use of the Welsh language in religious spheres, which was passed barely a generation after it was banned from secular life. In 1563, the bishops of Wales and Hereford were commanded by Act of Parliament to ensure that a Welsh version of the Bible and the Book of Common Prayer would be available in every parish church in Wales. The legislation sprang from the belief that, in an age of vicious sectarian conflict, religious uniformity was more important than linguistic uniformity. The Welsh Bible, the work of William Morgan, was published in 1588. Couched in superb, if somewhat archaic Welsh, it provided a standard of written Welsh which stood the test of time. The Bible never became available in Cornish; it was not available in Manx until 1773, nor in Scottish Gaelic until 1801. It was published in Irish in 1690 and in Breton in 1866, but the translations were not fully acceptable to the religious traditions of the majority of the Irish and the Bretons – traditions which were, in any case, less concerned with Bible-reading. Welsh was the only 'non-state' language of Protestant Europe to become the medium of a published Bible within a century of the Reformation, a central factor in its comparative resilience. In addition, the Welsh became literate in their own language, mainly through the efforts of Griffith Jones (1683–1761). Furthermore, when large numbers of them adopted a more radical form of Protestantism, they did so in a context replete with sermons, hymns and publications in Welsh.

The Welsh language had lost some of its linguistic territory in the Middle Age, following Flemish and English colonization in Pembroke, and English settlement in Gower, the Vale of Glamorgan and parts of the borderland. In 1536, however, at least 80 per cent of the inhabitants of Wales were Welsh-speaking; indeed, over the following two centuries, the proportion probably increased as the Welsh of the hills recolonized regions such as the Vale of Glamorgan. The main loss during those two centuries resulted from the increasing Anglicization of the gentry class, which meant that Welsh literary activity lost its aristocratic ethos and became dependent upon the lower middle and the lower classes. With the onset of the Industrial Revolution, there was a considerable influx into Wales of migrants from England and Ireland. Yet, where the Welsh language was concerned, the impact of industrialization was generally beneficent, for it permitted the inhabitants of the overpopulated Welsh countryside to find a livelihood within their own country – a marked contrast with the situation in Ireland. Thus, although between 1801 and 1901 the proportion of the inhabitants of Wales fluent in Welsh decreased from 80 per cent to 50 per cent, the absolute numbers more than doubled – the exact reversal of developments in Ireland, where, over that period, the numbers fluent in Irish more than halved. In the context of the history of the Celtic languages, therefore, Welsh is often considered to be uniquely fortunate. Yet, when it is compared with others of the

The title page of the first printing in 1588 of William Morgan's translation of the Bible into the Welsh language.

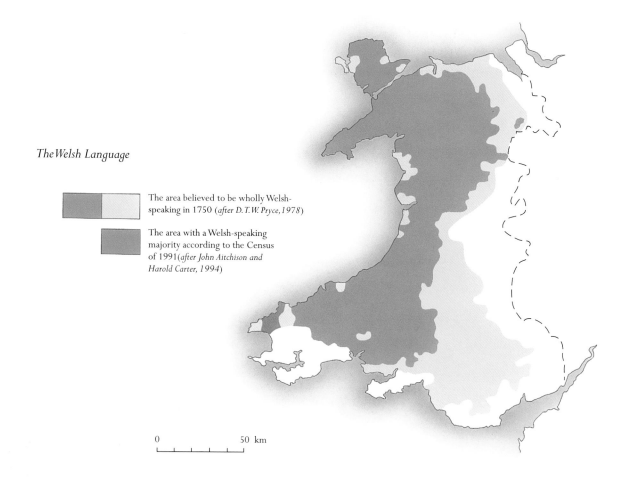

The Welsh Language

The area believed to be wholly Welsh-speaking in 1750 (*after D. T. W. Pryce, 1978*)

The area with a Welsh-speaking majority according to the Census of 1991(*after John Aitchison and Harold Carter, 1994*)

0   50 km

languages of Europe with a history of being denied full status – Slovene, for example, or Finnish – its resilience appears less obvious. Rather than claiming that Welsh has been uniquely fortunate, it would be truer to claim that other Celtic languages – Irish, in particular – have been uniquely unfortunate.

The progress of industrialization did much to undermine the viability of the traditional economies of the rural heartlands of the Celtic countries. It also led to the rise of large urban centres to which speakers of Celtic languages increasingly migrated. In the case of the Welsh and the Scottish Gaels, migrants had the choice of settling in towns within their own countries. In the case of the Irish, migration generally meant settlement in other countries, those of their fellow Celts among them. Thus, there was extensive migration from Munster and Leinster to the ports and iron-making districts of the south Wales coalfield, and from Connacht and Ulster to Clydeside. The migration to Wales was almost exclusively of Catholics, while the migration to Scotland consisted of members of both religious communities; indeed, the movement to Glasgow and elsewhere by Ulster Protestants represented a kind of inversion of the migration of the seventeenth-century Presbyterian settlers. The migrations rarely led to fervent expressions of inter-Celtic friendship, for in neither

Scotland nor Wales did Irish migrants find a warm welcome, particularly in the 1840s when they were fleeing their stricken island by the hundreds of thousands. Thus, although awareness of the kinship of the Celtic peoples was by then widespread, it did not give rise to a sense of a common 'Celtic' ethnic identity.

One of the ironies of the history of the Celtic peoples is that the major industry – in films, publishing, tourism, scholarship, spiritualism, mysticism and much else – spawned by their kinship has its origins in the work of a retiring Welsh scholar at Oxford. Edward Lhuyd (1660–1709) was the illegitimate son of Edward Lloyd of Llanforda near Oswestry and Bridget Price of Tal-y-bont, Ceredigion. After residence at Jesus College, Oxford, he was appointed in 1691 curator of Oxford's Ashmolean Museum. A botanist and a geologist as well as a linguist and an antiquarian, he won recognition as 'the finest naturalist now in Europe'. Inspired by William Camden's magnificent topographical survey, *Britannia* (1586) – he was much involved in the revised edition of 1695 – Lhuyd resolved upon the preparation of an exhaustive survey of the antiquities of Wales. In 1697, he began a two-year collecting sojourn in Wales. Then, in 1699, he sailed to Ireland, and subsequently to Scotland, Man, Cornwall and Brittany – where he was imprisoned as a spy. His motive for widening the sphere of his researches arose from a dawning realization that the languages of those five countries and that of Wales were closely linked, a realization towards which other scholars, the great philosopher Leibnitz among them, were groping. By 1701, when he returned to Oxford, Lhuyd was fully aware of those links, and over the following years he compiled his *Glossography*; published in 1707, it was intended as the first volume of his *Archaeologia Britannica*. It contained an analysis of the history, vocabulary, etymology and grammar of the six languages which he very tentatively described collectively as Celtic. As he died in his forties, Lhuyd did not complete any further volumes of his *Archaeology*. His manuscripts were sold and scattered; many

The title page of Paul-Yves Pezron's book on the Celts, together with a detail of the book's spine.

ANTIQUITÉ
DE LA NATION,
ET
DE LA LANGUE
DES CELTES,
Autrement appellez
GAULOIS.

Par le R. P. Dom P. PEZRON, Docteur en Théologie de la Faculté de Paris, & ancien Abbé de la Charmoye.

were burnt in various country-house fires, but substantial collections survive at the National Library of Wales, the British Library, Trinity College, Dublin, and elsewhere. As his *Geiriau Manaweg* (Manx Words) turned up unexpectedly in the 1970s, other surviving manuscripts may yet come to light.

While the *Glossography* was in the press, Lhuyd read *L'Antiquité de la Nation et de Langue des Celtes, autrement appelez Gaulois* (1703), the work of his Breton contemporary, Paul-Yves Pezron. Pezron's primary interest was Brittany. With Geoffrey of Monmouth's notions of the Trojan ancestry of the Bretons long discredited, he sought for them an even more ancient and distinguished genealogy.

The Celts, he declared, originated from the region around Mount Ararat in Asia Minor and were the descendants of Gomer, the grandson of Noah. All the languages of Europe had evolved from Celtic; thus words in Latin which were similar to those in Breton were the result, not of Breton loans from Latin, but of Latin's debt to Celtic. Only in Brittany had the language of pre-Roman Gaul survived. Therefore, the Bretons were the heirs of Vercingetorix and other Gaulish heroes, a notion which still reverberates in the adventures of Asterix.

William Stukeley's imaginative portrayal of a British druid.(Bodlean Library, Oxford)

Lhuyd's letters prove that he had warm admiration for Pezron's work, its absurdities included, an indication that scientific philology – to which his *Glossography* made such a distinguished contribution – was not yet securely established. His inscribed copy of Pezron's book is in Oxford's Bodleian Library and has been described by Simon James as 'the primary material relic of the creation of the modern Celts'. An English translation of Pezron's work was published in 1706. As it advertised Lhuyd's forthcoming book, there are grounds for believing that Lhuyd had a part in its publication. It was given the title *The Antiquities of Nations: more particularly of the Celtae or Gauls, taken to be originally the same People as our Ancient Britains* [sic]. Thus, between 1703 and 1706, the concept that the pre-Roman inhabitants of Britain were Celts took a major step forward. Lhuyd's *Glossography* was published in the following year. Its sternly academic content disappointed many of its subscribers, but it won admiration from Europe's small but increasing band of philologists. However, Pezron's book, which remained in print for more than a century, proved to be far more popular, as in the Welsh context did Theophilus Evans's reworking of Pezron's ideas, *Drych y Prif Oesoedd* (The Mirror of Past Ages), published in its final form in 1740.

Within a few years of the publication of the work of Pezron and Lhuyd, the word *Celtic* was winning increasing currency. Thus, Leibnitz in his *Collectanea etymologica*, published in Hanover in 1710, compared the Celtic, Germanic and Romance languages. He drew, not only on Pezron but also on the Dutchman Boxhornius, who in 1654 had published in Amsterdam part of the Welsh–Latin dictionary of Dr John Davies, the finest of Wales's Renaissance scholars. Much enthusiasm was aroused by the notion that, if the Brythonic and Goidelic-speakers were heirs to the Celts of Gaul, then their poets were successors of the druids described by Caesar. This was the theme of Henry Rowlands's *Mona Antiqua Restaurata* of 1723, in which he launched the druidomania which was to become inextricably intertwined with the development of Celticity. In 1724, William Stukeley published his *Itinerarium Curiosum*, in which he wrote of the 'Celtic' monuments of Britain. His notion that all pre-Roman remains were Celtic also inspired his later works on Stonehenge and Avebury, and was elaborated upon in France by Malo Tour-d'Auvergne and Jacques Cambry. Such works were indicative of the increasing desire to trace everything back to the Celts, which gave rise to the Celtomania that swept through the intellectual life of eighteenth-century Europe.

A self-portrait of William Stukeley (1687–1765), who contributed much to the development of eighteenth-century druidomania and who considered all British prehistoric monuments to be the work of the Celts. (Ashmolean Museum, Oxford)

The acceptance so rapidly won by the concept of Celticity has been the subject of much comment. The concept 'has no ancient pedigree', wrote Simon James. 'It is a modern interpretation, not an unambiguous historical truth.' James was much struck by the fact that Lhuyd's *Archaeologia* appeared in 'the very year that the Treaty of Union between England and Scotland saw the official creation of a new *political* identity called "British"'. 'The state usurpation of the name "Briton"', he argued, 'was the key reason for the success and speed of uptake of the label "Celtic"', for 'Lhuyd provided the terminologically dispossessed groups with a new collective name and identity.' As *British* had traditionally meant *Welsh*, James's argument may well be relevant in the Welsh context. Lhuyd could possibly have been seeking to provide his own people with an exalted pedigree and to satisfy some half-conscious need among them for 'Celtic' allies in resisting English hegemony. Yet, although there is no doubt about his Welsh patriotism, evidence that Lhuyd had some intentional 'political' agenda is scanty; the abiding impression given by his work is that it was inspired by a disinterested search for knowledge. Although the Irish and the Scottish Gaels were to embrace the word *Celtic*, it was not for them a substitute for the word *British* – a word they had never applied to themselves. In Scotland, the chief opponents of the 1707 Union came from the Lowlands, where, as Christopher Harvie and others have shown, the concept of Celticity received a very ambiguous welcome.

The word *Celtic* did eventually become popular as the term to denote the non-English peoples of the British state, and it was also adopted in Brittany, where it offered the Bretons the possibility of allies beyond the confines of the French state. Yet, the Celts of the British and the French states saw themselves primarily as Irish or as Bretons and so on. It was outsiders who identified them as a single ethnic, or – to use mercifully defunct terminology – a single racial group. That identification coincided with the rise of the cult of nature and the idea of the noble savage. Just as the Celts of prehistoric Europe had been defined by others rather than by themselves, so the Celts of the eighteenth century were bundled together and defined by those who found in them what Joep Leerssen has described as 'some mythical or primordial timelessness'. In consequence, Celticity has been compared with constructs such as Orientalism, constructs which, as Edward Said has argued, enabled outsiders to control that which they were defining.

The 'primordial timelessness' of the Celts seemed be confirmed by the publication in 1760 of James Macpherson's *Fragments of Ancient Poetry*. It was followed in 1762 by *Fingal* and in 1765 by *Temora*, works which Macpherson claimed he had translated from the Gaelic of the third-century poet, Ossian. He failed to produce the original manuscripts of the poems; as a result, they have long been considered to be the product of Macpherson's imagination, although modern scholarship has shown that they draw on much that is authentic in Gaelic tradition. Their publication coincided with the birth pangs of European romanticism and they came to be seen as representing the quintessence of the glories of the primeval world. Translated into twenty-six languages, the poems of Ossian were, wrote Madame de Staël, equal to those of Homer; William Hazlitt mentioned Ossian in the same breath as Homer, Dante and the Bible; Goethe found in the poems the melancholic romanticism which inspired his *Werther*; Napoleon read Macpherson with delight; Ossian inspired Mendelssohn's travels to the Hebrides; Keats's 'bards in fealty to Apollo' was a reference to Macpherson; the Ossian poems gave currency to the name Oscar, particularly among members of the Swedish royal family.

Scottish Gaeldom proved the most prodigious source of 'Celtic' romanticism and primitivism, a theme much embellished by Walter Scott, who considered that the use of the word *Celt* to denote a Highlander needed no explanation. The other Celtic countries also made their contribution. The Anglo-Irish, while oppressing the descendants of the creators of medieval Irish culture, were beginning to appreciate 'the profound antiquities of our culture', and to create that image of early Ireland as 'the island of saints and scholars' which was to become central to the concept of Celticity. Thomas Gray's *The Bard* (1757), a poem based upon the legend that Edward I massacred the poets of Wales, predated Macpherson's work and became the inspiration for János Arany's *Welski Bárdok*, the best loved of all the poems of the Magyars. The invention of tradition, so evident in the work of Macpherson, found practitioners among the Welsh – Edward Williams (Iolo Morganwg), the creator in 1792 of the Gorsedd of the Bards of the Island of Britain, pre-eminent among them. Iolo claimed to be the inheritor of the wisdom of the druids, and a literal belief in his theories did much to muddy the waters of Welsh scholarship. The notion that druidism represented as worthy a religious tradition as that of the Old Testament captured the imagination of no less a figure than William Blake. The Ossian inventions inspired similar activity in Brittany where, between 1836 and 1867, Hersart de la Villemarqué published his *Barzaz Breiz*. Purporting to be translations of ancient Breton epics, his work led Ernest Renan to write his 'Essai sur la Poésie des Races Celtiques' (1854). That article and Matthew Arnold's *On the Study of Celtic Literature* (1867) became the joint foundation documents of modern Celticism.

While literary studies, scholarly and fanciful, were furthering the concept of the Celts, there were remarkable developments in the field of linguistics. In 1767, James Parsons offered a thousand-word comparison of Welsh and Irish, thus building upon the achievement of Lhuyd. He also suggested that the languages of Europe, Iran and India were related, although, as his arguments were circumscribed by his insistence upon adhering to the biblical narrative, his perceptive comments received less attention that they deserved. The scholar generally acknowledged to have discovered the Indo-European family of languages is William Jones. The grandson of an Anglesey smallholder, he was related to the Morris brothers, the most distinguished intellectual family of eighteenth-century Wales. The son of a brilliant mathematician, he was brought up in London, and appears not to have been fluent in Welsh; indeed, he was introduced to the king of France as a man knowledgeable in every language but his own. In 1786, when Chief Justice of India, he addressed in Calcutta the Royal Asiatic Society, of which he was founder. After praising the richness of Sanskrit, he declared that its affinity to Greek and Latin could not have been produced by accident. 'No philologer could examine all the three without believing them to have sprung from some common source.' He then went on to argue, rather more tentatively, that other families of languages, Celtic among them, 'had the same origin with Sanskrit'. Yet, like Parsons, Jones was also circumscribed by the biblical narrative, and a generation was to go by before, to quote J. P. Mallory, 'the growth of a concept of linguistic affinity unfathered by Noah'.

It was in the early nineteenth century that philology became an established study, largely through the work of impressively erudite German academics. The term 'Indo-European' was coined in 1813 and, while its early scholars were convinced of the links between Sanskrit, Greek and Latin, they shared Jones's tentative approach to the status of Celtic as a member of the Indo-European family. Thus Rasmus Rask (1787–1832), who had a grasp of fifty languages, initially considered that Celtic had

A portrait of Edward Williams (Iolo Morganwg, 1747–1826), who in 1792 devised the Gorsedd of the Bards of the Isle of Britain. (Etched by Robert Cruickshank, the portrait appears as the frontispiece of Elijah Waring's Recollections and Anecdotes of Edward Williams, *London, 1850*

been spoken in Europe before the coming of Indo-European-speakers, a view supported by Franz Bopp (1791–1867) in the early stages of his researches. In 1831, however, the Welsh ethnographer, Samuel Evans-Pritchard (1786–1848) insisted that Celtic was a member of the Indo-European family, as did Adolphe Pictet (1799–1875) in his *De l'affinité des langues celtique avec le sanscrit* (1837). That view was eventually accepted by Rask and Bopp and was placed beyond doubt in 1853 with the publication of *Grammatica Celtica* by Johann Kaspar Zeuss (1806–56). Zeuss, as Matthew Arnold put it, 'stands as a model to all Celtic inquirers'. His achievement was not only significant for scholarly reasons. In an age when language and ethnicity seemed to be bound up with race, peoples not speaking languages belonging to the Indo-European or – to use the word then widely current – the Aryan family, were considered not to belong to the Aryan race. Thus, the Finns, as speakers of a language belonging to the Finno-Ugric family, had to submit one of their number for physical examination before they were deemed racially suitable to emigrate to the United States. Before Zeuss had established the 'Aryanness' of Celtic, there was a readiness to believe that the Celts were separated from the chief peoples of Europe by a wide racial gulf. As Lord Lyndhurst said of the Irish: they are 'alien in speech, in religion, in blood'.

Instrumentalists at a fest noz *– a Breton musical evening – at Carhaix in Brittany.*

Rigorous academic analysis of the Celtic languages coincided with increasing cultural contact between the Celtic countries. In 1821, the Welsh radical Thomas Roberts published an account of his travels in Brittany, the first of many Welsh-language Breton travelogues. Two years earlier, his fellow-countryman, John

Hughes, had made a passionate plea for the publication of the Bible in Breton, an issue which the man who can be considered to be the first pan-Celticist, Thomas Price (Carnhuanawc; 1787–1848), took up with enthusiasm. In 1827, encouraged by Price and the British and Foreign Bible Society, the Breton scholar, Jean-François Le Gonidec, published his translation of the New Testament and began working on the Old. So considerable was Price's assistance that Le Gonidec declared that the help of 'our learned Welsh clergyman' exceeded anything he had received from his fellow Bretons. Le Gonidec's association with Protestants aroused the suspicions of the bishops of Brittany, and he was also hampered by the lack of a recognized literary form of Breton and by the scarcity of readers literate in the language. The 1827 New Testament found more buyers in Wales than in Brittany, and so small was its circulation that the Bible Society refused to finance the publication of the entire Bible in Breton. Yet, despite his inability fully to realize his aspirations, Le Gonidec's achievements were considerable. To quote Rhisiart Hincks: 'It was his work above all which enabled nineteenth-century Bretons to feel confidence in their language.' The Breton Bible eventually appeared in 1866. Its publication owed much to the efforts of Villemarqué, who had been closely involved with Lady Charlotte Guest, the translator of the *Mabinogi* into English – even to the extent of plagiarizing her work. The meeting-place for the Welsh and Breton scholars – and also for Celtic enthusiasts from the other Celtic countries and from Germany, Denmark, France, and even Bengal – was the eisteddfod held annually at Abergavenny from 1834 to 1853, in which Thomas Price was the central figure.

Pan-Celticism had its roots in Breton–Welsh co-operation, although proto-pan-Celticism may perhaps be discerned in the 1790s, when the republicans of the Scottish Friends of the People sent delegates to the meetings of the United Irishmen. Too much should not be claimed, however, for sectarian antagonism and hostility to deprived migrants were much more prevalent than any desire to foster inter-Celtic fraternity. As the nineteenth century advanced, it was in the most detached of the Celtic countries – Brittany – that pan-Celticism found its greatest enthusiasts. (A comparison with other 'pan' movements is instructive: pan-Latinism became deeply rooted in Romania, and pan-Slavism in Bulgaria.) The trumpet-call of pan-Celticism was a book published in Nantes in 1864. The work of Charles de Gaulle (1837–80) – an uncle of the president – it called for the development of a common Celtic vernacular, a journal which would circulate in all the Celtic countries and the establishment of an annual Celtic Congress; it also hinted at some future federation of autonomous Celtic countries. Such ideas, once given expression, proved resilient. Some of them bordered upon the fantastic – for instance, any attempt to create a common Celtic vernacular was doomed to failure – but pleas for closer contact and collaboration were no more fanciful than the thinking which gave rise to the fruitful co-operation achieved by the peoples of Scandinavia.

De Gaulle was influenced by Ernest Renan, one of Europe's leading intellectuals. Renan's essay on Celtic literature was Macpherson's 'primordial timelessness' all over again. It was inspired, to paraphrase Joep Leerssen, by a sentimental attachment to the Breton homeland of his prelapsarian childhood. While Lhuyd invented the concept of a Celtic language, Renan invented the concept of a Celtic literature. Although a Breton, he had little knowledge of that or any other Celtic language; as Patrick Sims-Williams put it, 'his 'ignorance was an aid to generalization'. Renan found in France a ready audience for the virtues of Celticism, for the French had long taken pride in the Gauls, 'our ancestors'. Indeed, as he was writing, the Emperor Napoleon III was preparing to launch his vast study programme on Celtic Gaul, a campaign which culminated in his unveiling of the statue of Vercingetorix in Alesia in 1865.

Matthew Arnold, who held views similar to those of Renan, found in England a less sympathetic audience when in 1867 he delivered his lectures on Celtic literature at Oxford. The lectures coincided with the heyday of the notion that the virtues of the English sprang from the fact that they were a Teutonic nation – a belief firmly held by his father, the formidable Dr Arnold. In his lectures, Arnold had a complex agenda. To quote Timothy Champion: 'He was trying to persuade the English to be more receptive to an artistic element in their own background … to counter the increasing philistinism he saw pervading English society. On the other hand, he was concerned with the problem of Ireland … The artistic nature of the Celts provided something of value to complement the Anglo-Saxon virtues in the English heritage; the Celtic culture of Ireland was likewise something to be admired, but its ineffectualness in practical terms offered a rationale for English dominance to protect the Irish from the worst consequences of their own nature.'

Although he knew no Celtic language, and although the works he had read were mostly highly imaginative translations and re-creations, Arnold felt qualified to draw wide-ranging conclusions. The genius of the Celts lay in their spirituality, their awareness of enchantment and their sentimental wistfulness; it was an essential element in the eclectic imperial graces which lay at the root of Britain's greatness. The Celts were a childlike people, airy, insubstantial, loving bright colours, lacking 'the sanity of steadfastness' and failing 'to reach any material civilization'. Just as Renan referred to the Celts as 'an essentially feminine race', Arnold argued that 'the sensibilities of the Celtic nature [and] its nervous exaltation have something feminine in them'. Their great days had long passed – Arnold mentioned no literature later than the twelfth century. 'For ages and ages, the world has been constantly slipping ever more and more out of the Celt's grasp' and his duty was to recognize that fact, 'for the fusion of all the inhabitants of these islands into one homogeneous, English-speaking whole ... is a consummation to which the natural course of things irresistibly tends.'

Renan and Arnold were entirely wrong in their assessment of the character of Celtic literature. The jurist and Celticist, Whitley Stokes (1830–1909), considered early Irish literature to be 'strong, manly, purposeful, sharply defined in outline, frankly realistic and pitiless in logic', a view supported by Kenneth Jackson in 1951 in his discussion of Celtic literature in its entirety, who ridiculed 'the still widely held belief that the Celtic literatures are full of the mournful, languishing, mysterious melancholy of the dim "Celtic twilight" or else of an intolerable whimsicality and sentimentality ... Celtic literature is about as little given to mysticism or sentimentality as it is possible to be.' Yet, although authoritative scholarship has refuted the notions of Renan and Arnold, it is those notions which captured, and still capture, the public imagination. They were given a warm welcome by the aesthetes of the late nineteenth century, and found expression, above all, in the poetry of Yeats, whose *Celtic Twilight* (1893) is replete with primordial timelessness. In the twentieth century, the appetite for Celticity in the Arnoldian tradition became voracious, and it shows no sign of abating in the twenty-first. Indeed, the harder serious scholars work to demolish misconceptions, the greater the demand for such misconceptions.

The stereotype of the Celts had its darker side. If the Celts were primordial, they could not be expected to conform to the norms of civilized behaviour. J. W. Willis-Bund, writing in 1897, claimed that 'morality ... was never a characteristic of the Celts ... Among no Celtic nation has personal purity ever been considered an essential virtue.' By definition, the Celts were of stunted intelligence. In 1886, *The Spectator*, when commenting upon a Welsh radical's attack upon the royal family, attributed it to 'his simple Celtic mind'. As Celts, the Irish were too stupid to realize the benefits of being ruled from London. Thus, by demanding self-government, they were proving that they were unfit for it. Such notions were shot through with racism, partly because, as Joep Leerssen pointed out, 'from its beginnings, the science of comparative linguistics was a handmaiden of ethnological history'. Despite his comment that 'races and languages have been absurdly joined', Arnold's approach was essentially racist. He recorded, apparently quite seriously, the 'fact' that 'Germans have a larger volume of intestines [but] Frenchmen have more developed organs of

William Butler Yeats (1865–1939), the author of The Celtic Twilight *(1893) and the chief figure in the Irish literary revival. (The portrait is the work of Yeats's brother John: National Gallery of Ireland, Dublin)*

respiration'. The notion that the Celts were near the bottom of the evolutionary scale owed much to two Lowland Scots – Thomas Carlyle of Ecclefechan, whose attitude to the Irish marks him out as a proto-fascist, and the Edinburgh anatomist Ronald Knox, who made murderers of the Irishmen, Burke and Hare. Knox's *The Races of Men* (1850) spawned a virulent pseudo-scientific industry which 'proved' that the brachycephalic skulls of the Celts were unable to contain as much brain volume as the dolichocephalic skulls of the Teutons. The skulls of the fellows of the Royal Historical Society were measured in 1884, when it was concluded that the brains of the fellows with Anglo-Saxon names were larger than those of fellows with Celtic names. During the high noon of such studies, few scholars were sensible enough to accept the dictum of the German-born philologist Max Müller: 'To me, an ethnologist who speaks of [an] Aryan race … is as great a sinner as a linguist who speaks of a dolichocephalic dictionary or a brachycephalic grammar.'

Such, often contradictory, attitudes to Celticity coincided with the archaeological discovery of the Celts of mainland Europe. Those discoveries took some time to reach the communities in which Celtic speech was still current. Although the work initiated at Hallstatt predated Arnold's lectures by twenty-one years and that at La Tène by ten years, he was wholly unaware of them. Wales's chief academic journal, *Archaeologia Cambrensis*, did not discuss the Hallstatt discoveries until 1880. By the end of the nineteenth century, however, archaeological discoveries, a reassessment of classical sources, the increasing accessibility of early texts in the Celtic languages and a new appreciation of the glories of the golden age of Ireland were producing a rich Celtic melange. In particular, the publication of facsimiles of the great illuminated manuscripts aroused much enthusiasm, causing Celticism to be one of the elements which went into the making of Art Nouveau. Celtomania seemed to have returned, with an article in *The Fortnightly Review* in 1891 attributing almost every movement of the day to Celtic influence. 'The Celt', wrote its author, the Canadian Grant Allen, 'has lain silent for ages in an enforced sleep … [but now] the flood is upon us.'

The last two decades of the nineteenth century were the heyday of pan-Celticism. It was both a cause and a result of the resurgence in national consciousness apparent in all the Celtic countries. While the national question had dominated Irish history for centuries, it was not until the late nineteenth century that Irish patriots became concerned to safeguard and foster the Irish language. The Gaelic Union, the organization from which the Gaelic League later emerged, was founded in 1880, partly in the hope that cultural concerns would bridge the sectarian division which dominated Irish life. Few of the Irish-language enthusiasts were native speakers, and the gulf between them and the impoverished inhabitants of what was coming to be known as the *Gaeltacht* would be the subject of the delicious satire of Flann O'Brien and others. Nevertheless, the achievements of the Gaelic League were considerable. Chief among them were securing for the language at least a toehold in the education system and inspiring large numbers to consider it to be a central feature of their Irish and 'Celtic' identity. The Irish-language movement was consciously pan-Celtic, the manifesto of the Gaelic Union stating that it would 'stretch out the hand of fellowship to [our] Celtic kinsmen in Scotland, Wales, the Isle of Man, and Brittany'. Yet, the Irish, the most self-assertive of the Celtic peoples, frequently came near to assuming that the term *Celtic* was uniquely theirs, an assumption often shared by the Celtic enthusiasts of mainland Europe; it is surely significant that in 1888, the Irish of Glasgow, living alongside large numbers of migrants from Gaelic Scotland in what was probably the world's most 'Celtic' city, chose *Celtic* as the name of their football team.

Developments in Ireland were closely watched in Gaelic Scotland. Indeed, in what may be considered the only truly pan-Celtic novel – Compton Mackenzie's *The Four Winds of Love* (6 vols, 1937–45) – a Gael in Assynt advocates in 1900 the incorporation of the Highlands and Islands of Scotland with Ireland into a Gaelic state centred upon Belfast. The nineteenth century was not a good century for the Scottish Gaels. The inhabitants of Scotland fluent in Gaelic declined from some 335,000 in 1801 to 231,000 in 1901, and from 20 to 6 per cent of the population of the country as a whole. Yet, considering that the Gaels were suppressed following the Jacobite Rising of 1745, impoverished by the collapse of the kelp and fishing industries, dispossessed by the Highland Clearances and starved by the potato failure of the 1840s, it is surprising that they survived at all. Although all the well-known symbols of Scottishness – whisky, pipes, clans, tartan, kilts – belong to Celtic Scotland, the creators of those symbols had long been taught self-contempt by their

Attendants at a Gaelic service in the parish church at Crossbost, Isle of Lewis, Scotland.

The archdruid of Wales and two of his predecessors at the National Eisteddfod of Wales at Bridgend, Wales, in 1998.

fellow Scots of the Lowlands. The resurgence in Scottish Gaeldom owed a great deal to John Francis Campbell of Islay (1822–85), whose untiring efforts to record the rich Gaelic folk heritage saved much that would otherwise have been lost. It was aided too by the readiness of the Free Church to provide services in Gaelic and by the confidence created by the crofters' challenge to their landlords – a confidence indicated by the election to parliament of five members of the Crofters' Party in 1885. The Gaelic Society of Inverness, founded in 1871, succeeded in 1885 in securing the recognition of Gaelic as a school subject. An Comunn Gaidhealach (The Gaelic Society) was established in 1891, and in the following year it organized the first Mod, a competitive festival based on the Welsh eisteddfod. The Society subsidized Gaelic publications, sought to further the social and economic betterment of the Highlands and strove to encourage the study of Gaelic history, literature and music. Yet, too much should not be claimed. As Michael Lynch put it: 'Scottish culture gladly embraced a *Gaedhealtachd* with its linguistic teeth pulled.'

National resurgence in Wales proved more vigorous. It was also more populist, with its leaders coming from within the Welsh-speaking community itself, rather than – as was the case with the Gaelic League – from somewhat gentrified outsiders. The strength of Welsh-language culture is indicated by the almost nine thousand books published in the language in the nineteenth century, a figure far greater than the number published in all the other Celtic languages put together. As in Ireland and Gaelic Scotland, self-awareness owed much to the struggle against an Anglicized landowning class and to an identity shaped by a distinct religious tradition. Similar too were the attempts to win recognition for a Celtic language in the educational system, a victory partly won by Welsh in 1889. The chief milestones in the Welsh resurgence were the establishment of the University of Wales in 1893, the granting of charters to the National Library and the National Museum in 1907 and the disestablishment of the Church of England in Wales in 1920.

Breton culture also found enthusiastic advocates and in François-Marie Luzel it had its equivalent of J. P. Campbell. Kevredigez Vreizh (The Breton Association) was founded in 1895, with aims similar to those of the Gaelic League. The French state, however, proved less responsive to pressure than the British, and Breton failed to secure even a toehold in the educational system, despite the fact that it was, at the end of the nineteenth century, the most widely spoken of the Celtic languages. Neither did the French state use the census to gain information about the incidence of Breton, information available on Irish since 1851, Scots Gaelic since 1881 and Welsh

since 1891. Celtic enthusiasts among the Bretons were attracted by the inventions of Iolo Morganwg. In 1901, they established the Gorsedd of the Bards of Brittany, a borrowing which was copied by the Cornish in 1928. In both Cornwall and Man, that seminal era in the history of Celticism – the turn of the twentieth century – saw the founding of associations concerned with studying, fostering and reviving their cultural and linguistic traditions. Yn Cheshaght Ghailckagh (The Manx Gaelic Society) was established in 1899 and Kowethas Kelto-Kernuack (The Cornish Celtic Society) in 1901. In the history of Celtic resurgence, the story of Cornwall is perhaps the most remarkable. As Cornish lacked native speakers and had only a limited corpus of literature, the preparation of a full analysis of the language was a mammoth – and perhaps an impossible – task. Henry Jenner (1848–1934), the father of the Cornish revival, began the work when he was in his early twenties, and his address to the Union Regionaliste Bretonne in 1904 was the first time in over a hundred years that the language was publicly heard. Although doubt has been cast upon the authenticity of the revived Cornish of Jenner and his successors, there can be no doubt about the dedication of the Cornish revivalists.

In an era of rising national consciousness, it was natural for the Celtic peoples – speakers of among the smallest and most threatened of the language groups of Europe – to seek contact with each other. It is not surprising therefore that the late nineteenth and early twentieth centuries saw the flowering of pan-Celticism. Even more striking was the increasing contact – in the United Kingdom, at least –

The players of y corn gwlad (the horn of the country). Their fanfares precede the main ceremonies of the National Eisteddfod of Wales.

inspired, not so much by Celticism, as by an awareness that Ireland, Scotland and Wales all had an ambiguous relationship with the English-dominated British state. (English domination increased markedly in the nineteenth century; 73 per cent of the population of the United Kingdom lived in England in 1901, compared with 53 per cent in 1801.) In Wales, antagonism towards the Irish gave way to admiration as the Irish secured legislation on the Church establishment, land reform and education, issues central to the concerns of Welsh Liberals. On these issues, the Welsh MPs depended heavily upon the support of Irish members, and among MPs the proportion sympathetic to Irish Home Rule was higher in Wales than it was in Ireland itself. It was the Irish issue which caused the re-establishment of Scotland's parliament to be given renewed attention, and which placed a parliament for Wales on the political agenda. As Lloyd George put it in 1890: 'Wales is as distinct a nationality as Ireland.' The suggestion that Lloyd George should seek a parliamentary seat was first mooted by the great Irish land reformer Michael Davitt, who told a meeting at Blaenau Ffestiniog in 1886: 'You must get this fellow into parliament. He is saying in Wales what we are saying in Ireland.' Davitt was also a key figure in the contacts between Ireland and the Scottish Highlands. Indeed, so great was his support for the Scottish crofters that there were attempts to adopt him as parliamentary candidate for a Highland seat. Among Davitt's last activities was his campaign in Merthyr Tydfil in favour of the Scotsman Keir Hardie, elected in 1900 as Wales's first socialist MP. At the other end of the political spectrum, the resources to maintain the conservative wing of Scottish patriotism in the late nineteenth century came in the main from the vast income which the third marquess of Bute drew from his estates in Cardiff and the south Wales coalfield.

Such contacts developed side by side with more overt pan-Celticism. About half a dozen periodicals with the word *Celt* in the title came to be published, the most enduring of them being the Welsh-language weekly, *Y Celt* (1878–1900). Among such periodicals was *Celtia*, established in 1900 as the mouthpiece of the Celtic Congress, founded at the National Eisteddfod at Cardiff in 1899. The Congress caused division within the Gaelic League, partly because its founder was the Unionist, Lord Castleton, and partly because of the reluctance of many Irish nationalists to have dealings with what they considered to be their pusillanimous fellow Celts. The Congress organized a gathering in Dublin in 1900, and over the following century such gatherings were held almost annually. Thus Lord Castleton's foundation brought to fruition the hopes expressed by de Gaulle in 1864, although Celtic enthusiasts would argue that the congress held at St-Brieuc in Brittany in 1867 – a meeting which gave rise to a fascinating volume of 382 pages – represented the real beginnings of the movement. One of the issues which agitated the movement in its early years was the definition of a Celtic country. Was there any definition other than that it is a country in which a Celtic language is spoken? What therefore was the status of Cornwall? After much hesitation, Cornwall was accepted as a member in 1904; indeed, the need to receive the imprimatur of the Congress explains much of the activity of Cornish enthusiasts in the early years of the twentieth century. The Cornish debate foreshadowed that of the 1980s, when Galicia sought membership of the Congress, partly in order to reinforce its identity *vis-à-vis* Castilian culture. With some regret, Galicia's application was rejected, and the Congress accepted a definition based on that of the great Celtic scholar Henri Hubert: the Celts are the inhabitants of those countries in which people speak, or did speak in historic times, languages belonging to the Celtic family.

From the beginning, the Congress had quasi-political aims. Its proto- and early history coincided with an upsurge in Celtic research, which, although sometimes used for political ends, was motivated primarily by disinterested scholarship. The acheivement of Zeuss was built upon, and a new edition of *Grammatica Celtica*, revised by Herman Ebel, was published in 1871. There was considerable work on the early texts, particularly by such distinguished German scholars as Leo Thurneysen, Heinrich Zimmer, Kuno Meyer and Ernest Windisch. It was above all the Irish material which attracted them, partly because of its archaism and its copiousness, and partly because of the availability in the European heartland of the glosses written by the Irish *peregrini*; it was the glosses at Würzburg which brought Zeuss into Celtic studies. Much of the pioneering work of the Celticists of Germany and elsewhere appeared in the journal *Zeitschrift für celtische Philologie*, first published in 1897. However, it was in France that the earliest journal devoted to Celtic studies was founded. The *Revue celtique* began publication in 1870; it continued until 1934 and was succeeded two years later by *Études celtique*. The French and German journals were joined in 1904 by one mainly in English – *Eriu*, the journal of the School of Irish Learning founded in Dublin by Kuno Meyer in 1903. Wales followed in 1923 with the *Bulletin of the Board of Celtic Studies*, and in the later twentieth century other academic journals were founded, including the Irish *Celtica*, the Welsh *Studia Celtica*, the American *Celtic Studies Association Newsletter*, the Scandinavian *Lochlann* and the Japanese *Studia Celtica Japonica*.

Associated with the growth of journals was the establishment of chairs of Celtic, the foundation of research centres and the organization of regular meetings of Celtic specialists. The world's first chair of Celtic was founded at Oxford in 1877, largely as a result of Matthew Arnold's lectures. Its first occupant was John Rhŷs, whose academic interests included archaeology, ethnology and folk studies as well as philology. Born a few kilometres from the home of Edward Lhuyd's maternal ancestors, Rhŷs created a tradition of Celtic, and particularly of Welsh scholarship which built upon the achievement of Lhuyd. His ablest student was John Morris-Jones, the central figure in

St Patrick's cathedral on Fifth Avenue, New York. Built between 1858 and 1906, it is modelled upon the cathedral at Köln, Germany. The fact that it is dedicated to the patron saint of Ireland is indicative of the Irish roots of the Roman Catholicism of New York.

twentieth century Welsh studies; Morris-Jones's *Welsh Grammar* (1913) achieved for Welsh what the great German scholars had achieved for Irish. Other chairs followed – in Edinburgh and Paris in 1882, in Cardiff in 1884 and in Berlin in 1901. That the Cardiff chair was originally that of Celtic rather than of Welsh indicated a belief that Welsh did not deserve to have its own department; eventually, however, all the university colleges of Wales were to have departments of Welsh, as were all university colleges of Ireland to have departments of Irish. The Scots and Bretons, however, still share the timidity felt in Cardiff in 1884; the chairs in their universities continue to be denominated by Celtic rather than Gaelic or Breton. Cornwall and Man lack centres of higher education, but the University of Exeter has established a highly productive School of Cornish Studies. Where institutions are concerned, the most significant development was the foundation in 1940 of Dublin's School of Celtic Studies. Much has also been achieved by the Centre for Advanced Welsh and Celtic Studies at Aberystwyth, fully established in 1985; it is the home of the scholars now preparing a major Celtic encyclopaedia. Regular meetings of academic Celticists began in 1959, when the first International Congress of Celtic Studies was held in Dublin. The transactions of the Congress, which is held every four years, are a valuable indicator of the richness, the variety – and sometimes the abstruseness – of the world of Celtic scholarship.

North America also has regular gatherings of Celtic scholars, and has departments of Celtic at Harvard, Berkeley and elsewhere. Much of the concern for Celtic studies in North America arises from the fact that the continent has large numbers of inhabitants whose ancestors originated in Celtic countries. Indeed, population movements have caused Celticity in its various forms to become an almost worldwide phenomenon. Dissenters from Wales settled in Pennsylvania in sufficient numbers for publishing in Welsh to begin in Philadelphia at much the same time as it began in Wales. In the creation of the United States, the role of Ulster Presbyterian migrants was central, and a wholly disproportionate number of American presidents have come from the ranks of the so called Scots Irish. The flight from Ireland in the wake of the famines of the 1840s made many American cities bastions of Irishness. Admittedly, the various 'Celtic' immigrants showed little affection for each other. The Irish and the Welsh of the Pennsylvania coalfield were bitterly antagonistic to each other, and descendants of Scots and Scots Irish provided the bulk of the membership of the viciously anti-Catholic 'nativist' movements.

Where the United States is concerned, the fact that migrants from Ireland vastly outnumbered those from the other Celtic countries means that, there, Celtic is often considered to be synonomous with Irish. In Canada, however, the predominant Celtic element has Scottish origins, and Scots Gaelic still survives precariously on Cape Breton Island. Such Celticism as New Zealand has is also mainly of Scottish origin. So extensive was the migration from the Celtic countries to Australia that there is now an insistence upon describing the continent's settler population – at least as it was constituted until *c.* 1945 – as Anglo-Celtic. Among that population, there is a considerable Cornish element; indeed, the largest Cornish festival in the world is held in the vicinity of Adelaide. Of all the overseas colonies established by migrants from Celtic countries, perhaps the most fascinating is the Welsh colony in Patagonia. Initiated by a shipful of settlers in 1865, it is now experiencing something of a resurgence, at least where the Welsh language is concerned. Saturday-night visitors from Wales to Y Dafarn Las (The Blue Tavern) in Gaiman have claimed – probably with some exaggeration – that they felt they had hardly strayed from Caernarfon.

Irish overseas migration had political ramifications, for it brought to the host countries a strand of anti-Britishness which still has significance – in the current republican agitation in Australia, for example. The Irish diaspora's ability to pressurize American political leaders was a key factor in Britain's reluctant acceptance of the quasi-independence of the Irish Free State in 1922. The winning of self-government by a Celtic country – or at least part of one – was warmly greeted by Celtic enthusiasts everywhere. (The self-governmnent of the Isle of Man, although real enough, has a somewhat Ruritanian quality.) There were exaggerated hopes that the new state would foster, and even foment, pan-Celticism, rather as President de Gaulle fomented pan-Gallicism. Yet, although de Valera flirted with the notion, in particular by having meetings with the leaders of the Welsh and Scottish national parties and by providing lavish hospitalilty to the members of the Celtic Congress, Irish support amounted to little. The Irish fight for independence was an inspiration in

The proclamation of the Irish Republic read by Patrick Pearse from the steps of the General Post Office, Dublin, on Easter Monday, 1916.

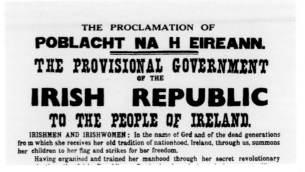

THE PROCLAMATION OF
POBLACHT NA H EIREANN.
THE PROVISIONAL GOVERNMENT
OF THE
IRISH REPUBLIC
TO THE PEOPLE OF IRELAND.

IRISHMEN AND IRISHWOMEN: In the name of God and of the dead generations from which she receives her old tradition of nationhood, Ireland, through us, summons her children to her flag and strikes for her freedom.
Having organised and trained her manhood through her secret revolutionary

particular to the more militant wings of the Welsh and Scottish movements, although the leaders of those movements considered the parliamentarianism of Parnell to be more relevant than the insurrectionism of Pearse. Indeed, to strongly Protestant Scots, the fact that the Catholic Irish had achieved statehood was an argument for 'repatriating' the Catholics of Clydeside, a stance which caused much of Glasgow to be difficult territory for the Scottish National Party.

The impact of the Irish struggle was most marked in Brittany. The political party Breiz Atao, founded in 1918, moulded itself on Sinn Féin and adopted a fervent pan-Celticism. Some of its members warmed to the clericalism present in elements of the Irish movement, for traditionalists among the Bretons saw Catholicism and right-wing politics as a defence against the centralism and the libertarianism of the Third Republic. In the 1930s, a handful of Bretons came to admire German racial ideology – despite that ideology's condescending view of the Celts – and adapted the Irish slogan, 'Britain's difficulty is Ireland's opportunity' to their own situation. During the Second World War, such notions led some of them to collaborate with the German occupiers, and the occupiers in turn showed some regard for Breton culture – by permitting Breton radio broadcasts, for example. Although the proportion of the inhabitants of Brittany who were collaborators was lower than it was in France as a whole, the fact that some of them were Breton nationalists provided an excuse, after the Liberation, for French centralists to defame the Breton movement as a whole. There were executions and lengthy gaol sentences; merely taking part in any Breton activity was considered a sufficient reason for persecution. There was a pan-Celtic reaction, with court sessions monitored by observers from Wales and with Ireland providing refuge for Breton exiles. The episode was disastrous for the Breton movement, since it caused the mass of Breton-speakers themselves to believe that even to advocate the teaching of Breton was to be tainted with Fascism. Overtly political pro-Breton activity did not reappear until the 1960s.

The repression in Brittany led to the call for a specifically political pan-Celtic movement, particularly in view of the fact that the gatherings of the Celtic Congress had become mainly social and cultural. The Celtic League was founded in 1961 and, over the following decade, published an annual volume of essays offering views varying from the highly practical to the wildly idealistic. Initially, the League was run by representatives of the various national parties, but there was controversy in 1969 when there were accusations that it was becoming an adjunct of one of those parties – Plaid Cymru, the Party of Wales. The League was reorganized in 1971 and since 1973 has published its quarterly journal

Supporters of Welsh devolution celebrating in Cardiff following the victory of the devolutionists in the referendum of 1997. Among the celebrators were visitors from Scotland and Cornwall.

Carn. It has had some successes, particularly on ecological issues relating to the Celtic Sea and in developing ideas concerning European confederation.

More tangible results have, however, been achieved through the co-operation in the British Parliament between Plaid Cymru and the Scottish National Party. That co-operation explains in part the readiness of the Labour Government elected in 1997 to prepare devolution plans for Scotland and Wales, a readiness which also owed much to the work of John Smith, the leader of the Labour Party from 1992 to 1995. His choice of Iona as his burial place is an indication of his Celtic sympathies. The year 1999 saw the re-establishment of the Scottish Parliament and the setting up of the National Assembly of Wales. At the same time, developments in Northern Ireland gave rise to the concept of the Council for the Isles, a concept very much in tune with the thinking of the Celtic League.

Yet while patriots in the Celtic countries consider these developments to be highly significant, Celtic enthusiasts rarely view Celticity in political terms. Indeed, the huge explosion in Celtophilia seen in the last few decades has only a tangential association with politics. That explosion can be seen in the growth of gatherings such as the pan-Celtic Festival at Killarney, the Inter-Celtic Festival at Lorient, the Cnapan at Ffostrasol, the Celtic Film Festival and the art exhibitions of Celtic Vision. There is delight in the music of Alan Stivell, the Chieftains, Run Rig, Ar Log and others. Even more fascinating is the universalization of Celticity indicated by the vast number of books on Celtic themes available in places such as Glastonbury, and the existence on the World Wide Web of thousands of sites with the word *Celtic* in their titles. In the United States, Australia, Germany and elsewhere the concept of Celticity has been 'un-anchored'. It is no longer linked with specific languages or ethnic groups. It is a state of mind associated with New Age philosophies, with a search for a natural religion and with the rediscovery of self. It almost seems as if the Celts are those who choose to see themselves as Celts – which brings us back to my friends on the way to Doolin.

A busy scene in Grafton Street, Dublin, redolent of the confidence and prosperity of the inhabitants of modern Ireland.

bibliography

The following list is limited to books and articles cited or quoted in the text. There is an admirable bibliography of all aspects of Celtic studies in Bernhard Meir, *A Dictionary of Celtic Religion and Culture* (Woodbridge, 1997)

Aitchison, John and Carter, Harold, *A Geography of the Welsh Language, 1961–1991* (Cardiff, 1994)

Allen, Grant, 'The Celt in English Art', *The Fortnightly Review*, February 1891

Arnold, Matthew, *Study of Celtic Literature* (London, 1867)

Binchy, D. A., *Celtic and Anglo-Saxon Kingship* (London, 1970)

Brown, Terence (ed.), *Celticism* (Amsterdam, 1996)

Buchanan, George, *Rerum Scoticarum Historia* (Edinburgh, 1582); English translation by James Aikman, *The History of Scotland* (Edinburgh, 1829-30)

Bujina, Jozef and Szabo, Miklos, 'The Carpathian Basin' in S. Moscati and others (eds.), *The Celts* (Milan, 1991)

Cahill, Thomas, *How the Irish Saved Civilization* (London, 1995)

Celtica, The Catalogue of the Exhibition of Celtic Books at the National Library of Scotland (Edinburgh, 1967)

Chadwick, Nora, *The Age of the Saints in the Early Celtic Church* (Oxford, 1961)

Chadwick, Nora, *The Celts* (Harmondsworth, 1970)

Champion, Timothy, 'The Celt in Archaeology' in Terence Brown (ed.), *Celticism* (Amsterdam, 1996)

Chapman, Malcolm, *The Celts: The Construction of a Myth* (London, 1992)

Charles-Edwards, Thomas, *Early Irish and Welsh Kinship* (Oxford, 1992)

Charles-Edwards, Thomas, 'Language and Society among the Insular Celts' in Miranda A. Green (ed.), *The Celtic World* (London, 1995)

Collis, John, 'Celtic Myths', *Antiquity* 71 (1997)

Cunliffe, Barry, *The Celtic World* (London, 1979)

Cunliffe, Barry, *The Ancient Celts* (London, 1997)

Dalrymple, William, *From the Holy Mountain* (London, 1998)

Davies, Norman, *The Isles: A History* (London, 1999)

Davies, R. R., *Domination and Conquest: The Experience of Ireland, Scotland and Wales, 1100-1300* (Cambridge, 1990)

Delaney, Frank, *The Celts* (London, 1986)

Dillon, Myles and Chadwick, Nora, *The Celtic Realms* (London, 1967)

Ellis, Peter Beresford, *The Celtic Dawn: A History of Pan Celticism* (London, 1993)

Evans, D. Ellis, 'The Labyrinth of Continental Celtic', *Proceedings of the British Academy* 65 (1978)

Falc'hun, Francois, *Histoire de la Langue Bretonne d'apres la Geographie Linguistique* (Paris, 1963)

Filip, Jan, *Celtic Civilization and its Heritage* (Prague, 1962)

Fleuriot, Leon, *Les Origines de la Bretagne* (Paris, 1982)

Fox, Cyril, *The Personality of Britain* (Cardiff, 1933)

Green, J. R., *A History of the English People* (London, 1877-80)

Green, Miranda A., *Exploring the World of the Druids* (London, 1995)

Green, Miranda A. (ed.), *The Celtic World* (London, 1995)

Harvie, Christopher, 'Anglo-Saxons into Celts' in Terence Brown (ed.), *Celticism* (Amsterdam, 1996)

Hawkes, Christopher, 'Culminative Celticity in pre-Roman Britain', *Etudes Celtique*, 13, 2 (1973)

Henebry, Richard, 'Whitley Stokes', *The Celtic Review*, VI (1909-10)

Hincks, Rhisiart, 'Hanes Ysgolheictod Llydaweg' [A History of Breton Scholarship], University of Wales Ph.D. dissertation (1983)

Hindley, Reg, *The Death of the Irish Language: A Qualified Obituary* (London, 1990)

Hubert, Henri, *The Rise of the Celts* (London, 1934)

Humphreys, H.L.I., 'The Breton Language' in Glanville Price (ed.), *The Celtic Connection* (Gerrards Cross, 1992)

Jackson, Kenneth, *A Celtic Miscellany* (London, 1951)

Jackson, Kenneth, *Language and History in Early Britain* (Edinburgh, 1953)

Jackson, Kenneth, *The Oldest Irish Tradition: A Window on the Iron Age* (Cambridge, 1964)

Jackson, Kenneth, 'The Celtic Aftermath in the Islands', after Joseph Raftery, *The Celts* (Dublin, 1964)

Jacobsthal, Paul, *Early Celtic Art* (Oxford, 1944)

James, Simon, *The Atlantic Celts: Ancient People or Modern Invention?* (London, 1999)

James, Simon, 'Celts, Politics and Motivation in Archaeology', *Antiquity* 72 (1998)

Jones, Michael, *The Creation of Brittany: A Late Medieval State* (London, 1967)

Keay, John and Julia (eds.), *Collins Encyclopaedia of Scotland* (London, 1994). The entry on George Buchanan.

Koch, John T. with John Carey (eds.), *The Celtic Heroic Age: Literary Sources for Ancient Celtic Europe and Early Ireland and Wales* (Maldon, Mass., 1995)

Kruta, Venceslas, 'In Search of the Ancient Celts' in S. Moscati and others (eds.), *The Celts* (Milan, 1991)

Kruta, Venceslas, 'Celtic Writing' in S. Moscati and others (eds.), *The Celts* (Milan, 1991)

Leersen, Joep, *Remembrance and Imagination* (Cork, 1996)

Leersen, Joep, ' Celticism' in Terence Brown (ed.), *Celticism* (Amsterdam, 1996)

Lloyd, J. E., *A History of Wales from the Earliest Times to the Edwardian Conquest* (London, 1911)

Loth, Joseph, *L'Emigration Bretonne en Armorique* (Paris, 1883)

Lynch, Michael, *Scotland, a New History* (London, 1991)

Mac Cana, Proinsias, *Celtic Mythology* (Feltham, 1983)

Mallory, J. P., *In Search of the Indo-Europeans* (London, 1989)

McEvedy, Colin, *The Penguin Atlas of Medieval History* (Harmondsworth, 1961)

McNeill, John T., *The Celtic Churches: A History, A D 200-1200* (London, 1974)

Megaw, Ruth and Vincent, *Celtic Art* (London, 1989)

Megaw, Ruth and Vincent, 'Ancient Celts and Modern Ethnicity', *Antiquity* 70 (1996)

Moscati, S. and others (eds.), *The Celts* (Milan, 1991)

O'Faolain, Sean, *The Irish* (West Drayton, 1947)

O'Luing, Sean, *Kuno Meyer, A Biography* (Dublin, 1991)

Piggott, Stuart, *The Druids* (Harmondsworth, 1974)

Powell, T. G. E., *The Celts* (London, 1958)

Pryce, W.T.R., 'Welsh and English in Wales, 1750–1971', *Bulletin of the Board of Celtic Studies* 28 (1978)

Raftery, Barry, 'Dispelling the Celtic Mists', *Times Literary Supplement*, 12 June 1998

Rankin, H. D., *Celts and the Classical World* (London, 1987)

Renfrew, Colin, *Archaeology and Language* (London, 1987)

Renfrew, Colin, *Before Civilization: The Radio-Carbon Revolution and Prehistoric Europe* (London, 1973)

Richter, Michael, *Medieval Ireland: The Enduring Tradition* (Basingstoke, 1988)

Roualet, Pierre, 'The Marnian Culture of Champagne' in S. Moscati and others (eds.), *The Celts* (Milan, 1991)

Seton-Watson, R. W., *Masaryk in England* (Cambridge, 1943)

Sims-Williams, Patrick, 'The Invention of Celtic Nature Poetry' in Terence Brown (ed.), *Celticism* (Amsterdam, 1996)

Tolkein, J. R. R., 'English and Welsh' in *Angles and Britons: The O'Donnell Lectures* (Cardiff, 1963)

Toynbee, A. J., *A Study of History* (London, 1934-61)

Webber, Eugene, *Peasants into Frenchmen* (London, 1977)

Whatmough, Joshua, 'Continental Celtic', *Proceedings of the Second International Congress of Celtic Studies* (Cardiff, 1966)

Williams, Gwyn A., *Excalibur: The Search for Arthur* (London, 1994)

Willis-Bund, J. W., *The Celtic Church of Wales* (London, 1897)

Withers, Charles W. J., *Gaelic in Scotland, 1698-1981* (Edinburgh, 1984)

▦ index

Page numbers in *italics* refer to illustrations

ACKNOWLEDGEMENTS

My first debt is to Mervyn Williams of Opus Television who suggested that I should write this book. Other members of Opus, Caryl Ebenezer in particular, have also been superbly supportive. I wish to thank S4C, especially Helen Howells and Huw Walters, for their interest in the project. Stuart Booth, commissioning editor at Cassell & Co has been a delight to work with, as have the book's editors Monica Tweddell and Chris Westhorp. As always, my greatest debt is to my wife, Janet Mackenzie Davies, with whom I have discussed every paragraph.

To dedicate the book to my younger daughter brings me great pleasure.

John Davies

ILLUSTRATIONS

Nearly all photographs in the book were supplied in digital form as copyright by Opus Television from their production of the accompanying S4C television series *The Celts*. In this context, appropriate locations and sources are also acknowledged, with associated copyright, within each caption.

Permission to reproduce here in is gratefully acknowledged.

In addition, other sources are gratefully acknowledged for permission to reproduce copyright illustrations as detailed in the captions.